OCCASIONAL PAPERS OF THE SOCIETY
OF ANTIQUARIES OF LONDON, NO. 19

'The Remains of Distant Times'
Archaeology and the National Trust

'The Remains of Distant Times'

Archaeology and the National Trust

Edited by David Morgan Evans, Peter Salway
and David Thackray

Published by

THE BOYDELL PRESS

for

THE SOCIETY OF ANTIQUARIES OF LONDON

and

THE NATIONAL TRUST

First published in 1996 by
The Boydell Press
an imprint of Boydell & Brewer Ltd
PO Box 9, Woodbridge, Suffolk IP12 3DF
and at PO Box 41026, Rochester NY 14604-4126
for
The Society of Antiquaries of London
and The National Trust

British Library Cataloguing in Publication Data
A catalogue record for this book is available from the British Library.

ISBN 0 85115 671 1
ISSN 0953–7155

This publication is printed on acid-free paper

Typeset by PPS, London Road, Amesbury, Wilts.
Printed in Great Britain by
St Edmundsbury Press Ltd, Bury St Edmunds, Suffolk

CONTENTS

THE CONTRIBUTORS

Gareth Binns
Countryside Education Officer, National Trust

Priscilla Boniface
Tourism consultant, freelance writer and lecturer

Professor Richard Bradley
Department of Archaeology, University of Reading

Professor R. Angus Buchanan
Professor for the History of Technology, University of Bath; Member of the
National Trust Properties Committee, and Archaeology Panel

Jo Burgon
Coast and Countryside Adviser, National Trust

Philip Claris
Archaeological Adviser, National Trust

Rosamund M.J. Cleal
Joint Curator, Alexander Keiller Museum, Avebury, National Trust

Professor Timothy Darvill
Professor of Archaeology and Property Development, Department of
Conservation Sciences, Bournemouth University; Council for British
Archaeology Nominated Member of the National Trust Council, Member of
the National Trust Archaeology Panel

Susan Denyer
Historic Buildings Representative, North-West Region, National Trust

David Morgan Evans
General Secretary, The Society of Antiquaries of London

Paul Everson
Head of Royal Commission on the Historical Monuments of England, Keele;
Member of the National Trust Archaeology Panel

Professor Peter Fowler
Department of Archaeology, University of Newcastle; Member of the
National Trust Executive Committee and Council

Katherine A. Hearn
Adviser on Nature Conservation, National Trust

Tiffany Hunt
Regional Director, Northumbria Region, National Trust

Simon Jervis
President, Society of Antiquaries; Historic Buildings Secretary, National Trust

Nicholas Johnson
County Archaeologist, Cornwall Archaeological Unit; Chairman of the National Trust Archaeology Panel, Member of the National Trust Properties Committee

Richard Keen
Historic Buildings Representative, National Trust, South Wales Region

Dr Marilyn Palmer
Department of History, University of Leicester

Michael Pitts
Stones Restaurant, Avebury

Julian H. Prideaux
The Chief Agent, National Trust

Dr Oliver Rackham
Botanist and historical ecologist, Corpus Christi College, Cambridge

Isabel Richardson
Holnicote Estate Office, National Trust

Emeritus Professor Peter Salway
The Open University; All Souls College, Oxford; The Society of Antiquaries of London Nominated Member of the National Trust Council

Sir Angus Stirling
Director-General, National Trust

Christopher Taylor
Landscape historian (retired)

Dr David Thackray
Chief Archaeological Adviser, National Trust

Angus Wainwright
Regional Archaeologist, East Anglia, National Trust

Professor Geoffrey Wainwright
Chief Archaeologist, English Heritage

Introduction

Peter Salway

The National Trust for Places of Historic Interest or Natural Beauty has in its care approximately 40,000 archaeological sites in England, Wales and Northern Ireland, including around 1,000 Scheduled Ancient Monuments and all or part of five World Heritage Sites. It owns 234,000 hectares of land, with protective covenants over another 31,000. Nor do the figures stand still. New land continues to be acquired, a large proportion of it with a higher than normal likelihood of including features of archaeological significance. Meanwhile, new discoveries are constantly being made on existing properties. In addition, a number of important sites owned by the National Trust but previously looked after by English Heritage are being transferred to Trust management. The huge responsibility of the Trust for the archaeology of its own possessions is therefore obvious. The potential importance of what it does as an example to other owners and to planning authorities is perhaps less well recognized.

There is no doubt that there were periods in the Trust's history when archaeology played little part in its consciousness. Outside the Trust, there are many quarters in which this image has persisted. The celebration of the Trust's Centenary in 1995 seemed an opportunity to bury that misconception. It is, moreover, a misconception that exists alongside two other unjustifiable notions about the Trust today. One is that the Trust 'preserves in aspic'. Many of the papers included in this volume give the lie to that. The other is that the National Trust's conservation of 'countryside' is highly meritorious (an opinion extended in certain circles to include vernacular buildings), but that its preservation of country houses is somehow élitist and should not be pursued by 'excessive' expenditure on existing properties of this sort or by acceptance of new. Such a view reveals a lack of understanding of the extent of the manmade nature of the landscape and of the intimate relationship between land and structures. It particularly underlines an ignorance of the part estates played in the creation of much of what is now valued by the public as 'natural beauty', and (often coincidently and unintentionally) in the preservation of historic landscape on the large scale. And it displays a perception of 'historic interest' that is too much rooted in the fashion of the moment for the National Trust to follow, since the Trust's fundamental obligation under the National Trust Acts is to preserve for the distant future as well as for the present.

The Centenary Conference, entitled *Figures in a Landscape*, was primarily intended to raise the public profile of the place of archaeology in the National Trust as currently practised. In the process, the contributions published here should help to demolish those misconceptions. One of the most important features highlighted during the Conference was the vital part archaeology now plays in the management of National Trust properties, through archaeological evaluation property by property, by the creation of accessible systems of recording archaeological data, and by research on topics relevant to the understanding and care of monuments, buildings and landscape. The results are fed back to Trust committees and staff taking decisions, both at policy level and in everyday action on individual properties. Sometimes there is direct intervention by archaeologists, whether in rescue mode (as at Uppark), or in conservation (in the repair, for example, of earthworks eroded by visitors), or through research excavation to improve the understanding of particular properties before restoration and informed presentation to the public. Perhaps the most significant current development is the gradual introduction of 'whole farm plans', in which all aspects of the conservation needs of individual holdings are worked out in close consultation with their agricultural tenants, and the latter compensated when farm incomes are reduced by consequent changes in practice. What emerges is a picture of properties undergoing change, directed by innovative policies in which archaeology – alongside the other conservation arts and sciences – plays a very important part.

The Society of Antiquaries has for some time past been very aware both of the need to collaborate with other national bodies where interests overlap, and to maximize the usefulness of the Society's intellectual and (in the broadest sense) political resources. The Antiquaries have a direct institutional link with the National Trust, being one of the national bodies that nominate 26 of the 52 members of the Trust's Council (its board of trustees). The community of interest is very wide, since the Society's concerns extend beyond archaeology in the narrow sense to all aspects of enquiry into the past as revealed by its material remains, very many of which disciplines – the study of the decorative arts, for example – are of everyday importance to the Trust. It was a happy coincidence that the Conference took place at a time when the newly-elected President of the Society was about to take up the post of Historic Buildings Secretary of the National Trust, while his predecessor in that post – another Fellow – had just become Director-General Designate. Those who developed the idea of *Figures in a Landscape* cannot claim to have arranged events to fall out so neatly, but they are very pleased to report that at the time of writing the Conference has already stimulated moves towards further co-operation between the two institutions. In its third century of existence the Society of Antiquaries of London is sure to share even more common ground with the National Trust, as the latter moves into its second.

Note

In order to avoid confusion with John Gaze's book *Figures in a Landscape*, which provided the inspiration for the conference, these papers come out under the title *The Remains of Distant Times*. This is taken from a letter of June 1709 from John Vanbrugh to the Duchess of Marlborough giving reasons for preserving some part of Woodstock Old Manor in the park of Blenheim. It starts, 'There is perhaps no one thing, which the most Polite part of Mankind have more universally agreed in; than the Vallue they have ever set upon the Remains of distant Times.' Thanks are due to Martin Williams FSA for providing, in another context, this reference.

Acknowledgements

Special thanks are due to Linda Viner whose meticulous organization and enthusiasm made the conference such a great success; to Caroline Thackray for the production of the exhibition 'Figures in a Landscape' and its accompanying booklet, which so ably set the scene for the conference; and to the Society of Antiquaries' Managing Editor, Janet Clayton, whose efficiency, hard work and cajoling has kept the production of these Proceedings running so smoothly.

1   Archaeology and the National Trust

Sir Angus Stirling

Amongst the many opportunities for celebration and reflection that are being provided by this Centenary Year, we especially welcome the privilege of sharing with the Society of Antiquaries in the conference on the National Trust's work in archaeology. We are very grateful to the Society for the invitation.

The title of the conference, *Figures in a Landscape*, is borrowed, with proper acknowledgements, from the title of the history of the National Trust written in 1988 by the late John Gaze, a former Chief Agent. In this book John Gaze devoted a chapter to archaeology entitled 'Archaeological Sites and Historic Buildings'.

The chapter reviews the organization's early acknowledgement of the importance of the preservation of archaeological sites, especially those major monuments in its ownership. It reflects on the middle decades of the century when the Trust gave only marginal acknowledgement to archaeology and the ensuing period of redress from the 1950s onwards when Sir Mortimer Wheeler, Sir Cyril Fox and Professor Richmond, all past Presidents of the Society of Antiquaries, acted as Honorary Advisers.

The book goes on to record the pioneering role of Miss Phyllis Ireland who, working primarily as a volunteer, produced hand-lists of archaeological sites on the Trust properties for the Area Agents.

The chapter on archaeology concludes with the statement: 'Details of the way in which, during the last ten years, the Trust has got its archaeological house in order must come later. At this point its early perception of its task and its latter confusion need to be seen against the major place which archaeology has come to take among its preservation achievements.' Sadly John Gaze died before he was able to write the concluding section bringing the Trust's archaeological work up to date. We hope that this Conference and the publication of the proceedings will help to do that.

Our various archaeological activities relate to many facets of the Trust's work, and this variety is reflected in the number of agencies, organizations and groups at both national and local level in England, Wales and Northern Ireland with whom we have been fortunate to establish close relationships. Amongst these I would like to acknowledge the excellent assistance we have received from English Heritage, Cadw and the Department of the Environment, Northern Ireland. Their administration of the heritage legislation, experience and skills of management in support of the protection of the cultural heritage are essential aids to the Trust's work.

Similarly we derive enormous help from our colleagues in local authorities on matters of planning and conservation. The staff of the Royal Commissions on Ancient and Historic Monuments for England and Wales have provided support and encouragement to our archaeologists and architectural historians over many years. Without their exceptional skills in site recognition, survey and analysis, and without the substantial inventories of the various national records, our understanding of our properties would be diminished.

The Council for British Archaeology has played a significant role since the 1970s in persuading the Trust to take its archaeology seriously, and in supporting us by the creation in 1975 of a network of Honorary Archaeological Advisers for each of our regions – the forerunners of our present Archaeology Panel. We also derive considerable help from a number of university departments, archaeological societies and archaeological units with whom we work closely, particularly in gaining access to relevant research, and in carrying out recording in the field.

It is important to emphasize this co-operation with others, because without it the Trust's purposes could not be realized.

The Trust's statutory purpose is the preservation of places of historic interest or natural beauty for the benefit of the nation. The management of properties, including coast, countryside and historic buildings and their contents, is based on detailed property management plans, for which archaeological and historic landscape surveys are being prepared. These surveys, which are crucial to the understanding of the significance of the place, are by no means complete for the whole of the Trust, but the process is a continuing one.

The Trust has now appointed a number of archaeologists both to its Advisers Office in Cirencester, where the two national advisers are based, and to the Regions. All are involved in integrating the conservation of archaeological sites, structures and historic landscapes into the Trust's conservation responsibilities as a whole.

Our archaeologists now work alongside nature conservationists, forestry advisers, advisers on access and visitor management, tenant farmers and property managers in the countryside, buildings managers, architects, gardens advisers and conservators, on our historic houses, their gardens and designed landscapes.

The Trust's developing national Sites and Monuments Record will play a significant part in informing our Regional staff of constraints on developments, and in planning for the best use of existing resources. The development of this major database will soon enable us precisely to quantify the scale of the Trust's archaeological responsibilities, as the owner and curator of the largest number of archaeological sites and structures in Britain. Perhaps even more important, it will help with the analysis and understanding of their landscape contexts and settings, the preservation of which is as critical as the preservation of the sites themselves.

The Oxford English Dictionary gives as a definition of archaeology: the study and systematic recording of antiquities. I would be bold enough to apply to that definition, in the light of our present approach, some words of Thomas Jefferson: 'The new circumstances under which we are placed call for new words, new phrases and for the transfer of old words to new objects'.

It is, I believe, essential that the Trust should interpret its responsibility towards archaeology not in a strictly limited sense, meaning the conservation of specific ancient sites. That remains, of course, vital. But an understanding of archaeology must surely imply a deeper knowledge of the historical development of our landscape and the way human occupation and activity has brought it to its present condition. It is crucial to the Trust's integrated management philosophy that this deep appreciation of the past informs the principles of management and interpretation for the future.

The conference programme has provided us with the opportunity to look at some of the many areas of archaeological activity with which we are involved, and to assess those against wider, national archaeological trends. It will be of particular value, and no doubt constructive in our future planning, to understand further the perceptions of the Trust's work from our eminent friends and colleagues who have contributed from outside the Organization. To all of them and to the speakers from within the Trust, I would like to extend my gratitude for so generously contributing to this milestone event.

I would also like to thank all the archaeological staff who have worked so hard in preparing for the event with its exhibition. I hope that we will be able to raise the profile of this important, but perhaps still little appreciated area of the Trust's activity.

2   Shared history, shared purposes: Opening address by the President of the Society of Antiquaries of London

Simon Jervis

The association between the Society of Antiquaries and the National Trust is a long one. Our first representative on the Council of the National Trust, a seat that Professor Peter Salway now holds with distinction, was Dr Edwin Freshfield. He only lasted until June 1897 when, as a result of failing to be elected President, he resigned and was replaced by Mr Philip Norman. It is probably not without significance that both these gentlemen were Treasurers of the Society. I say 'not without significance' because of the very first reference to the National Trust which can be found in the Society's records – ninety-nine years ago. At a meeting of Council on 25 November 1896:

> Read – an application from the National Trust for places of Historic Interest or Natural Beauty for a grant in aid of the preservation of the so-called Pre reformation Clergy House at Alfriston, Sussex.
>
> Resolved – that the National Trust etc. be informed that the Society has no funds available for such a purpose.

The hand of the Treasurer seems apparent. The statement that the Society has no funds for such purposes becomes more poignant if we go back to the 1850s.

In the summer of 1854, the opening of the Crystal Palace caused John Ruskin to issue a pamphlet in which he deplored 'modern' ideas of 'unrivalled mechanical ingenuity' and looked to ways of conserving monuments of the past. Ruskin proposed that 'an association might be formed . . . with active watchers and agents . . . who should furnish the association with . . . an account of every monument of interest in its neighbourhood, and then with a yearly or half-yearly report of the state of such monuments, and of the changes proposed to be made upon them'. Ruskin then went on to propose that such an association should 'furnish funds, either to buy, freehold, such buildings or other works of untransferable art as at any time might be offered for sale, or to assist their proprietors, whether as private individuals or public bodies, in the maintenance of such guardianship as was really necessary for their safety'. All this was proposed by Ruskin in order 'to prevent unwise restoration and unnecessary destruction'.

These ideas soon found their way to the Society of Antiquaries. In November of 1854 the Executive Committee of the Society considered the proposal 'that the Society should undertake the management and disposal of a Fund to be subscribed for the preservation of Medieval Buildings, Mr Ruskin offering to contribute the annual sum of £25 towards that purpose and believing that his friends would contribute a considerable further amount'. The Executive Committee, recognizing 'that this proposition involved very important considerations' duly passed it to Council, who in the best of traditions, sent it back for further study.

The upshot was that the Society of Antiquaries decided that it could administer such a fund, that initially it would be confined to Great Britain and Ireland, that a list of existing ancient buildings or other monuments be drawn up and that the conservation of these buildings or monuments should be without any attempt to add to, alter or restore them. This last principle caused the usual row. Nearly one hundred and fifty years ago my predecessor as President received a letter from the Reverend E. T. Yates of Aylsham in Norfolk. The reverend gentleman amongst many other matters wrote, 'men doing what they trust to be good work do not like to be shown up in the public papers, particularly if they are using all proper means to effect their object'. The Reverend Yates's church had been, according to Pevsner, 'drastically restored in 1852'.

From this small acorn of the 1850s there arose at most a twig, but unfortunately not even a small sapling. Though a few grants were given by the Conservation Fund, the committee administering it were, to say the least, lacking in energy and the opportunity was lost. Ruskin went on to proselytize others and was, of course, one of the key influences leading to the creation of the National Trust. It is interesting to imagine what the situation might have been today had the Society of Antiquaries been more active. Would the care of monuments and buildings have started off in the 'private' sector? Would there have been the need for state guardianship? But 'cut is the branch that might have grown full straight' and further speculation would be fruitless.

Sir Angus Stirling mentions as a statutory purpose of the National Trust 'the preservation of places of historic interest or natural beauty', and clearly links the Trust's archaeological activities to that central inspiration. The Society of Antiquaries of London, founded or refounded in 1707, does not incorporate its 'mission statement', if you will forgive the phrase, in its title, but our Royal Charter of 1751 charges us with 'the encouragement, advancement and furtherance of the study and knowledge of the antiquities and history of this and other countries'. The grand sweeps of our purposes and ambitions have much in common. In the National Trust, I have been told, those who are concerned with looking after the land are known as 'boots' while those who care for the great houses and their contents are known as 'lilies'. I know of no such brief formulation of difference for the Fellows of the Society of Antiquaries, but the Society always tries to maintain a balance between the interests of those whose emblem is the trowel and those whose hands, gloved to handle manuscripts or goldsmiths' work, never get dirty. But of course these distinctions have no ultimate substance. In 1974 I attended the Mentmore debate in the House of Lords, a sad but interesting occasion. One noble and intelligent Lord, now deceased, questioned whether Mentmore could be considered as part of the national heritage because it had never been seen by the public and no one had known about it. Would he have applied the same argument on the discovery of Sutton Hoo or the Mildenhall treasure? Of course not, and a great country house is as much an archaeological site as the most battered of barrows, and its contents, splendid though they may be, are finds to be awarded the same interest and study as the most unprepossessing and squashed medieval coin (during my time at the Fitzwilliam Museum we collected not a few of the latter). And it is worth mentioning at this point that in Kelmscott Manor, Oxfordshire, the Society has its own country house, to which, with advice and assistance from the National Trust, we have devoted much care and attention in recent years. We are planning, I am glad to report, in the spirit of this conference, to have a hard archaeological look at the small estate which goes with Kelmscott, in close consultation with our National Trust neighbours.

Another crucial mutual concern is Stonehenge, where we have been working together with the National Trust and English Heritage to find the best way of securing the future. A testimony which has not been cited before is recorded in a minute of the Executive of the Society of 1897. It records:

> The Assistant Secretary called attention to a proposal on behalf of the Government to permanently appropriate a large extent of Salisbury Plain for cavalry manoeuvres. In view of the possible damage to Stonehenge through the concussion of near artillery fire or other causes he had written to Lt. General Pitt-Rivers, who thought it 'quite possible', though he would not say 'probable', that the firing of cannon close by might bring down some of the stones, especially those that are hanging to one another by the mortises at the top.

The Society of Antiquaries is very glad to be collaborating with the National Trust in this conference. It is, I think, a happy coincidence that in the National Trust's Centenary Year its President should be appointed Historic Buildings Secretary to the Trust. I would like to associate myself very warmly with the welcome to the conference given by Sir Angus.

3 Landscape: personality, perception and perspective

Peter Fowler

Remove not the ancient landmark, which thy fathers have set (Proverbs 22.28)

Introduction

'Archaeology' and 'The National Trust' are two set landmarks which we shall keep in view as we move around a familiar landscape. We shall doubtless perceive their personality from time to time in different perspectives. My guides are the above quotation, already invoked, and another one, equally authoritative if perhaps not quite so celestially inspired (but then, who knows?).

The second quotation is from the *Centenary Handbook* (National Trust 1995, 6). It is the third of the nine points which state in half a page what the Trust does: 'The National Trust looks after buildings representing the breadth of the nation's cultural history'. The point is then elaborated, implying that the word 'buildings' here includes '1,000 scheduled ancient monuments; over 200 historic houses; 160 gardens; and 25 industrial monuments, including mills and mines'. Further, the implication is that such structures embrace 'the breadth of the nation's cultural history.

Both quotations embody thoughts that silently run through the tenor of my remarks. One is the idea of ancestral landmarks – is that perchance what the Trust all unknowing is actually about? Another is the concept of breadth in whatever it is that any one of us might mean by 'cultural history' – does the Trust really believe that its portfolio truly ranges right across the nation's cultural history? Some of my thoughts might jar, in that they may not usually resonate in what others perceive to be proper Trust contexts; but of course, it is the role of a first foray into our figurative landscape to provoke reaction and stimulate discussion. Indeed, we merely follow the spoor of self-critical appraisal imprinted so clearly for us by Merlin Waterson (1994, 269) in the centennial history of the Trust. 'The Trust's Centenary provides an opportunity for its past and future role to be assessed,' he observes, 'for its achievements and ideals to be scrutinised.' From such critique can come reaction. We come to celebrate the Trust but stay, I trust, to cerebrate.

Future heritage

Before the next centennial a lot of heritage, as yet unmade and indeed unconceived, will have been created. Indeed, for it to have become posterity's heritage, it will have had to be made, used, become redundant, survived in some relic form, been discovered, recognized as being of value, been recorded, been selected for preservation and then had something done to it to keep it in some form of authentically acceptable existence. If the heritage lobby believes that out there is a self-defining and already-made heritage, in the landscape for example, deriving from a past that *has already happened*, then it is selling us and the future's heritage short. Some of our children's grandchildren's heritage has not yet happened and, if there is any hope for our species and the world, then more heritage has to be in the pipeline than has already gushed through the stopcock of history. And the Trust thinks it is already overloaded! The real challenge is yet to come.

That has to be true of landscape in particular, and we should already be thinking about the nature and relationship of heritage and landscape in the first half of the twenty-first century (Countryside Commission 1994). The cover of the Trust's own forward-looking book about the next century (Newby 1995), though a beautiful image, suggests nostalgic fogeyism rather than dynamic renewal as the vision. Since, however, we do not actually know what that heritage is going to be, we cannot know the main requirement for successful heritagism over the next few decades. But we can be reasonably clear about one thing: it will not be only, and perhaps not at all, about what we now regard as our heritage. The past of the future will not be the same as ours, so heritage – a collective noun merely expressing the result of a process of selective evaluation from versions of pastness available at any one time – will be different too. This is of course a common-place in heritage discourse, but too characteristically Trust discussion of such issues seems to start from the unstated assumption that 'our heritage' is self-evident, known and permanent.

Yet concepts of and policies deriving from unquestioning beliefs in an unchanging past have dangers for institutions perhaps even more than mere individuals. While there are perfectly legitimate occasions for seeking refuge in a cosy pastness, on the whole the future surely lies in *not* slumping back into an easy-riding nostalgia of, for example, arcadian landscapes that never were; lies in *not* becoming entrapped in an intellectually inert triumphalism of the Little Englander sort not entirely unknown in bucolic heritage park and country house; lies in learning *not* to freeze-frame on a particular sort of heritage. Just look at so many 1980s versions of heritage: not only already dead as dodos conceptually and commercially but dead too in that popular taste, never mind academic revisionism, has changed too in the fashionably directionless decade of the nineties. Was populist 'heritage' ever more than a medium for a day-out? In a mid-nineties milieu already identified as 'post-heritage' (Fowler 1994), should we be surprised therefore if it is replaced by the Sunday shopping mall?

Some institutional versions of the past will prove to be based on concepts that the twenty-first century is going to find anachronistic and even redundant.

Best-guessing which those are going to be could well be a worthwhile activity. Much of our heritage perspective is strongly influenced, for example, by nationalism: whither that concept? Will that be a viable posture for heritage policy come 2050? – we do not yet know but surely it is not too early to ask the question.

Similarly, much heritage thinking is based on militarism in one form or another; it is certainly important in landscape preservation and interpretation. Will it continue to be an acceptable model in a mid twenty-first-century society which may be either unbelievably violent or, by today's standards, incredibly 'soft'? Either way, is it wise to get too caught up in the present vogue for heritage weekend warfare? What happens when heritage peace breaks out, that is when people get bored with spurious battles?

An advertisement by English Heritage (EH) suggests a different angle. Appearing in the national press in spring/summer 1995, it was designed to boost visitor numbers to EH Properties in Care under the slogan 'A Legendary Day Out'. Ostensibly it showed what many would think of first and foremost as a military, even militaristic, monument, Hadrian's Wall. The exact location was not given, nor did it matter; reproduced in a gritty, nostalgic shade of black and white, image was all. The implications are interesting. The length of Wall divides a man (presumably Father) with child on shoulders from three other children on the south side. They wave, he smiles, they all express happiness; though their flimsy summer clothes suggest a designer concept of Northumbrian weather and landscape even though snow appears to lie on the background hills. But of Mother there is no sign. Can this be a deliberate decision to invoke an attractiveness about a well-known piece of heritage by linking it, like current TV advertisements, to contemporary issues of gender and sociological change? Not only 'Where is the mother?', perhaps, but 'Where are the mothers?' Whatever happened to the 'happy family' of both the adperson's world and the historic doorway into gladsome membership of the heritage institutions?

The advertisement betokens 'other' perceptions of the familiar which themselves clearly signal change. Here is another viewpoint, something different from the perspective of 'landscape and heritage' which tends to result from perceptions of them by heritage professionals appraising them within well-understood frameworks. 'The unspoken comment about the non-present mother' is actually quite an interesting way of looking at Hadrian's Wall in contemporary terms. At least it makes a change from assumptions that everybody is interested in, let alone approves of, the military achievement which the Wall is primarily presented as representing. But, it could now be remarked in 1995, such is the pace of heritage change, that some would see such a politically correct remark as of dubious acceptability.

Take another familiar topic. Will landscapes based on concepts of social hierarchy survive as attractive heritage? However historically correct their bases may be, if interpretation of them ignores issues such as gender, resource exploitation and social inequality which already interest quite a lot of people, will they be viable heritage two or three decades into the next century? Those will probably not be the specific issues in 25–50 years' time; but issues of that sort will be of interest to people two generations hence, in looking at their landscapes and in appraising what heritage guardians tell them about *how* they should see them. Whatever the particulars, we can be certain that heritage in 2045, never mind 2095, will be very different indeed from today's. Perceptions and presentations of it will change, and woe betide those in the heritage business who want their version to remain of the late twentieth century. They will of course themselves become historical, but whether they become heritage, that is, something worth saving, is another matter. Curiously, most of our reference points to heritage lie in the future, not the past.

One justifiable retrospective reference, however, is the starting point one hundred years ago. If only the National Trust had kept to its originally proposed title, how much easier we would be now. The invitations to the meeting from which it sprang, on 16 November 1893, were headed: 'National Trust for Historic Sites and Natural Scenery' (Waterson 1994, 14). Archaeologists could live with that; landscape archaeologists and indeed environmentalists too. Especially is that so when we read that the meeting was to set up 'a Corporation for the holding of lands of natural beauty and sites and houses of historic interest to be preserved intact for the nation's use and enjoyment.' That is even better, though it is a pity the drafters did not stick to 'scenery' instead of changing to 'natural beauty'. Scenery, after all, is scenery whereas beauty is in the eye of the beholder. Nevertheless, there is nothing in those phrases about cultural aesthetics, for example, fine art and neo-classical architecture, and, most importantly, nothing about importance or significance – just the 'historic *interest*' of places to be held for enjoyment.

That all seems close to a current definition of landscape and the role of historic landscape in contemporary circumstances now. Why on earth has archaeology, and particularly historic landscape other than stately, mannered parks, played therefore such a lowly role in the Trust's thinking until very recently? Why have archaeologists been made to feel awkward? – my predecessor, Professor Ian Richmond, for example, as recorded by John Gaze (1988, 86). Gaze himself percipiently put it down to the 'confusion that existed between the Trust's scientific and aesthetic reponsibilities', despite the absence of the latter from the documentary evidence of its originators; and he then goes on to remark that probably archaeology would not have survived as a Trust concern 'were it not for the accident that so many of the properties it acquired were encumbered with archaeological remains.' Let us acknowledge that Gaze's phrase has been silently rethought by many a Trust land agent both before and since. Nevertheless, at the very least archaeology now shares the stigma of 'encumbrance' with other land-based academic disciplines. More positively, nuisance though it is to have to be holistic sometimes, now we have all come to see these things as resources and opportunities, have we not?

Post-industrial landscape

Industrial landscape of the twentieth century is a sort of landscape heritage the Trust has not so far seriously touched. Perhaps what I really mean is a landscape of full industrialization, of an industrial society. This is something different from long-dead plant of often marginal eighteenth- and nineteenth-century industry and ruinous collectables of industrial activity, so often rural and agrarian rather than truly industrial. To say as much is not to comment on a particular failure by the Trust but, in drawing attention to the speed at which our own society is moving on from its industrial base, to suggest that thought should be given to the philosophical and conservation consequences of this rapid socio-technological change to post-industrial times. That it is happening before our very eyes should not blind us to its *historical* significance.

We can no longer just assume that because something is 'only' of twentieth-century date, it is of no historical importance, even if we enter the caveat 'yet'. As others have already recognized in their own fields – the archaeology of Second World War air and sea defences, and early 'Welfare State architecture', for example – the recent past comes crowding hard upon the present in terms of landscape heritage in particular. This is especially so when the material, such as an American aerodrome of the early 1940s, not only represents a new and significant development but is also now completely dead and unrepeatable except as conscious, imitative anachronism. This applies above all to industry for, from the vantage point of 1995, we can already clearly see that what in archaeological parlance we can properly call 'The Industrial Period' was, far from being the norm, a brief century of an unusual form of mass activity 1850–1950, declining to decreasing economic and relatively minor cultural significance in a 'Late IP' of 1950–85.

A third generation electricity power station called Stella typified this. It was built in what became a very unlovely urban fringe edging the west side of the Tyneside conurbation. Indeed, Stella could well be taken as metaphor for all that the Trust was set up to enable people, however briefly, to escape from; yet just 6 miles (10km) away, on the same side of the same river valley, is Cherryburn, quite properly acquired by the Trust for its associative value. It was the home of Thomas Bewick, one of Tyneside's all-time greats like Hadrian and Sting, but Cherryburn itself is otherwise a charmingly arcadian irrelevance in terms of Tyneside's history and material culture. Far more representative is Stella; yet it would not (so far) have occurred to the Trust to think of acquiring a redundant twentieth-century power station even if it were threatened. For its period either side of 1950, however, Stella was theoretically no different in principle from what might be called run-of-the-water-mill acquisitions from the eighteenth and nineteenth centuries. Frankly, Stella would have stood a better chance of being Trust-worthy if it were a 200-year-old lime-kiln on a country-house estate. As it was, watched by thousands of silent Tynesiders in the cold grey light of a damp dawn on Sunday, 29 March 1992, so apparently permanent a monument was spectacularly blown up and ceased to be a landmark except on film and in the mind. As Stella deconstructed in less than half a minute, it was not just a power station that disappeared. The watchers knew her demise was a metaphor for the passing of industrial Tyneside, a passing from what had been perceived as the nobility of manual labour to the hopelessness of no work. Therein lies one of the great landscape challenges for the Trust over the next few decades.

Few would deny that one of the most significant landscape developments of the nineteenth century and more has been the growth of urbanization. The Trust can go on acquiring more and more arcadian villages until the cows come home, but can it, should it, address the logistical issues inherent in a monument-led representation of urbanism? Fairly obviously, it cannot, and many would argue that it should not; but a consequence is that the Trust, in seeking self-justification, should be careful in not stretching credulity beyond what it actually is – for example, in claiming that its portfolio of buildings represents 'the breadth of the country's cultural history'. To do so was not the intention; the Trust's acquisition policy has never been based on building up a representative sample of anything; and what it has is not representative in any scientifically defensible sense. Fine; but do not pretend that it is. Let us rather glory in the diversity of serendipity and personal foible.

My own instinct is nevertheless that in ways which are not yet clear, somehow an important part of the Trust's future lies in those post-industrial landscapes. And surely not just with the landscapes; surely also with the people left within them and, equally disorientated, with those who moved away and now, on a non-Reptonian landscaped estate, seek a new identity with a neo-Georgian door. Fortunately, one way into that sort of post-industrial socio-complex through landscape is already there and working within the Trust's remit through such urban fringe properties as Tatton Park and Lyme Park, both in Cheshire, but both situated just outside one of England's largest conurbations, Greater Manchester. Lyme is super: just over 6 miles (c. 10km) south-east of Stockport on the Glossopdale 361 bus with 1,377 acres of parkland affording 'Magnificent views of Pennine Hills and Cheshire Plain' (National Trust 1995, 56). Gibside was acquired, over and above its undoubted historic landscape, associative and architectural attractions, with contemporary and future social functions very much in mind: 6 miles (*c.* 10km) south-west of Gateshead with the Northern 745 Newcastle–Consett bus passing nearby, it is a local lung for Tyneside, now with new purposes giving it a completely new lease of life (National Trust 1995, 251). A landscape designed for private delectation, for exclusivity, finds its twenty-first-century role in inclusivity, as a sort of people's park.

Such landscape properties seem to me to contain a considerable chunk of habitat where the Trust's soul should reside next century, different habitat but the same soul as sought to convert concern for our fellows into practical help via 'open air sitting rooms' a century ago. But why not put the sitting room close by where people live rather than in distant arcadia? We already have some, the Lymes and Gibsides, in the suburban fringe; others exist in the urban jungle.

They are called parks. They are the town and city parks dotted around our urban centres and just off-centres. Mostly great and altruistic legacies of Victorian vision marrying social need, they mark local points in time when populations exploded into the really big figures of the urban landscapes of the second half of the nineteenth century. But today, such parks characteristically lie semi-derelict and inadequately managed, subject to vandalism and often violence. The results of years of declining local authority care, of lack of resources, and of middle-class emigration to the suburbs, show all too clearly. Yet the need for them has never been greater: perhaps not primarily for frequent mass entertainment, as was often an original role, and perhaps not now for large numbers, for many of the descendants of those for whom the parks were built have left the inner city. They are needed because those who can and want to use them are by definition largely the carless in a motorized society, the pedestrian inhabitants of the inner city, the users of public transport – in other words, they tend to be the underprivileged, who cannot leave, and those who choose to lead an urban life.

These urban parks are not just green spaces; they also are a hundred years old now, and indeed more in many cases, so they too, like the NT, have a history. As historic parks they were and are of far more importance to more people in their daily lives, and for many people on their holidays too, than yet another emparked landscape, five social classes, £4.50, two centuries and 50 miles (80km) away. Perhaps more surprisingly to a suburban and rural population, people living near these parks actually, *mirabile dictu*, love them. An urban park can be as lovable in the eyes of its inner city locals as is the familial park to an ancestral duke. Spirits and semiotics reside in both, not just in the ducal acres. We should never, as trustees of heritages for all, confuse hierarchy with humanity.

If the Trust is looking for a mission, a way in which to express in practical terms its concern for the less fortunate in our society through landscape, then here is an opportunity, a challenge, to do so in a way which is absolutely four-square with its purpose. As H. E. Bracey remarked (1970, 220), 'Octavia Hill was as much, probably more, concerned with the physical and mental well-being of the urban masses as she was with preservation of the natural beauties of the Lake District'. A long-term urban park project offers an unexplored way back to that ethic and, building on the Trust's recent mini-urban experiences and longer term provision around the urban fringes, into the future.

Such a project would undoubtedly be useful but the real reason for presuming to fly the kite in an NT context is that the Trust could do it superbly well. After all, in essence we are talking about heritage and history, about made landscapes and often exotic and bizarre buildings, about land and its management, and about people and their needs. Is not that the Trust personified? That the locus is urban rather than rural should not deter the Trust: rather would it be to seize an opportunity, to accept a challenge with new partnerships, notably local authorities, and different people, notably urban locals. Conceptually this could be the urban equivalent of Enterprise Neptune, and as relevant to the needs of landscape and people in the early part of the twenty-first century as is Neptune in the second half of the twentieth.

The conservation landscape

'The rate, extent and completeness of the destruction of archaeological sites of all periods is increasing so rapidly that few intact examples will remain by AD 2000' (Fowler 1972, 103). Since those sorts of predictions some twenty and more years ago, there has been both a steady degradation of many aspects of our landscapes and a long chapter of specific disasters. But the fact of the matter is that by 1995 we can already be certain that the worst of those sorts of apocalyptic visions of the future will not happen. We will not finish off destroying the countryside in the next five years. I would even go so far as to deconstruct my propheteering and suggest that there will probably be more intact archaeological sites being well looked after in 2000 than there were in 1970. So we doom and destruction merchants got it wrong; but in so doing, how have we all managed to get it right?

A profoundly important point, not least for both conservation archaeologists and the Trust, is that somehow we both edged alongside and then have haltingly begun to articulate a point of view which is minimally acceptable to many and good sense to some. Bracey (1970, 222) put his finger on it: of the Trust he wrote that 'until recently [it] has not had to concern itself overmuch about public reaction to its policy and actions .... The public ... has a big financial stake in the Trust's operations. The ordinary tax payer is entitled to question whether he [*sic*] is able to enjoy access to the Trust's properties ...'. The point and the argument are familiar, not only within Trust councils but to archaeologists too as the performance of their tasks and its products have increasingly come, through funding, into the public domain. But we not only have to dance to tunes of our pipers' calling through obligation; somehow we are all aligning along the same message. That is, the growing awareness that, behind all the particularist issues, such as the archaeological one quoted, there is the generality that we cannot go on like we have been doing. Hence the positive reactions, initially of the conservation ethic, then of 'greenery' and now of sustainability. Catch-words, slogans, maybe, but all saying the same: not just that we cannot continue thoughtless exploitation but that we must do something else instead.

How does that affect the land and our visions of it as landscape? In Britain the siren cries of urban swamping of the countryside have not been realized either: about 13 per cent of UK land is in urban use and that proportion has not significantly altered in recent history, nor will it. The real change has been in use, designation and attitudes as what we can already identify as the creation of a 'conservation landscape'. This has progressively developed since the 1960s and with increasing bite in the 1980s and 1990s, incorporating not just fairly static, status-laden designations such as World Heritage Sites and National Nature Reserves but also working countryside designations like the National Parks and the proliferation of more dynamic, land-management income-producing schemes such as Environmentally Sensitive Areas and Countryside Stewardship. Some thirty such designations now exist, more if you take local designations into account as well. National Trust inalienable land and, though it is not officially designated as conservation land, the many hectares of Forestry Commission land effectively managed for amenity, recreation and conservation, could also be added.

The total of such conservation land recognized in one way or another in what is already a recognizable national conservation landscape must be approaching the sort of percentage of land area in urban use. Perhaps it is conservation not urbanization which now threatens the countryside? – not have we gone too far, but have we now gone far enough?

That cannot be answered in isolation, for an outline of what is likely to happen in the countryside anyway is already to hand. The most significant trends from our viewpoint, and particularly the Trust's, are that income from land – rents, and profits from land production – are likely to continue to decline within a framework whereby the well-off get richer and the small farmers get smaller. Land values are forecast to fall as a long-term trend within an industry of which a characteristic for a decade already has been a decline each year in capital investment. Over recent decades the only major profits in land have come from development rights on it rather than from the land itself. In future, as land-use in general becomes less intensive for food production, the major player on the British landscape is likely to be not the owner or the UK Government or conservation interests but Europe and in particular, of course, the European Union.

However much we may think 10–12 per cent of the national estate for land-based conservation is quite enough, however much we may believe that the

Trust owns quite enough for the good of itself and all of us, as we move into the next millennium there are going to be both needs as well as opportunities for more rural land to be put to useful conservation, amenity and recreational purposes. Countryside, and those parts of it for all sorts of other reasons dignified as 'landscape', are central in this respect, not just to look at and walk through but because of their capacity, through the delightful mechanism of the Trust, to engender doubtless illusory but nevertheless real sensations of ownership. Thanks to the Trust we can all share not just in experiencing our history but in owning our own land, the land with the ancient marks of our ancestors on it. The English, perhaps much more so than the other ethnic groups making up the British, are a nation, not of shopkeepers, but of wannabe country landowners.

Conclusion

Archaeology should be interesting and can be exciting but the real point is that it is part of a highly complex socio-intellectual matrix which is rather more about today and the future than it is about the past. In other words, it is more about what we do with it, as archaeologists and Trust staff and as heritage consumers of landscapes, than it is about what they, our ancestors, did to produce the material and the evidence which underpin our concept of 'past' and, now, increasingly our leisure-pleasure time. 'It is our purpose,' states our Director-General (National Trust 1995, 5), 'to offer enjoyment to everyone'. Admirable; but possible?

The Trust has to recognize that archaeology has rapidly matured during the later twentieth century from an antiquarian and largely introspective activity into a theoretically complex, ethically based, professionally led, publicly accountable function of society.

'Landscape' is a relative concept, not a self-evident fixture; it is also a very recent concept, but one which has now very dangerously come to be almost synonymous with what used to be called countryside: what on earth, literally, does the Trust think it is doing, both in owning 600,000 or so acres of the stuff and in managing it in the way that it does? Is this tenure and activity intellectually defensible, never mind justifiable? And what role, if any, does archaeology have in providing answers to theoretical and social critics and in helping hard-pressed land-agents on the ground? Correspondingly, what does all that green and brown stuff do for archaeology?

Landscape may well in the perspective of time come to be perceived as truly Britain's major world-class resource, for natives as much as visitors. All must learn to respect it for what it actually is, and that can best come from reading it. It was a novelist, Henry James, who remarked that 'It takes a great deal of history to produce a little literature'. It also takes a great deal of history to produce an historic landscape.

The author acknowledges the help of Priscilla Boniface, Professor Martin Whitby and Dr David Thackray.

References

Bracey, H. E. 1970. *People and the Countryside*, London

Countryside Commission [undated but 1994]. *Views from the Past. Historic Landscape Character in the English countryside* (Draft policy statement). Cheltenham

Fowler, P. J. (ed.) 1972. *Archaeology and the Landscape*, London

——, 1994. 'The nature of the times deceas'd', *International J. Heritage Stud.* 1 (1), 6–17

Gaze, J. 1988. *Figures in a Landscape: A History of the National Trust*, London

National Trust 1995. *Handbook for Members and Visitors 1995*, London

Newby, H. (ed.) 1995. *The Next Hundred Years*, National Trust, London

Waterson, M. 1994. *The National Trust. The First Hundred Years*, National Trust/BBC Books, London

4 A is for Archaeology

Julian H. Prideaux

Property Management is at the heart of all the Trust's activities. It is a complex and delicate balancing act calling for an ability to assimilate information, formulate objectives and assess priorities for an almost infinitely variable range of properties. These include historic houses and their estates, gardens, woodland and open country, farmland in the uplands and the lowlands, coastal cliffs and estuaries, properties in villages and in towns. All these broad categories require specialist skills in management, and are underpinned by the Trust's ability to declare its properties inalienable. All also have another factor in common; they are concerned with people. Those who manage the Trust's property are involved with local communities, farm tenants, donors and tenants of historic houses, with residents and visitors, with supporters and critics, with those who have statutory interests in the properties, local authorities, agencies and government departments, with historians and scientists and an endless list of specialists of all sorts who can and do contribute to the understanding of the properties. All have different perspectives and perceptions and all require something different from their relationships or encounters with the Trust. The Trust's purpose laid down by Parliament is the preservation, in perpetuity, and for the benefit of the nation, of land and buildings of historic interest or natural beauty. Thus place and people are inextricably linked. These are our cornerstones.

But what about archaeology? Well, it is there throughout all these activities as a reminder to the managers that an understanding of and respect for the history of the very fabric of these places is one of the keys to conservation, for without it no specification would be complete; it is at the heart of understanding the character of the properties, without which no manager would be properly equipped, and I suggest it is inherently there in the interests and desires of all those people, visitors and others with whom the Trust is involved. We may not always use the word 'archaeology', but we are constantly required to recall and promote its values; including its scientific importance, history and continuity, diversity in landscapes, and regional and local distinctiveness. What is important is that we recognize and keep what Pope called 'the genius of the place'.

In fact, it was amongst the Trust's original concerns; Sir Robert Hunter, one of the Trust's founders, took a lead in drafting and promoting new Ancient Monuments legislation to improve on the 1882 Ancient Monuments Protection Act. In 1899 the Duke of Westminster, the Earl of Rosse and Sir Robert Hunter wrote to archaeological and other learned societies urging co-operation in an attempt to influence local authorities to help in preventing 'wanton and careless disfigurement to interesting features' (Gaze 1988) – shades of our current concern with 'local distinctiveness'.

Early acquisitions by the Trust included Duffield Castle, Derbyshire (1899), Tilshead White Barrow, Wiltshire, bought by subscription in 1909, the Roman fort, *Galava*, at Ambleside, Cumbria (formerly Westmorland) on the edge of Lake Windermere, and the Castlerigg Stone Circle, Cumbria (formerly Cumberland) in 1913. The Cerne Giant, Dorset, was acquired in 1914, Chedworth Roman Villa (Gloucestershire) in 1920, Cissbury Ring was acquired by an appeal for £20,000 in 1924 and Coldrum Long Barrow in 1926. The history of events leading up to the acquisition of Stonehenge Down in 1927–8 after a major national appeal to protect the setting of Stonehenge is fascinating. The first acquisition at Hadrian's Wall was made in 1930 when J. M. Clayton gave $5\frac{1}{2}$ acres (2 ha) including Housesteads Fort. This was followed by a major bequest of 913 acres (369 ha) in 1942 by George Trevelyan of Wallington, Northumberland. The description of the Trust's prehistoric and Roman sites given by Grahame (later Sir Grahame) Clark in 1945 gives a picture of the extent of the Trust's archaeological holdings at the time of its fiftieth anniversary (Clark 1945), and it is remarkable that the Trust held such an important collection; I doubt that this and subsequent developments could ever have been predicted by our founders.

A fascinating review in *Antiquity*, by R. C. C. Clay, of the National Trust's annual report for 1928–9 (Clay 1930), is quoted by John Gaze (Gaze 1988, 86). It recalled that the number of Trust subscribers had for the first time exceeded 1,000. It goes on to state:

> The Trust is becoming the possessor of places of archaeological interest, and therefore archaeology should be more adequately represented on its councils. Furthermore, the funds accruing from the ownership of places of archaeological interest, such as the White Barrow, or the land around Stonehenge, should not be engulfed in the common fund, but should go to form the nucleus of a fund for purchasing and preserving other sites of archaeological interest. In short, there should be an archaeological branch of the Trust with its own central committee with separate sub-committees for individual sites and its own special fund.

These were, and indeed still are, worthy reminders and the Trust has gone a long way in responding to them, consciously or otherwise, but, despite Grahame Clark's review in 1945, it was over thirty years before the Trust began to appreciate again the range and quality of the archaeological sites it owned. What happened to the subject during those years? It would probably be true to say 'not a lot'.

It would perhaps be unfair to say that the Trust's attitude to archaeology during this period is truly reflected by James Lees-Milne in his diaries, but it is interesting to recall his thoughts, which do give us a clue.

On Tuesday 2 April 1942, James Lees-Milne, who described himself as 'an unqualified historic buildings secretary', and Eardley Knollys, described by Lees-Milne as 'an unqualified land agent', visited Avebury and the Long Barrow known as White Barrow, at Tilshead. The visit is recorded in Lees-Milne's *Ancestral Voices*, a diary recording all the passion and excitement of working for the Trust, then almost fifty years old and deeply immersed in the Country House Scheme. He wrote:

> I drove with Eardley straight to Avebury. He took me round the Circle. He is madly keen on Avebury and rather peevish about my lack of enthusiasm and disrespect for the ugly stones which Keiller has dragged from the ground into the light of day. I cannot approve of the proposal to destroy the old village inside the Circle. I admit that the empty sections of the Circle are impressive where the terraces have been cleared of scrub and are neatly cropped by sheep; but to remove medieval cottages and clear away all traces of habitation subsequent to the Iron Age seems to me pedantic and a distortion of historical perspective. We walked round the Manor garden. Eardley was bored by the house because it is not classical and is romantic. Today's fashionable distaste for the romantic in English country houses is as overemphasised as was the Edwardians for the classical and regular.

They lunched at the inn off cold beef and potatoes in skins and a trifle, then drove on in the company car, a baby Austin, to Tilshead.

> At Tilshead we walked to the Long Barrow. I agreed with Eardley that the scrub and untidy spruce trees ought to be eradicated in order to reveal the simple contours of the Barrow. The undulations of these tumuli along the backs of the down against the sky are their only point and beauty. To hell with Archaeology! (Lees-Milne 1942)

Despite Lees-Milne's final invective, we now have no problem in agreeing with his concern about Keiller's policy of removing the buildings from within the Circle at Avebury, a policy incidentally that had ceased by the 1960s as the importance of the historical continuity of the site and its surroundings was recognized. Whether we would agree so wholeheartedly with his statement that the aesthetics of the site, White Barrow, in the landscape is its only point is less certain, and few would agree with his positive dislike of the stones of Avebury. But it captures an attitude at a certain moment.

From the 1960s, the Trust became increasingly exposed to archaeology. Initially, this was through the work of the indomitable Miss Phyllis Ireland, its first Archaeological Correspondent, who worked tirelessly, largely as a volunteer, from 1964 to 1980, to produce lists of known sites on the properties from the records of the Ordnance Survey in Southampton. Subsequently, from the early 1970s, the Trust was influenced by the Council for British Archaeology to obtain more professional advice. This came through the CBA's Officers and its Countryside Committee, who were instrumental in establishing a committee in 1974 of Honorary Archaeological Advisers, one for each Trust Region, under the chairmanship of Professor Grimes. At last this was what R. C. C. Clay had advocated almost forty-five years earlier!

The Committee of Honorary Advisers has played a key part in the Trust's archaeological development, and has now evolved into an Archaeological Panel in line with a number of other Trust specialist panels, such as Estates, Nature Conservation, Architecture, Gardens and Arts, whose chairmen sit on and advise the Trust's Properties Committee. Nicholas Johnson is Chairman of the Panel, having taken over from Peter Fowler. Peter Fowler, one of the CBA's prime movers in awakening the Trust to its archaeological responsibilities in the 1970s is still, I am delighted to say, actively involved in the Trust's Executive Committee and Council. In addition, both the CBA and the Society of Antiquaries have active nominees on the Trust's Council, and a number of other archaeologists are involved in these Head Office Committees and on many of the Regional Committees.

Archaeology in the Trust today embraces *inter alia* industrial archaeology, cultural landscapes, the archaeology of standing buildings, garden archaeology and maritime archaeology. It also has a significant place in promoting the historic environment in the Trust's broad work on environmental issues.

I find the mechanics of all this is interesting, and worth recording briefly. Archaeology is one of the curatorial disciplines within the Chief Agent's Department, which also includes nature conservation, forestry, agriculture, gardens and designed landscapes, buildings management and fire, access and coast and countryside management and volunteers. The structure of the Department allows, and indeed promotes, an interdisciplinary, integrated approach for property advice and management, and policy development. Archaeology is also an inherent discipline in the Historic Buildings Department, where its concerns relate more particularly to artefact and structural fabric conservation.

Amongst the curatorial responsibilities within both Departments are the creation and management of data-bases containing national records of, for example, archaeological sites and structures – the Sites and Monuments Record – the catalogues of our internationally important plant collections, ecological and habitat records, environmental records, architectural historical records, house contents' inventories and conservation records. As these evolve, and many are still in their infancy, they will encourage further integration and provide reasonably comprehensive data for property management purposes. We must know what we have got.

At Regional and property levels, the staff of the Department, particularly the Advisers in each discipline – including two national Archaeological Advisers and one Research Assistant – are involved with the provision of advice on property management, and with monitoring of conservation activities against a national background. The archaeological activities are carried out by a growing network of regionally-based archaeologists who are closely involved with their regional colleagues in property management matters. Their responsibilities include the preparation of property-based archaeological surveys, including buildings surveys, and regional archaeological inventories which feed into the national Sites and Monuments Record. They are also closely involved in regional development-related project work, and in promotion and staff training. More and more they are providing direct, daily advice on archaeological elements of property management, in conjunction and co-operation with their colleagues in other disciplines. This is a particularly important development which I want to encourage to spread, so that the expertise is directly available in all Regions.

A further, recent, and significant development is the appointment of archaeologists as wardens at property level. There have been, for many years, wardens with backgrounds and experience in nature conservation, and it is exciting to see archaeologists gaining experience in the wide field of countryside conservation so that they can bring their special skills to the day-to-day management of properties. The Trust has two such appointments so far, the Property Manager, formerly Head Warden, at Avebury, covering North Wiltshire properties, and the Warden for the Upper Plym Valley, Devon, who also has a wider archaeological responsibility in the Region. Other, specific, regional archaeological appointments include the posts of curators at the Alexander Keiller Museum, Avebury, the Archaeologist/Property Manager at Chedworth Roman Villa, Gloucestershire and other regional contract, research, curation and support posts. This increasing regional recognition of the value of having archaeologists on their staff will allow the national Advisers in the Chief Agent's Department to maintain an overview, to develop liaison with other national and international bodies in order to keep abreast of professional developments, to set and monitor standards nationally and to develop policy. These functions are at the core of the Department's work.

As a result of the initiative of the Director General, over the last three years the Trust has been carrying out a Countryside Policy Review, co-ordinated and managed by David Russell, Chief Forestry Adviser. This was established to develop a contemporary interpretation of the Trust's purposes in the countryside, and to consider the best way to provide a comprehensive definition of policy which serves its aims (National Trust 1994).

This review, which drew on experience throughout the organization and involved external specialists, including the General Secretary of the Society of

Antiquaries, examined the diversity of the Trust's activities and its strengths, weaknesses and tensions. A series of Working Groups reviewed the Trust's objectives, its priorities now and for the future, its relevance and its values under a series of related headings. An Historic and Cultural Working Group chaired by the Chief Archaeological Adviser examined its attitudes to the historic environment, to continuity and change. Other subject areas included the Trust's responsibilities past and present, and attitudes to Aesthetics, Ecology and the Environment, Land Use, Social and Economic Activities and Visitor Values and Perceptions. The importance of partnerships at local and national levels was emphasized as was the need to respect community requirements and local distinctiveness.

The review was a profound and objective examination of the Trust, and its outcomes, published as a consultation report, *Linking People and Place*, will guide policy development into the future.

At the same time that we have been allowed the luxury and privilege of critical examination, the Trust has maintained its active and continuing involvement with developments in the politics of the countryside, with agricultural review and reform, on-farm diversification, rural employment, the politics and practice of the rapidly developing tourist industry, with planning issues, most notably road development schemes and sustainable transport policies, with the development of the environmental movement and with relevant social and economic policies. A thread throughout all these debates is change, the dynamics of which were considered by the Countryside Policy Review. The Trust should seek to manage change sensitively, respecting both its own special responsibilities for the preservation of its properties, the living needs of the communities and places with which it is involved, and the requirements of sustainable, cultural tourism. What is most important is that it does not fossilize communities, particularly rural communities, but provides appropriate support. In the countryside, initiatives like Whole Farm Plans will enable the Trust to work with its tenants to accommodate its conservation requirements whilst supporting the livelihood and continuity of the agricultural community, and the needs of visitors. On a wider, regional front we will pursue partnerships with other agencies to develop conservation strategies, acknowledging responsibilities, not just for our own properties, but for their wider landscape and environmental context.

With these broad and other more specific initiatives the Trust will work flexibly to respect and enhance the link between 'people and place', and the process of continuity between 'past and future'. Our responsibilities in the historic environment are fundamentally important to this. Archaeology is here to stay.

References

Clark, J. G. D. 1945. 'Ancient Sites', in *The National Trust, A Record of Fifty Years'
  Achievement* (ed. J. Lees-Milne), London, 29–41

Clay, R. C. C. 1930. 'The National Trust for Places of Historic Interest or Natural Beauty.
  Report for 1928–1929', *Antiquity* 4, 136

Gaze, J. 1988. *Figures in a Landscape: A History of the National Trust*, London

Lees-Milne, J. 1942. *Ancestral Voices*, London

National Trust 1994. *Linking People and Place*, Countryside Policy Review Consultation
  Report, London

5   National landscapes, National Parks, national figures and the National Trust

David Morgan Evans

Much of the content of John Gaze's book on the history of the National Trust, *Figures in a Landscape* (Gaze 1988), is of particular relevance to any archaeologist or historian considering the treatment of the historic landscape over the last one hundred years, especially in terms of the relationships between archaeology, architectural history and natural history.

He also considers in passing the evidence of attitudes and opinions amongst politicians and those who advise government, and the effect that these have had on legislation both in its enactment and enforcement. It is these relationships that are now examined in more detail, concentrating particularly on the period from the 1920s to the 1950s.

It is not without interest that the founders of the National Trust gave it a title with alternatives, namely the National Trust for Places of Historic Interest or, and this is emphasized, Natural Beauty. In composing this title, and in enacting the first National Trust Act in 1909, one wonders whether this was really viewed as an alternative or if and might have been as appropriate. There is, however, evidence of tensions which seem to have arisen from an uncertainty about what the Trust should be acquiring.

In the early days of the National Trust 'historic interest' was expressed by acquisitions of houses such as the Alfriston Clergy House, in 1896; Eashing Bridges over the River Wey in Surrey, in 1901, said to date from the time of King John; and the earliest acquisition of a proper 'ancient monument', White Barrow, near Tilshead in Wiltshire, in 1909, purchased with 2.75 acres for £60. 'Natural Beauty' was represented by Toy's Hill near Brasted, Kent, acquired in 1898 – a gift which formed 'the first realisation of the idea, suggested by the Trust, that memorials should sometimes take the form of beautiful scenery' (National Trust 1923, 14) – Derwentwater, the Brandelhow Park Estate and the summit of Kymin Hill at Monmouth, both purchased in 1902. But even from the earliest years of the Trust certain acquisitions lay uncomfortably between these two classes. Wicken Fen, acquired in 1899, was part purchase and part donation, but was important as 'almost the last remnant of the primeval fenland of East Anglia' and 'is of special interest to entomologists and botanists, on account of the rare insects and plants found there' (National Trust 1923, 14). Burwell Fen in Cambridgeshire was acquired in 1907 and Blakeney Point was presented to the Trust on condition that the natural flora and fauna should be preserved. While there is every reason for an organization to be flexible, there did seem to be some confusion over exact objectives which resulted in the inter-war years in the Trust handing over the care and management of many of its ancient monuments to the government, in the form of the guardianship of the Ministry of Works.

John Gaze recognized these problems and tensions when he referred 'to the confusion in the collective mind of the Trust between its romantic, aesthetic and scientific objectives' (Gaze 1988, 85). The tensions which are inherent in the title of the National Trust perhaps did not become a major issue because of the very small size of the Trust membership and the apparent absence of 'single-issue factions'. It is worth recalling that in 1924, the year that Hatfield Forest was acquired, there were only some 630 members and 106 properties. But in 1930 the chairman of the executive committee, John Bailey, while reporting a growth in membership to 1,700, lamented the fact that the 'younger' National Art Collections Fund had 10,000 members and 'precious as are Titians and Rembrandts, the face and the History of England are more precious still' (Bailey 1930). John Bailey would have been pleased to know that the National Arts Collection Fund had about 27,000 members in 1991 to compare with the 2 million that the Trust has today.

In 1929 G. M. Trevelyan wrote his seminal essay 'Must England's Beauty Perish?' with a sub-title, 'A Plea on Behalf of the National Trust' (Gaze 1988, 48). His assessment of landscape beauty could well have formed part of the Department of the Environment Policy Planning Guidance Note Number 15 paragraph 6.40, 'Identifying the Historic Environment' – referring to early nineteenth-century England Trevelyan wrote:

> It was all good to look at, not least the 'improvements' of the eighteenth century, the thatched and gabled houses, the cornfields, hedges, lanes, stone bridges, new plantations of oak and beech all harmonized well together, and harmonized with the wilder parts of the nature in which they were set, the still remaining wrecks of the old English forest, thicket, moorland and marsh. (Gaze 1988, 56)

We are fortunate that this integrated approach to what can be called our 'historic environment' was an implicit part of the National Trust philosophy of preservation in the inter-war years – a time of great importance for archaeological legislation. This was promulgated in the Ancient Monuments Act of 1931 and was the first major change since the late nineteenth century, remaining as the main archaeological legislation until the 1979 Ancient Monuments and Archaeological Areas Act. The 1931 Act has to be viewed together with other concerns which arose from changes in the countryside.

In his book, John Gaze has painted the broad picture of the unregulated change and development of the countryside in the 1920s and the reactions this engendered, with events such as the conference in February 1926 when Lord Crawford, President of the Society of Antiquaries (also an honorary member of the Trust, having given over £100) eventually also became President of the newly founded Council for the Preservation of Rural England, and so on (Gaze 1988, 6off). Two particular themes stand out, the moves towards National Parks and the battle for Stonehenge.

In September 1929, Ramsay MacDonald appointed:

> a Committee to consider and report if it is desirable and feasible to establish one or more national parks in Great Britain with a view to the preservation of natural characteristics including flora and fauna, and to the improvement of recreational facilities for people; and to advise generally an in particular as to the areas, if any, that are most suitable for the purpose. (HMSO 1931, 3)

The Right Hon. Christopher Addison was appointed chairman. None of the committee members appears to have been a member of the National Trust although one, Mr Frederic Raby, was a Fellow of the Society of Antiquaries. He also happened to be a senior official in the Office of Works and a considerable scholar in his own right (*Who was Who* 1972, 925).

The National Trust gave evidence to the committee (HMSO 1931, 52–5). In its report this evidence was singled out in the general survey (paragraph 6, p.5): 'in particular, the National Trust formulated proposals for the preservation of areas "large enough for the nation to enjoy and important enough to justify the intervention of the State"'. The National Trust was also cited when it came to considering the perceived problem of the break-up of landed estates under the pressure of taxation. In addition, its evidence referred in particular to the loss of parks and hedgerows and unwelcome development – 'promiscuous advertisements disfigure our fields and roadsides and even disgrace some of the most historic and beautiful spots in the country'.

The evidence pointed out the special position of the Trust, as its properties provided almost the only, and certainly the most numerous and recent, illustrations of what may be called National Parks. The threat to the 'ordinary' country of the most characteristic part of England was emphasized rather than that to the great moorland districts. The motor car with the construction of new roads was a major cause of damage and 'the nation itself, which through its chief spokesmen, is always deploring these irremediable losses, is itself by its public action, one of their chief causes'. The National Trust also stated that preservation was the primary need; access, however important, only comes second.

In defining National Parks there was also the need to allow for smaller scale areas with variety to contrast with the uncultivated areas of mountain and moor.

The Trust urged the provision of adequate sums for purchase and maintenance and a system of local management such as they practised. They indicated their willingness to place their experience at the disposal of the government. It is interesting to find the Manchester and District Joint Town Planning Advisory Committee suggesting the National Trust as the central controlling body for National Parks (HMSO 1931, 83). It is tempting to consider the possibility that if there had not been a national financial crisis at this time the role of the National Trust might have become much larger and the concept of National Parks not so monolithic.

This report is also of interest to archaeologists for the written evidence given by Dr Cyril Fox and O. G. S. Crawford, amongst others. Fox urged the choice of Snowdonia and Pembrokeshire as National Parks, pointing out the continuity of history that could be found in those areas. He urged that any governing body should include at least one geologist, botanist, zoologist and archaeologist (HMSO 1931, 76). Crawford, along with Cecil Curwen, proposed a scheme for the preservation of the South Downs and part of Hampshire. In this evidence the value of the archaeology, flora and wild birds was stressed (HMSO 1931, 77ff).

Appendix III of the report (pp. 104–7) lists areas suggested as National Parks. The National Trust supported the Norfolk Broads, the South Downs, Dartmoor, the Cornwall and Devon coastline, the Peak District, the Malvern Hills, the Lake District, Snowdonia, the Brecon Beacons and the Black Mountains. Crawford supported the South Downs, Dartmoor and, on his own, the Marlborough Downs. One of Crawford's Editorial Notes in *Antiquity* compiled near the time he must have been preparing his evidence summarizes his views:

> In most instances nothing short of the purchase of land is of the slightest use, although an intelligent application of the Town-planning Act may suffice. The need is really urgent; for with the approaching electrification of Southern England, the coniferous activities of the Woods and Forests Department and of private planters, the demands of the Services for land for aerodromes and manoeuvres, the spread of bungaloid eruptions, and the threat of arterial roads and ribbon-development – with all these terrors imminent, it is unlikely that any open country or downland will be left in Southern England in a hundred years' time. Salisbury Plain is already ruined; the Sussex Downs are threatened. Dorset and Dartmoor, however, survive, and the Cotswolds, though less prolific of prehistoric sites, are still entirely agricultural and unspoilt. (Crawford 1929, 3)

The use of the words such as 'bungaloid eruptions' and 'arterial roads' introduces us to another figure – Lord Curzon, that 'most superior person' who has not had a good press but who did a great deal for conservation in this country and in India, as John Gaze rightly recognizes (Gaze 1988, 88ff). He was also responsible for introducing the concept of the 'octopus', the spread of roads and ribbon development whose frustration formed one of the aims of the constitution of the Ferguson Gang, whose activities are summarized by John Gaze (Gaze 1988, 110). Of course, these days we do not so much have arterial roads and ribbon development but by-passes and in-fill.

To return to the Addison report. Due to a financial crisis, seen now as probably more perceived than real, the outcome of the report was negative; no action, no legislation. However, the work that had been started was sustained and emerged again, in official terms, during and just after the Second World War. The next report of significance resulted from a committee set up by Lord Reith on Land Utilisation in Rural Areas (HMSO 1942). This is commonly known as the Scott report after the chairman, the Right Hon. Lord Justice Scott. Familiar names on the Scott committee included Dudley Stamp, the geographer, and Lord Radnor, Lord Lieutenant for Wiltshire. In examining the future of the countryside the committee considered, amongst various factors, 'the preservation of amenities'. 'Amenities' were defined in the introduction to the report by lines from H. G. Wells and G. M. Trevelyan the flavour of which has already been given above.

The body of the final report contained a detailed account of the historical development of the British countryside which bears the mark of Dudley Stamp. No archaeologist appears to have given evidence but the National Trust was represented by D. M. Matheson, Secretary of the Trust from 1934 to 1945. He is described in Gaze's book as sensitive, shy and often ill, and he had taken the job as being less stressful than his previous one (Gaze 1988, 98). The recommendations of this committee (paragraph 160, p. 47) included:

> the preservation of amenities – we regard the countryside as the heritage of the whole nation ... the citizens of this country are the custodians of [this] heritage ... a duty incumbent upon the nation to take proper care of that which it ... holds in trust .... In large parts the beauties of Britain are man-made ... the countryside cannot be preserved ... it must be farmed if it is to retain those features which give it distinctive charm and character. We regard this principle as of fundamental importance. This principle is recognised in the management of the properties of the National Trust.

This is a clear indication of the way that the Trust has, by its example, influenced national thinking. The words and concepts of this report are still current, even if unacknowledged, and can be found in use today. Due to wartime conditions nothing practical resulted, but 1945 saw the Dower report on National Parks (HMSO 1945). John Dower, as it happened, was married to Pauline, the niece of Trevelyan (Gaze 1988, 119) and had been involved, in 1936, with the detailed work which led to the centre of the Lake District being freed from the threat of forestry. The Dower report was not necessarily helpful to the National Trust. In its conclusions (paragraph 90, p.54) it proposed a statutory authority for the National

Parks on the grounds that 'keen and useful as they have been and will be the unofficial advice and activities of . . . the National Trust is not enough'. Dower examined the role of ancient monuments and National Parks in which he saw no need for the transfer of the responsibilities of the Ministry of Works to the National Park authority. He also looked at a role for the National Trust: 'it should be recognised that the acquisition by the Trust of further properties in National Park areas, particularly by means of public appeals, will be less likely to occur on any large scale once a National Park policy has been adopted' (HMSO 1945, 49). In effect he saw the National Trust withdrawing from National Parks. Important though Dower was in setting up the National Parks and Countryside Commission, there are some doubts about his concepts and influence especially in his view of the relationships between 'natural beauty' and historical human activity in the United Kingdom, or even the Old World as compared to the New, given his appreciation of American national parks (HMSO 1945, 6). The Dower report gave rise directly and indirectly to two further reports both coming out in the summer of 1947.

The first of these was that of the National Parks Committee (HMSO 1947a). The National Trust gave written and oral evidence, Lord Esher, chairman, Mr George Mallaby, briefly on secondment from the Civil Service, secretary, and Mr Hubert Smith, chief agent, attending. Something of the approach by the National Trust can be seen in one of the essays in the volume produced in 1945 to celebrate the first fifty years of the Trust (Lees-Milne 1945). In the first essay entitled 'National Trust and National Parks', Ivor Brown starts with the words, 'One sentence, whose author, I must confess, I cannot remember, has summed up the qualities and duties of two epochs with a brevity and acumen beyond criticism. It was the function of the nineteenth century to liberate: it will be the function of the twentieth to control'. The Trust barely receives a mention in the report, although ancient monuments have two paragraphs which at least acknowledge the need to protect their surroundings (HMSO 1947a, 39). This report did result in administrative and legislative action being taken and is the foundation of our present National Parks and Countryside Commission system.

In terms of ideas, and lost opportunities, the more important report was that on the Conservation of Nature in England and Wales (HMSO 1947b). No archaeologist was on this committee although the names of Dr J. S. Huxley and Professor A. G. Tansley will be familiar to some. The National Trust gave evidence, but the report does not record who by and the only real reference to the Trust is that it already has nature reserves which could be counted in the general number. The name which is of significance amongst those acknowledged as helping the committee is that of O. G. S. Crawford. The influence of his views can be seen in the report which refers twice to the usefulness of aerial photography (HMSO 1947b, 153, 253), makes the bold suggestion that in the selection of sites of special scientific interest those other than strictly biological ones could be considered, 'such as archaeological sites'. The report, in its most archaeologically significant paragraphs, on pages 30 to 32, states:

> (paragraph) 86 Mention has already been made ... of the biological and economic importance of studying flora and fauna of sites that have at varying times been subjected to varying degrees of disturbance by man. This interest is not confined to recent or even historic actions, but stretches right back into prehistoric times and so joins with the interests of the archaeologist. In prehistoric times, it becomes impossible to draw any sharp line of demarcation. Some practical division can ... be made ... constructions and sites ... do not lie within the terms of reference to the ... Committee ... but in those areas of natural or modified soil which owe their present condition to prehistoric or early human activity there is often ... a very close connection between their archaeological and biological interest.

> (paragraph) 87 This connection is well illustrated in the chalk regions of southern and eastern England [typical earthworks are then described] bounded by lynchets, ploughed in the Iron Age and in the Romano-British period, and now covered with the chalk grassland vegetation traditionally used as rough grazing. These sites present special habitats in the general chalk grassland .... For this reason the concern of archaeologists and prehistorians for the preservation of these sites is shared by naturalists and ecologists, and areas specially rich in such earthworks could with great advantage be treated as reserves or conservation areas. The continuous turf covering the Neolithic pits at Maiden Castle in Dorset, for instance, was probably established in the Bronze Age, and the charcoals found at different levels throw light on the vegetation of the neighbourhood at different times, so that both archaeological and botanical evidence, coupled with the evidence to be derived from the sub-fossil remains of snails and other animals, contribute to the elucidation of human biological and climatic prehistory. Moreover, the archaeological dating of certain sets of conditions throws much light on wider problems of plant and animal distributions. Thus, these different lines of research interlock, and the preservation of the evidence is vital to both sciences.

In paragraph 88 the agencies which destroy sites, including building, ploughing, tree-planting and 'neglect resulting in overgrowth by self-sown bushes and trees' are considered.

> The first three could be excluded by reservation or conservation, but without scientific management the last danger remains and is, for example, capable of destroying completely the delicate outlines of disc-barrows while at the same time radically altering the soil and vegetation. Where earthworks are scheduled as 'ancient monuments' ... it is understood that the Ministry of Works has no power to interfere if the landowners take no action to clear the bushes.

In paragraph 89 the importance of peat for the archaeologist as well as the biologist is remarked on.

> (paragraph) 90. In making our selections for reservation and conservation we have borne these biological values in mind, but we have not been able to cover a sufficiently wide field. There are a great many sites which, though of value to the biologist, may be of even greater importance to the archaeologist. Though the Ministry of Works has fairly wide powers, we are not satisfied that these conjoint interests are sufficiently met. We understand that the law at present permits the scheduling of any area which can be shown to have a 'work' upon it, and that 'Celtic fields' could thus be scheduled as ancient monuments, but in fact most of them are not. We are neither directed nor qualified to consider archaeological values; but, as we have tried to show, the interests with which we are concerned are closely involved, and we should like to see applied to archaeology principles of reservation and conservation similar to those we are seeking to apply to our own sciences. We therefore strongly recommend that a special committee fully competent to advise on those aspects should be set up without delay; and meanwhile, that in any proposed legislation provision should be made to include archaeological features in the general conservation machinery. We therefore strongly recommend that a special committee fully competent to advise on those aspects should be set up without delay; and meanwhile, that in any proposed legislation provision should be made to include archaeological features on the general conservation and planning machinery.

This section of the report contains much that it still very relevant today. The integration of biological and archaeological matters is of the first order and compares very favourably with its comparative absence in the National Parks report. However, the report does make depressing reading when one considers the years of positive conservation which might have been gained if the recommendations had been acted on. The people who did not appreciate and act upon them must, in history, bear a heavy burden for wasted opportunities. We are only now coming somewhere near this approach with measures such as the Department of the Environment Policy Planning Guidance Note 15 and the *Natural Heritage* (Scotland) Act 1991.

The second theme is the preservation of Stonehenge in the 1920s and 1930s from the 'octopus' and to look at some of the people who figured in the matter. Having mentioned the Ferguson Gang above it is worth remembering their resolution 'that England is Stonehenge and not Whitehall' (Gaze 1988, 111). The National Trust's involvement in the battle during the years 1927 to 1929 to save the Stones from development is described by John Gaze (Gaze 1988, 81ff), but some additions can be made to the account. Crawford in Antiquity editorials, sums it up:

The latest area threatened (from progressive disfiguration) is the immediate area
of Stonehenge. It might seem incredible that it should have been seriously suggested
to erect a row of bungalows in the Avenue field immediately opposite the old stones,
but a tea-shop, complete with flags, has already been built there, and plans are
actually in existence for extending waterpipes and drains to the Amesbury road . . .
it is proposed to buy out the owners of the land, vesting it in the safe-keeping of
the National Trust. (Crawford 1927, 259)

   the first stage of the Stonehenge campaign has been completed and the land
on which the aerodrome stands has been acquired by the National Trust . . . that
the threat was no imaginary one is shown by the facts . . . had not one of the options
been secured when it was . . . the land would have been acquired for a factory!
(Crawford 1927, 386)

Both editorials were accompanied by an appeal for funds to be sent to the National
Trust. In its annual report for 1927–8 the Council writes 'perhaps one of the most
important movements with which the Trust has been connected was launched
. . . to purchase the land adjoining Stonehenge . . . the solitude of Stonehenge
should be restored' (National Trust 1928, 12). The object was to clear all the
existing developments and to prevent future encroachment.

   The aerodrome was cleared but then the Ministry of Works was given land
for a car park, and it was not without adverse comment that the National Trust
tried to keep the tea-room but were stopped by the Ministry of Works and so
on (Chippindale 1985, 193ff). Any National Trust member should remember why
and for what purpose this land was purchased by popular appeal.

   The human figures in this 1920s Stonehenge landscape are worth consideration, especially when it is remembered that the letters which were involved in
the appeal for funds were signed by the then Prime Minister, Stanley Baldwin
and the leader of the opposition, Ramsay Macdonald. The President of the Society
of Antiquaries, Lord Crawford and Lord Grey of Falloden, Vice-President of the
National Trust, also signed. What is more, Baldwin and Macdonald were Honorary
Vice-Presidents of the Trust. While it is perhaps still fashionable to deride Baldwin
as an appeaser, and Macdonald as a traitor to the labour movement, it is also
quite clear that they had a profound sympathy with the countryside and its past
and were prepared to give their personal support. Some of the details of this
interest can be found elsewhere (Elton 1939; Jenkins 1987).

   In conclusion, in its Centenary Year the National Trust can be proud of the
role that it has played in the cause of conservation and the people that it has
attracted to that cause. It has set high standards which it will have to fight hard
to maintain.

References

Bailey, J. 1930. Appeal letter included with the National Trust Report of Council, 1929–1930

Chippindale, C. 1985. *Stonehenge Complete*, London

Crawford, O.G.S. 1927. *Antiquity* I

——, 1929. *Antiquity* III

Elton, Lord 1939. *The Life of James Ramsay Macdonald*, London

Gaze, J. 1988. *Figures in a Landscape: A History of the National Trust*, London

HMSO 1931. *Report of the National Parks Committee*, Cmd. 3851, London

HMSO 1942. *Report of the Committee on Land Committee on Land Utilization in Rural Areas*, Cmd. 6378, London

HMSO 1945. *National Parks in England and Wales*, Cmd. 6628, London.

HMSO 1947a. *Report of the National Parks Committee (England and Wales)*, Cmd. 7121, London

HMSO 1947b. *Conservation of Nature in England and Wales*, Cmd. 7122, London

Jenkins, R. 1987. *Baldwin*, London

Lees-Milne, J. (ed.) 1945. *The National Trust: A Record of Fifty Years' Achievement*, London

National Trust 1923. *Report of Council, 1922–1923*, London

——, 1928. *Report of Council, 1927–1928*, London

Who was Who 1972. Volume VI, 1961–1971, London

6   Ancient landscapes and the modern public

Richard Bradley

A recent paper by Peter Fowler (1995) raises an interesting question. Why has archaeological writing on the countryside had so little impact? Why have archaeologists failed to communicate with the public when biologists and natural historians have done this so successfully? I would like to put forward my own answer to this question. It has less to do with the shortcomings of archaeological writing than it does with the nature of the discipline itself. I shall contend that the public's perception of the landscape has something in common with the concerns of people in the past. Unfortunately, we cannot always say the same about our own research.

I begin with a question of my own. Do archaeologists choose their field projects, or do those projects choose them? I am not talking about the day to day demands of public archaeology, but about the more delicate processes by which research projects are formulated. Why are certain areas of England studied rather than others? Why are particular fieldworkers driven to conduct one project after another in the same part of the country? More often than not, this has little to do with access to suitable funding. There is another issue at stake.

I could quote many examples of this identification between an archaeologist and one particular region. There is the work of George Jobey in Northumberland, Francis Pryor's research in the Fenland or Barry Cunliffe's involvement with the archaeology of the Hampshire chalk. We recognize such allegiances in others, and we may see them in our own work. What is so striking is that they are very rarely expressed in the archaeological literature. Of course there are exceptions. Stuart Piggott devoted much of his career to the archaeology of the Wessex landscape, and it figures in his poetry. As he has admitted in print (Piggott 1983), he did not feel at ease with the highland landscapes in which he worked.

Perhaps we are so reluctant to talk about our identification with particular places because it detracts from our credentials as scholars. I remember talking to an environmental scientist who had worked with a well-known archaeologist in a study of an important prehistoric landscape. Their project was successful and productive and yet, he told me, he felt that his collaborator was motivated by the simple desire to 'be there'. That experience of participating in a landscape is what we so rarely convey to our readers. The demands of academic writing set us on another course and we suppress our subjective response in favour of description and documentation. That is not to deny the importance of accurate analysis, but the absence of any personal equation is what makes such writing so dull. The great merit of books like Andrew Fleming's account of the Dartmoor reaves (Fleming 1988) is that that they convey the personality of the landscapes that they study.

I chose the term 'personality' advisedly, for it evokes the influence of human geography on archaeological fieldwork. There have been numerous exchanges between archaeologists and geographers since Cyril Fox published *The Personality of Britain* in 1932, but in the course of these encounters two things seem to have happened (Goudie 1987). The notion that particular landscapes possess a distinctive personality eventually went out of favour, and for a decade or so we were more likely to talk the language of the 'New Geography' with its consciously scientific vocabulary of resources, energy expenditure and the friction of distance. The second feature of these exchanges is that the relationship was almost always one-sided, so that archaeologists were essentially consumers of other people's ideas. During the crucial period in which unfamiliar methods were adopted, they went of fashion with those who had developed them in the first place.

Our current predicament is typical of that process. I find this particularly ironic since it results from a theoretical stance that has already lost its attraction outside archaeology. Modern geography pays more attention to the ways in which people respond to different places and landscapes. The title of another book is very revealing here: Tuan's *Space and Place: The Perspective of Experience*, published in 1977. That is why the glossary of *Interpreting Archaeology*, the collection in which Peter Fowler's essay is published, defines landscape as 'a social construction of space' and refers to it as an amalgam of 'practices, meanings, attitudes [and] values' (Hodder *et al.* 1995, 239). There is no mention of resources here, no talk of food production. A change is taking place in archaeological theory which could bring it into line with the public's response to the countryside.

If recent thinking in geography emphasizes the experience of living in a particular landscape, its influence on archaeology has been confined to a small number of academics. Field archaeologists have taken a different path. The traditional approach to the landscape is epitomized by the work of the Royal Commissions and includes some of the most accomplished research ever carried out in Britain. Although the scope of this work has been changing, its basic features remain the same: the accurate identification, mapping and analysis of the archaeological remains visible on the surface, from fortifications and buildings to field systems and land divisions. The analytical approach is basically the same whether they are dealing with the earthworks of ceremonial monuments or those of ornamental gardens. In this sense ancient landscapes represent the sum total of the visible remains in any one area, refined by a detailed appreciation of their chronological development and their relationships with one another.

There are two problems with this approach. First, it favours certain kinds of archaeology at the expense of others. It is an archaeology in which the emphasis is on what is fixed: on well-established settlements and on lasting boundaries in the landscape. Thus my own work in the Salisbury Plain Military Training Area was an attempt to reconstruct the territorial organization of the early first millennium BC (Bradley *et al.* 1994), but before that time there was little to discuss apart from a poorly understood distribution of round barrows. Even if we were to map the occurrence of surface artefacts, as the Stonehenge Environs Project did so effectively (Richards 1990), we would still be confronted with a problem. Human activity did not seem to form itself into sites as we might have expected, and there can be little obvious relationship between the distribution of portable artefacts and the positions of identifiable earthwork monuments like henges. One reason for this problem is that we are better equipped to study sedentary communities than those that practised a more mobile occupation of the landscape.

Our second problem is that we have tended to divide the ancient landscape into foreground and background, so that the character of the terrain only features in our work when it seems to account for the location of archaeological material. By that stage it has been reduced to a distribution of resources. This was the premise of site catchment analysis in the 1970s, and it continues to direct much of our thinking even now. Thus the distribution of monuments may be explained by plotting them on soil maps, whilst an equally strong relationship with natural landforms might go unobserved. In the Stonehenge Environs Project, for example, the distribution of flint artefacts is far more closely related to the topography of King Barrow Ridge than it is to the agricultural potential of this particular area (Richards 1990).

It may be that our approach has been altogether too rigid, for in fact the very notion of landscape is a peculiarly modern one (Cosgrove 1984). This is a word that has changed its meaning (Olwig 1993). It originally indicated a territorial division: a piece of ground that had been cleared for agriculture and which belonged to a particular group of people. From the seventeenth century onwards it came to indicate an area of land as it appeared to an outside observer, and this change of meaning is encapsulated by the genre of landscape painting. That is the perspective that we adopt today. It is the perspective of an onlooker, not that of a participant. As I said at the start of this paper, that is often misleading, for archaeologists are not the dispassionate observers that they claim to be. Often they are drawn to particular landscapes in a more intuitive way than they might care to admit.

At that level the landscape is much more than a distribution of archaeological evidence. It is an entire network of paths and places: a system of natural landforms that change their configuration according to the position of the viewer. As Tilley has shown, the archaeologist's more limited perspective is rare outside Western society (1994, chapter 2). The papers in a recent volume called *Sacred Sites, Sacred Places* (Carmichael *et al.* 1994) only emphasize his point. These studies come from many different parts of the world, but very often it is the natural features of the terrain that hold the greatest significance: trees, streams, lakes, mountains, cliffs, outcrops, caves, clearings and rock fissures.

It would be easy to object that such a landscape is the landscape of mobile communities, and quite different from the perspective of settled farmers, but this is not quite true. The easiest illustration of my point is to consider English place-names, for virtually all of these must date from a time when the landscape was already occupied by permanent settlements. Professor Kenneth Cameron has published a list of the 160 most common elements among these names, some of which exist in different versions (1977, 212–28). I find it very revealing that fewer than a third refer to features that we would think of as parts of the archaeological landscape, yet the very fact they were so often given names must mean that they had a particular significance. They include names for hills, valleys, rocks, streams, paths and forests. These are precisely the elements that are missing from the literature of field archaeology. Worse still, they are features of the terrain that receive no legal protection on specifically archaeological grounds. This is because they are not antiquities and were not necessarily modified by human endeavour.

That is a crippling limitation, for it suggests that some of the features which are most apparent to the modern visitor can play little part in public archaeology. Worse still, the archaeologists' emphasis on sites and monuments means that, all unwitting, they are caught up in this process, with the result that these preoccupations stand between them and some of the landscapes that they study. Those ancient landscapes that survive intact do so because our public have come to terms with the features whose significance we as archaeologists seem so reluctant to research. It is their response that has given the ancient landscape some measure of security, through the formation of the National Trust and the creation of National Parks.

Before I suggest a way forward, let me summarize what I have said so far. I have made two points. Archaeologists discount their personal reactions to the landscape even as human geographers are making them their object of study. At the same time, those archaeologists may be working with a concept of landscape which is far too limited. They do so because to break with tradition would seem subjective and lacking in scholarly method. As a result of these inhibitions they find it difficult to communicate with the general public.

How can archaeologists expand their horizons? How can they come to terms with the features of the unaltered topography, and how are they to consider the relationship between human activities and the natural terrain without losing their capacity for reasoned argument? I do not suggest that they give up what have been very real advances in methods of analysis and recording. Rather, I would advocate a broadening in the scope of landscape archaeology until it comes closer to the concerns of the people who visit those areas today.

What is it that animates the visitor's response to different places? And how can we be sure that this is any more than a reflection of modern aesthetics? I would suggest that two elements are particularly important here. One is the idea of a high place with a view that overlooks the surrounding area. The other is the simple principle of following a path through the landscape. As we do so, the view changes all the time. It may be no coincidence that these two features seem to be the main elements by which mobile people define their worlds (Ingold 1986).

Both those elements are present in the recent work of Christopher Tilley. He has argued that in parts of Sweden neolithic passage graves could be laid out to imitate features of the natural landscape (Tilley 1993). In south-west Wales megalithic tombs were sometimes built beside rock outcrops, along paths whose significance was already established during the mesolithic period (Tilley 1994, chapter 3). The long mounds of the Black Mountains, on the other hand, drew attention to other components of the landscape and were often orientated on prominent hills (*ibid.*, chapter 4). The views from and between all these monuments were of particular significance.

Such ideas are exciting, but they raise a potential problem. How can archaeology come to grips with such intangible elements? Is there any way of assessing these suggestions apart from repeating the exercise on the ground? I believe that this can be done by following a fairly stringent methodology, by which our intuitive perceptions of place are measured against a control sample. By that means we can police our imaginations without losing confidence altogether. We can also provide the evidence by which other people can check our findings.

My own experience of venturing into this rather difficult terrain arises from a project that I conducted with Mark Edmonds on a National Trust property in the Lake District. We were studying the important series of quarries based on Great Langdale, which produced many of the stone axes used during the neolithic period. By employing entirely orthodox methods – technological analysis of the debitage, excavation and radiocarbon dating – we came to the conclusion that the character of stoneworking may have changed over time and that the most intensive activity took place in the most dangerous and remote areas: amongst the narrow ledges on the south face of Pike o' Stickle (Bradley and Edmonds 1993, chapters 4–6). The form of the mountain is most distinctive. It can be identified from many miles away, and the sites of the quarries command an enormous view. We were already aware that other exposures of suitable rock had been worked on a smaller scale, in those cases in which they had been used at all. We also knew that some of the products of the Cumbrian quarries had been employed in very specialized transactions far away from their source. Were we entitled to suggest that part of their importance was due to the spectacular locations in which they were made?

It was not difficult to make this suggestion, for some of the very same features attract thousands of visitors to the mountain every year, but was there any way in which we could develop this subjective impression? The alternative was to suggest that the intensity with which stoneworking was undertaken in different locations reflected subtle differences in the quality of the rock and its suitability for making tools. This could be checked by the methods of materials science, which allowed us to assess the strength of different samples of the stone and their response to stress (Bradley *et al.* 1992). As a result we could compare them on a numerical scale. If the most suitable sources were those with most evidence of exploitation our more ambitious hypothesis could be abandoned. But this is not what happened. Although the rock on Pike o' Stickle was of high quality, we found that sources of rather poorer stone had been exploited just as intensively. Rock with virtually the same physical properties had been under-used, despite the fact that a stone source of this kind had to be crossed in order to reach the remote locations where more of the raw material was worked.

This study suggested that the distribution of stone quarries was not entirely determined by the physical characteristics of the rock. Could that suggestion be taken any further? Was there indeed a preference for using inaccessible and remote locations? My student, Aaron Watson, has been investigating this question, and I am grateful to him for allowing me to summarize his results. If such claims were to be substantiated, we would need to know that such patterns could not have happened by chance. He examined the entire outcrop which was used for making axes, recording its characteristic topography every 500m. Fortunately, these samples included an almost equal number of locations with and without evidence of prehistoric stoneworking. This meant that he could compare the two groups directly. The results of this exercise show that the sites that were used in the neolithic were not located for easy access. They are higher than those in the control sample and the ground below these sites is steeper than it is elsewhere. There is only a 10 per cent probability that these differences could have arisen by chance.

The results of this exercise align the modern visitor's reaction to the Langdale Fells with the archaeologist's. Although the location of axe sources was influenced by practical considerations, those were by no means paramount. The striking form of the mountain, the dangerous and remote position of the quarries, the immense views that they commanded over the lower ground: all these seem to have influenced prehistoric attitudes to the landscape. I have tried to show how such features can be recovered by disciplined analysis.

The importance of paths is more difficult to determine, but it can be approached obliquely, provided the analysis is undertaken following an equally disciplined procedure. In this case my example is not on National Trust land. In fact it lies just outside the Northumberland National Park.

For the last few years I have been conducting a study of prehistoric rock art in the British Isles, and this work led me to visit a large group of carvings on the edge of the Fell Sandstone near Rothbury. The carved rocks seemed to cluster on either side of a valley leading from the coastal plain to the higher ground. That route provides easy access between the two areas and that is why it is followed by a Roman road and by its modern successor. The rock carvings seemed to command views along this axis, but was their topographical setting of any significance?

In this case we searched the entire area on a 100m grid, recording the extent of visibility from the nearest exposed rock to the points where the grid lines intersected. We adopted the same procedure with all the carvings. This allowed us to compare the views from the petroglyphs with those from a control sample of uncarved rocks. Again the two groups showed a significant contrast. Within 500m both commanded very similar views, but as the distance increased it became apparent that the views from the carved rocks were wider than those in the other sample. With the most distant views, those extending for more than 5km (3 miles), there was only a 1 per cent probability that this difference could have arisen by chance. We also studied the directions of the views in both the samples, and this highlighted an equally striking contrast. Most of the rocks in the control sample commanded a view in only one direction, but those with any decoration overlooked both axes of the valley: they were directed towards the coastal plain to the south and into the Cheviots to the north (Bradley *et al.* 1993).

Elsewhere in Northumberland there are indications that the main sites with carved rocks were intervisible. This echoes some of the results of Tilley's fieldwork in Wales, but how can we be sure that such links were really significant? The sites in Northumberland seem to be ranged along a major route leading towards the monuments in the Milfield Basin, and the pattern of connections between them is very striking indeed. Each major concentration of carvings commands a view towards its neighbour, so that anyone visiting those sites would be likely to encounter them in a prescribed sequence. As each new complex was visited, the view over the landscape would have changed.

In this case my original idea came from looking at contour maps, but it has now been checked on the ground by another Reading student, Ruth Saunders, who has kindly allowed me to summarize her results. She also visited an equal number of locations in the same area selected by random sampling and has recorded any visual links between these places. They show far fewer connections than the sites with rock carvings, and in this case there is no suggestion that these views followed a common axis across the landscape. What started as an intuitive interpretation of features of the local topography is strengthened by comparison with a control sample.

Both these examples make the same point. We have used very little of the landscape in our studies, but it is possible to extend the scope of archaeological fieldwork without losing sight of the need for disciplined procedures. At one level such analyses may provide some novel insights into topics which we have not considered before. They may allow us to incorporate the features of the natural terrain into our research in a way that gives them equal status with sites and monuments. That poses worrying problems for the management of ancient landscapes. But a second result of this approach is to suggest that we can move outside the rather narrow framework in which landscape archaeology is conducted. If we can do so, then we may find that we have more common ground with members of the public. It is a singular irony that prehistorians should have found it so difficult to think about the importance of landmarks, paths and viewpoints when it is those elements that lead so many people to visit the countryside today.

References

Bradley, R. and Edmonds, M. 1993. *Interpreting the Axe Trade*, Cambridge

Bradley, R., Entwistle, R. and Raymond, F. 1994. *Prehistoric Land Divisions on Salisbury Plain*, English Heritage Archaeol. Rep. 2, London

Bradley, R., Harding, J., Mathews, M. and Rippon, S. 1993. 'A field method for investigating the distribution of rock art', *Oxford Journal of Archaeology* 12, 129–43

Bradley, R., Meredith, P., Smith, J. and Edmonds, M. 1992. 'Rock physics and the Neolithic axe trade in Great Britain', *Archaeometry* 34.2, 223–33

Cameron, K. 1977. *English Place Names*, 3rd edn, London

Carmichael, D., Hubert, J., Reeves, B. and Schance, A. (eds) 1994. *Sacred Sites, Sacred Places*, London

Cosgrove, D. 1984. *Social Formation and Symbolic Landscape*, London

Fleming, A. 1988. *The Dartmoor Reaves*, London

Fowler, P. 1995. 'Writing on the countryside' in *Interpreting Archaeology* (ed. I. Hodder, M. Shanks, A. Alexandri, V. Buchli, J. Carman, J. Last and G. Lucas), 199–209, London

Fox, C. 1932. *The Personality of Britain*, Cardiff

Goudie, A. 1987. 'Geography and archaeology: the growth of a relationship' in *Landscape and Culture* (ed. M. Wagstaff), 11–25, Oxford

Hodder, I., Shanks, M., Alexandri, A., Buchli, V., Carman, J., Last, J. and Lucas, G. (eds) 1995. *Interpreting Archaeology*, London

Ingold, T. 1986. 'Territoriality and tenure: the appropriation of space in hunting and gathering societies' in T. Ingold, *The Appropriation of Nature*, 130–64, Manchester

Olwig, K. 1993. 'Sexual cosmology: nation and landscape at the conceptual interstices of nature and culture; or what does landscape really mean?' in *Landscape: Politics and Perspectives* (ed. B. Bender), 307–43, London

Piggott, S. 1983. 'Archaeological retrospect', Antiquity 57, 28–37

Richards, J. 1990. *The Stonehenge Environs Project*, English Heritage Archaeol. Rep. 16, London

Tilley, C. 1993. 'Art, architecture, landscape' in *Landscape: Politics and Perspectives* (ed. B. Bender), 49–84, London

——, 1994. *A Phenomenology of Landscape*, London

Tuan, Y-F. 1977. *Space and Place: The Perspective of Experience*, London

7 Hatfield Forest

Oliver Rackham

Just as no [national] park is purely a natural area without any historical relevance, so all historical parks have some natural values. (Chase, *Playing God in Yellowstone*, 1986)

In 1924 the National Trust was given Hatfield Forest, Essex, by Edward North Buxton and his family. The Forest was ceremonially opened by Lord Ullswater, vice-president of the National Trust. A report in *The Times* celebrated the Buxton's generosity; Lord Ullswater was photographed talking to an old man who remembered the Forest under the previous regime before the Enclosure Act of 1857.

Seventy years later almost to the month Hatfield Forest became a National Nature Reserve. The Forest was ceremonially declared such by Lord Cranbrook, chairman of English Nature. A report in *The Times* celebrated the National Trust's management of the Forest; Lord Cranbrook was photographed talking to Mr Ron Monk who remembered the Forest under the previous regime before 1924.

The history of the Forest between these two events was not tranquil. In 1924 the Forest's disputatious days were by no means over. This was one of the first attempts by the Trust (or any other conservation body) to conserve an entire landscape. The Centenary of the Trust is not merely an occasion for empty self-congratulation, but for studying how well this has succeeded and the lessons for the future and for other sites.

What was Hatfield Forest?

The Norman kings of England declared certain areas to be Forest, places where the king might keep deer to kill and eat. Hatfield became a Forest in *c.* 1100. The king's deer were added to, and did not replace, whatever was previously going on on the site, which was usually common-land. Many Forests were not wooded: those that were, such as Hatfield, involved arrangements of land-use known as wood-pasture, which reconciled the king's deer and the commoners' cattle and sheep with the maintenance of the trees (Rackham 1990).

Hatfield Forest (originally 1,115 acres) is divided into *coppices* and *plains*. (fig. 7.1) Each of the seventeen coppices was a wood, from 25 to 60 acres in extent, with a woodbank round it. Each wood was supposed to be felled every eighteen years and then fenced for six years against deer and three years more

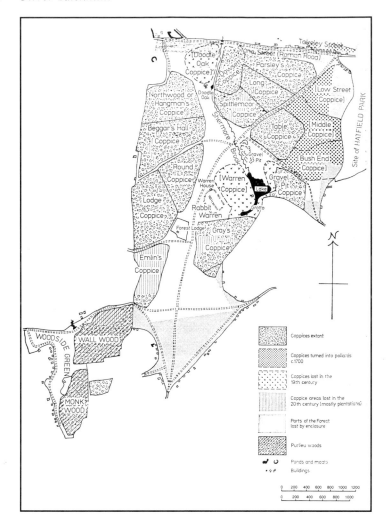

Coppices extant

Coppices turned into pollards c.1700

Coppices lost in the 19th century

Coppice areas lost in the 20th century (mostly plantations)

Parts of the Forest lost by enclosure

Purlieu woods

Ponds and moats

Buildings

7.1 Hatfield Forest and the adjacent Woodside Green and Wall Wood (also National Trust properties) and Monk Wood. The latter were 'purlieu woods' to which some provisions of Forest Law applied. The parts of the Forest not shown as coppices were plains.

against other livestock, lest they eat the young shoots sprouting from the stools. The plains, originally some 435 acres in extent, were accessible to deer and domestic livestock all the time. The trees in them were not coppiced but pollarded at about 10ft (3m) above ground so that the animals could not reach the young shoots. New trees in the plains arose in the protection of patches of thorny bushes called *scrubs*. This arrangement had apparently reached its full development by the fourteenth century, and persisted with only minor changes until the nineteenth.

7.2 Old pollard hornbeam. Any ancient tree is a complete ecosystem with hollows, roots and debris, and dead wood and loose bark each being the particular habitat of a suite of creatures. Ancient trees remain important even if decrepit or dead. March 1994.

Hatfield Forest is a microcosm of English history. Five of its landowners suffered for high treason. Robert the Bruce, the Wars of the Roses, the Civil War, and the founders of the Bank of England all played their part. The seventeenth and eighteenth centuries are a story of comic squabbles between the landowner, the lord of the manor and the commoners; because of the historical researches that they did, very extensive Forest archives survive.

The last private owners, the Houblon family, bought out the commoners under an Enclosure Act in 1857. Privatization would ordinarily have been followed by destruction, but the Houblons realized that the Forest was a special place and preserved it as an annexe to their park. Only about one-sixth of the area was lost; this, being mainly round the edges, resulted in the loss of most of the Forest's distinctive shape.

The biological interest of the Forest lies in the many habitats which it brings together; these are more valuable in combination than any would be singly. There are dry and wet grasslands; different types of woodland; a lake and fen. Specially important are the ancient pollard trees, significant not only for their beauty and historic significance but also as a habitat for many insects and other animals which do not occur on young or middle-aged trees (fig. 7.2). Hatfield has eight species of pollard trees – only one other site in Britain has so many – including the largest number of ancient hawthorns (and in consequence the biggest concentration of mistletoe) known in England.

I have described Hatfield as the Last Forest; and such it is, in the sense of the last English royal Forest to remain in nearly full working order. Although

7.3 Removal of scrub for a plain and creation of new pollards; ancient pollard oaks in background. South-east of Forest Lodge, May 1995

what remained of the social fabric was abolished in 1857, under the Houblons nearly all the physical fabric survived: coppices, plains, scrubs, pollards, grazing and woodcutting. In the New Forest, Sherwood, Dean and Epping some of the components survive but others do not.

Hatfield in the National Trust period

The Trust did not fully appreciate what it had acquired. As the last fully-functioning English royal Forest (and the most complex wood-pasture known in Europe), Hatfield must have been the Trust's most significant Place of Historic Interest when it was acquired; few Trust sites surpass it even today. Instead, it seems to have been regarded merely as a minor place of natural beauty. Two historic buildings, Forest Lodge (the only medieval Forest lodge in England of which any fragment remains above ground) and Warren Lodge (a seventeenth-century brick rabbit-keeper's cottage) escaped notice until my own researches for *The Last Forest*. Even today the Forest gets less than its due prominence in catalogues of Trust properties – although this may be done to avoid attracting even more visitors.

The Forest's local management committee was content, at first, to follow roughly the Houblons' style of management. Grazing and coppicing were kept up; there was an attempt to prevent elms from invading the coppices (a natural change). Deer were mildly disapproved of. This was a sensible if uninquisitive policy, but two mistakes were made. Pollarding was abandoned; and the committee, unfamiliar with wood-pasture practices, failed to fence the coppices after felling, with the result that cattle got in and ate gaps in the regrowth.

In 1955 the National Trust was denounced in a letter to *The Times* by Anthony Buxton, son of the donor. He objected to a proposal to lease some of the coppices to the Forestry Commission to convert to oak plantations. This was followed (as one would expect) by reassuring letters from the Trust's secretary and chief agent, and then by controversy from an unreassured public and a number of experts. In the face of this opposition the Trust dropped the project, but quietly resumed it in a slightly modified form whereby the Trust would do the work but be subsidized by the Commission.

This was not the only intrusion of Progress in the 1950s. There was a short period of fertilizing, weedkilling and draining which permanently spoilt the ancient grassland. (The Forest had just been scheduled as a Site of Special Scientific Interest on the strength of its grassland insects!) Coppicing was abandoned as 'no longer an economic proposition', but quite large monies were spent on planting trees in the plains; sites and species seem to have been picked at random, regardless of their appropriateness for the Forest.

When I first knew the Forest in 1969 the most memorable activity was bulldozing. The woods were being grubbed out and replanted, though with diminishing energy as the meagre results were becoming apparent. Woods were also being 'opened up' by bulldozing swathes through them to create strips of grassland, known as 'motorways' by the inhabitants. This was apparently a substitute for restoring the patterns of woodland rides carefully laid out in the eighteenth century and recently overgrown. Somebody was employed to cut down and burn any tree that was dead or might be thought 'unsightly'; this doubtless explains why the Forest lost more than one-third of its pollards in the first fifty years of Trust ownership.

In the last twenty years the Forest has been rediscovered and rehabilitated. The first step was to resume cutting the pollards (which saved them from massacre by storm in 1987). Next came re-coppicing, and fencing newly-cut areas against cattle. Cars and motorcycles, originally allowed to use the Forest until they got bogged down, have been restricted. The grasslands are regaining some of the species lost in the improvement period, although forty years are too short for a full recovery. Pollards are treated with respect, and every one (living or dead) bears a number. At long last new pollards have been started in order to continue the succession of ancient trees (fig. 7.3). There is a programme of reducing the scrubs in order to recover the grassland in the plains. The latest advance has been to bring back sheep for the first time in 150 years. Much of this is due to the efforts of the National Trust's ecological advisers and of three able Wardens, Nigel Hester, Lawrence Sisitka and Jeremy Wisenfeld.

Changing management of conservation sites

What went wrong? Many long-standing conservation sites have a similar story of unstable management, for reasons which were often not recorded. A principle that seemed too obvious at the time to be worth explaining is baffling to a later generation.

At first – indeed even in the 1980s – Hatfield was described as 'a fragment of the Forest of Essex', a splinter from a once much greater whole. This is a misconception. In the twelfth and thirteenth centuries nearly all Essex was royal Forest, but only in the technical sense that people could be prosecuted for infringing Forest Law anywhere in the county. This did not mean that Hatfield Forest itself was bigger than it had been in 1857, nor that Hatfield had once joined up with Epping Forest 10 miles (16 km) away. Not realizing that Hatfield was a complete Forest, nobody asked how it had worked as a Forest, what kind of Forest it was, and how this should affect modern management.

This misunderstanding has discouraged attempts to restore the Forest to its original extent. To recover a hypothetical 'Forest of Essex' would be impossible, but at times over seventy years some of the 200 acres of land lost in 1857 could have been bought back if their significance had been realized. This would have restored the full integrity of the Forest, and would have provided a buffer zone on to which car parks and some of the more generalized kinds of public recreation could now have been shifted.

The earliest fashion in the modern conservation movement was for letting Nature take her course. In 1878, when the City of London Corporation acquired Epping Forest, they abolished pollarding as 'unnatural', without a thought that this would destroy the character of a unique historic landscape, lose special wildlife habitats, and create grave problems for their successors a hundred years on. In the same spirit the National Trust had acquired Wicken Fen in 1899 and had abandoned traditional management, with the result that it ceased to be Wicken Fen and turned into a wood – from which it has now partially, and with great labour, been recovered.

Hatfield Forest, fortunately, was acquired after that philosophy had fallen from favour in England (though it continues in other countries). It fell into the next trap of conservationist fashion.

Just before its acquisition the Forest had passed through the hands of timber merchants, who had felled many trees. In reality this made up for previous decades of abnormally little felling, and few if any important trees were cut down. But the Trust was haunted by the thought that action was needed if the Forest were again to 'grow fine trees'; this fear continued for fifty years, long after the problem had solved itself by natural means. The Forest was thus an early victim of the 'Plant Trees Anywhere' movement, the notion that there is nothing more to conservation than planting trees.

In the 1950s the idea was gaining ground that the countryside was no more than the creation of farmers and foresters in the past, and the future even of special places like forests lay in contemporary 'good estate management practices'. Naive as this view now seems, the Trust was not slow to adopt it by converting ancient woods to plantations. The historic Frithsden Great Copse in Berkhamsted, Hertfordshire, was not allowed to have a life of its own, but was usurped by 'Queen Elizabeth Wood, planted 1952'. Replanting in Hatfield was justified on the curiously contradictory pleas that the Forest was overgrown and impenetrable, and lacking in young trees.

The Trust today would no doubt insist that Hatfield Forest had been given to it precisely in order that it might escape from modern agriculture and forestry. Such obstinacy in the 1950s would have led to collision with the Ministry of Agriculture and the Forestry Commission, both then at the height of their powers. The clash would have been exciting, and the Trust might have had to invoke its special legal status. In the event the matter was apparently not thought worth making a scene about. Let us not blame the Trust: the replanting of ancient woods was being defended in the conservation press in the 1960s and by the Nature Conservancy (predecessor of English Nature) even in the 1970s.

This fashion reigned in Hatfield when I first knew it. Visitors objected – or were assumed to object – to dead wood or 'misshapen' trees, and this was thought to be a good enough reason for summarily burning the offending objects. Hatfield was treated as if it were a garden or a landscaped park, and subjected to standards of tidiness which were a solecism in a Forest.

Conservation and public access

In 1826 there was trouble with 'idle and disorderly' nutting parties using Hatfield Forest for 'all sorts of Debauchery'. In the early National Trust years such scenes were rare; but (with the growth of Bishop's Stortford town and Stansted Airport nearby) visitors have steadily increased until the Forest is a major place of public resort, which it was never intended to be. This strains both its management and the National Trust's conservation philosophy.

The Trust has a stout principle: 'preservation is its first task which must always take precedence over public access'. This was enunciated by John Bailey, the Trust's chairman, in the 1920s, and repeated in the Trust's booklet *Conservation and Access* in 1980. Other conservation bodies sometimes take the less robust view that the public that finances and supports their activities has the right to see their sites, even at the cost of damaging them.

Even if the principle can be agreed on, applying it is more difficult. How is the precedence of preservation over access to be sustained in face of a gradual increase of public use that never gives rise to a decisive conflict? Visitors, at first harmless, increase in numbers until something has to be done. A decision is not reached until considerable damage has already happened.

At least as important as the direct effect of visitors are works done to cater to the needs – or often, rather, the supposed needs – of visitors. For example, it is easier to drain a path (which is usually detrimental to a site) than to explain to visitors that the wet state is normal and they should bring gumboots. Every site has to be given a car park; this is usually done, as at Hatfield, by sacrificing part of the site, rather than acquiring an adjacent piece of land.

It is hard to resist stretching the rules about alteration in order to allow disabled visitors to enjoy a site, but such alterations are often not devised by disabled people themselves. It is easy to instal hard paths, in place of woodland rides, when inquiry might have revealed that what is wanted are logs on which infirm visitors can sit.

The most recent fashion is obsession with safety. This objective is hard to resist; but safety arguments tend to be accepted unquestioningly, without considering whether they would really result in fewer accidents. Safety considerations get separated from the real world, for example when experts pronounce about 'dangerous' trees, ignoring evidence about how trees actually behave. Management becomes dominated by excessive responses to imaginery hazards. When I am told that muddy paths are dangerous I believe that safety is getting out of hand: what can be safer to fall on than soft mud?

Conservation bodies are secretive about accidents, possibly for fear of legal repercussions. Accidents are not failures to be lived down and forgotten; they need to be reported and collated, together with any legal or insurance claims. Until this is done, safety policies will be based on guesswork rather than evidence.

Learning the lessons

If this paper is construed as an attack on the National Trust I shall have failed. My message is that conservation, like all long-term human activities, has weaknesses which need to be studied. Many of the issues in the conservation of sites – over-restoration, disabled access, safety – have already been debated in connection with the conservation of buildings.

Let not other conservation bodies flatter themselves that they would have done better than the National Trust. Yellowstone National Park in the Rocky Mountains is one of the world's largest and longest-running nature reserves, declared in 1872. The objectives were simple. Yellowstone had not long been discovered; it was thought – ignoring the contribution of the Sheep-eater Indians to the landscape – to be a 'wilderness' in the American sense of an area unaffected by civilized human activity; and it was intended to preserve it as such. In practice, Yellowstone received an ever-increasing amount of human intervention. According to Alston Chase (1986), Yellowstone has failed as a wilderness, largely because of generations of managers bowing to the whims of conservationist fashion. He gives a catalogue of amazingly un-wilderness-like interventions. The authorities, although forbidden by statute, set out to exterminate wolves, cougars and coyotes lest they eat the deer. They introduced exotic fish and European grasses, as though God had not given Yellowstone fishes and grasses enough. Fire, like carnivores, was bad, so they suppressed it. They built roads and towns for visitors regardless of what lay in their path. They later lost confidence and pretended that wolves and cougars were still present half a century after the last had been shot. The result, according to Chase, was that 'elk' (red deer) proliferated at the expense of all other large mammals and ate up the more palatable trees and other plants. Just after he wrote, Nemesis struck – or, as many would say, the balance of nature was partly restored: in 1988 unsuppressable conflagrations devoured the fuel that had accumulated over half a century of fire suppression.

What happens to a site if it does not fall into the hands of conservationists? (Chase claims that in some American national parks vertebrate animals are worse conserved than in the surrounding country.) Private landowning families often have a most tenacious sense of continuity – but then comes an heir who commits high treason, or dies for his country, or is an enthusiast for planting eucalyptus, or loves money, or takes to drugs, or gambles away the estate, and undoes in one generation centuries of his ancestors' work. At first it seemed that semi-public ownership would assure continuity; but, as we have seen, this is not guaranteed in practice even by the National Trust.

Hatfield Forest has a twin, Writtle Forest near Chelmsford. This was the same kind of Forest (although the environment is different) and had a very similar history. It still belongs to the descendants of the henchman to whom Henry VIII granted it. Writtle Forest is not quite as well preserved as Hatfield, but it belongs in the second rank of surviving royal Forests. It would be invidious to compare their conservation point by point over the last seventy-one years; suffice it to say that Writtle has not fared outstandingly worse than Hatfield. In 1991 Essex County Council made it the first example of a new designation of Ancient Landscape.

It is essential to begin by understanding the history of a site. This should be obvious for the National Trust, whose business is with places of historic interest; but for any site the conservation objectives cannot even be defined without understanding how it got into its present state.

One meets the argument that all natural sites are forever changing, and changes should not be opposed. The fact (or presumption) that there has been one type of change in the past is used as an argument for not opposing a different change in the future. The phrase 'shouldn't [or can't] be preserved in aspic' rises to the lips of those who present this point of view. To this I cannot reply fully, being ignorant of the preservative qualities attributed to aspic, but I offer the following response.

Historical ecology shows that some sites are inherently changeable – some, like ecosystems developing on bombed buildings of the Second World War, to the point of being unconservable – and others not. It is a platitude that all living systems change, but not all changes are the same. Some are within the normal dynamics of a site, and it is foolish – an offence against the *genius loci* – to oppose them. The historical ecologist's job is to find out the limits to the normal dynamics.

Hatfield Forest turns out to have had a remarkably stable history and has resisted many vicissitudes. Not being closely dependent on any specific social environment, it is a very suitable site for a conservation body to maintain. The question 'What stage in the site's development is it intended to preserve?' is (in this case) not critical. There is little to be said for perpetuating the rather run-down state which the National Trust took over in 1924, or preserving the random artefacts thrust into the Forest's fabric in the 1950s and 1960s. Landscaping and tree-planting in the Houblon period are a legitimate part of the Forest's history, neither to be eliminated nor allowed to dominate the Forest's character.

At Yellowstone, we are told, wolves, cougars and fire (including the occasional great conflagration) are part of the natural dynamics: without them it ceases to be Yellowstone. At Hatfield the historic dynamics include timber-felling, sheep-grazing, visitors (up to a point), and probably Dutch Elm Disease. Wolves, continuous shade, tree-planting, coppicing without fencing, off-road motorcycling, and bulldozing are not.

At Hatfield two recent major changes are the coming of grey squirrels and the increase of birch, said to have been absent in 1924 but now the fifth commonest tree. These are unhistoric – the site would probably be better off without them – but cannot be resisted.

Conservation as a profession

Conservation is now professionalized: people make it their careers and get qualifications in it; they become respectable and have proper training. Making conservation a career, as if it were engineering or cuisine, has drawbacks as well as advantages. Conservation becomes much more dependent on money. Wildlife trusts' finances become dominated by salaries; they have to raise more money; they have to pay the raisers of money; and they wonder uneasily what will happen when the money runs out.

Engineers and chefs can practise almost anywhere; but with conservation local experience is at least as important as general knowledge. A good conservationist takes up a post for a few years, begins to get to know the site, and then moves on to pursue a career elsewhere, leaving the site in the hands of a successor who may have different ideas.

Trusts develop general policies which are allowed to override the conservation objectives of their earlier-acquired sites. There is a danger that there will emerge 'rules of good conservation' which will be applied uncritically to all sites, much as were the 'rules of good forestry' which did so much damage in the 1960s. For example, conservationists trained in the 1970s tend to think coppicing is good for all woodland.

Conservation sites are traditionally administered by local management committees which include professional ecologists. Some have secured the services of very distinguished scientists, like Sir Harry Godwin at Wicken Fen. They also, where possible, include people who knew the place before it became a conservation site. In the last fifteen years local committees have often been treated with disrespect by the increasingly professionalized central organizations of bodies like county wildlife trusts; they have been overruled, allowed to decay through natural wastage, or sometimes abolished. One trust sacked the local committee of a major reserve because they insisted on putting the site's conservation above the trust's policy of attracting more visitors. A local committee, if properly advised by ecological scientists, is more likely to be right than a distant central organization. Hatfield Forest provides an example. The replanting fiasco was imposed by the National Trust's executive committee; it was not the fault of the local committee.

Transmitting plans to future generations

The real problems of conservation are anthropological. In a rational world each generation would add to its predecessors' knowledge, and management would progress towards a practical ideal. In the real world unreason often triumphs, and knowledge can diminish as well as grow. Landscape conservation is seen in terms of technical solutions – coppicing, scrub-clearing, wolf-slaying – which are thought to be predictable. The study of human fallibility is no less important in conservation than the study of techniques.

Conservationists carry out their own ideas and enthusiasms without looking at the ideas of their predecessors. In 1878 it was envisaged to 'protect the timber and other trees, pollards, shrubs, underwood, heather, gorse, turf, and herbage' of Epping Forest. The early Conservators pursued their own enthusiasm, which happened to be for timber trees. They failed to protect, indeed actively destroyed, other features. These were required to be protected by an Act of Parliament but still were ignored, probably because nobody read the Act. The Conservators, and those who opposed the changes they made, agreed that the management of Epping Forest was a matter of taste (Rackham 1978).

With the frequent changes of personnel that follow from professionalization, it is essential to have a good management plan. This means a management plan that is read, and therefore that is readable. The management plan of Hatfield Forest is, of course, a very detailed document, even though the level of detail is not excessive compared to that involved in the conservation of a country mansion. Unfortunately many management plans are written to a prescribed form, are platitudinous, written in officialese (all ancient woods are described as W8 or W10), or are loaded with conservationists' claptrap. They are therefore not read. To write a good management plan is not easy. There is a temptation to leave out the details as inessential, but this should be resisted; it is the details that are fun to read, not generalities and platitudes.

Management plans are normally written for only five years at a time. Re-writing them becomes an industry in itself, and diverts energies that would be better spent in conservation. Any fashionable idea, however hare-brained, can be introduced the next time the management plan comes up for review.

An amusing parallel is what happens to public maps of complex sites like Hatfield Forest. These are updated every few years by revising the previous map. At each revision the previous errors are copied and new errors introduced. After a few revisions it becomes impossible to tell coppices from scrubs.

Usually a management plan should be published. This gives some independent check that it is being carried out, as well as setting an example for the treatment of similar sites elsewhere.

Conservation, like forestry and other long-term human activities, is beset by the sin of triumphalism. Successes are remembered and put on record. Failures are not treated as experiments from whose outcome future generations may learn, but as mistakes to be lived down and forgotten – and thus to be repeated by their perpetrator's grandchildren. The post-1955 replanting of Hatfield was not the first. Replanting had been tried in the 1750s and 1850s, and each time had damaged the fabric of the Forest and had ended in failure. I was disconcerted to find that by 1985 the controversy of thirty years before had again been laid to rest. 'Those who cannot remember the past are condemned to repeat it.'

I am indebted to Ann and James Hart for discussing many of the issues in this paper.

References

Chase, A. 1986. *Playing God in Yellowstone: The Destruction of America's First National Park*, San Diego

Rackham, O. 1987. 'Archaeology and land-use history', in *Epping Forest – the Natural aspect?* (ed. D. Corke), *Essex Naturalist* (ns) 2, 16–75.

Rackham, O. 1990. *The Last Forest: The Story of Hatfield Forest*, London

8   The archaeology of gardens and designed landscapes

Christopher Taylor

The use of archaeology to help understand the history of gardens and in particular, from the viewpoint of the National Trust, to display them better, is a very recent development (Brown 1991). Although garden archaeology began in earnest in the 1960s, it is only in the last few years that is has been widely applied. Indeed it seems to have burst upon the gardening world suddenly and to have been accepted with all the fervour of a new religion, apparently affording a novel and fascinating way of finding out even more about the history of gardens as well as making possible the accurate restoration of some of our most historic gardens. Institutions and private landowners have been quick to accept this new discipline and garden archaeology is now used in many places.

As someone who has been responsible, at least partly, for beginning garden archaeology (Taylor 1983; 1991), I am sometimes appalled at what I have helped to start. It is therefore an appropriate moment to take stock of the situation and especially to examine the position of the Trust in relation to garden archaeology, for the Trust, together with English Heritage, has been a leader in the use of garden archaeology and there is no doubt that some of the results have been spectacular. This is especially true of the work by English Heritage at Audley End, Essex, by the Royal Palaces Agency at Hampton Court (Dix 1994; Thurley 1995), and, at first sight, by the Trust at Wimpole in Cambridgeshire and at Biddulph in Staffordshire. Yet in the excitement it may be that all the implications of the use of garden archaeology are not being taken on board.

What is garden archaeology? It is the use of archaeological methods, in all their varied forms, to recover details of the structures and layouts of former gardens and, to a lesser extent, some of the planting arrangements therein. There are two quite distinct types of garden archaeology. One is that which most people think of when the word archaeology is used, excavation, or the digging up of the structures and layouts of former gardens. This can be termed, crucially, destructive archaeology, for in the course of making the discoveries required or hoped for these very discoveries are themselves destroyed, together with all the associated evidence relating to both earlier and later land-use on the site. The excavations at, say, Audley End not only destroyed the evidence for the 1830s garden which was being sought and then recreated, but also removed the evidence for the later gardens there. It also damaged or destroyed part of the evidence of the underlying monastic house on the site, as well as earlier gardens. Likewise at Wimpole the

8.1 Wimpole Hall, Cambridgeshire. The slight remains of Victorian parterres are picked out by a light snow cover, 9 April 1975. These parterres have now been replaced by modern flower beds. (Cambridge University Committee for Aerial Photography copyright reserved)

creation of the new parterres has destroyed the evidence for the earlier, Victorian, ones (fig. 8.1).

The other type of garden archaeology is non-destructive. It includes analytical ground survey, various geophysical techniques for identifying sub-surface features as well as aerial photography. These methods produce information related to former gardens and other features without destroying the evidence but not necessarily as accurately or in as much detail as excavation. A good example of this type of work is the recovery of the arrangement of the unfinished garden of the 1590s of Sir Thomas Tresham at Lyveden New Bield, Northamptonshire, a notable Trust property (Brown and Taylor 1973).

These two types of garden archaeology employ very different methods and produce very different results. Excavational archaeology is vastly expensive, not only to carry out but also to publish properly the results. It is also time-consuming and, to judge by some recent examples, can produce information of such complexity that it is difficult to interpret. The quite unsuspected sub-structures revealed by excavations by English Heritage at the seventeenth-century gardens at Kirby Hall, Northamptonshire, is a good example (Dix 1994). In contrast, some excavation can produce either very little evidence at all, as was the case at Basing

House in Hampshire, not a Trust property, or fairly limited evidence as at Hanbury Hall, Worcestershire. At Basing House it is difficult to see what the excavations achieved and certainly they played little part in the restoration of the gardens there which were largely based on historical evidence. At Hanbury the excavations did indeed lead to some discoveries but did not apparently alter to any great extent what was already clear from historical sources (Currie 1993; National Trust 1994; Allen and Turtin 1995). Elsewhere excavation seems to have led only to the discovery of innumerable drains or culverts, as at Prior Park, Bath, or again merely confirmed what was already known from other sources, as at Dinefwr Park, Dyfed (Thackray 1995, 13, 15).

Non-destructive archaeology, although not cheap, is relatively inexpensive compared to excavation and much can be achieved in a relatively short time, as Mr Everson shows in the case of Bodiam in the following paper. The results of both forms of archaeology are, of course, part of a process of academic research into garden history. But the Trust is not a research body and its use of archaeology has to be justified on other grounds.

There are two types of Trust properties where the use of garden archaeology may be of value. The first is the flagship properties where the emphasis is on informing and entertaining visitors and where the Trust's public image is at its most prominent. The second type, and by far the greater number, are the tenanted estates and other lands whose management and incomes underpin the former. These two each require different information from garden archaeology. The principal properties usually require the results of archaeology to assist in the restoration or improvement of existing gardens the better to educate, inform, interest or merely increase the pleasure of its members and visitors. Elsewhere the archaeology is needed to inform the Trust's own staff and tenants of the location and significance of former gardens and thus to improve management systems and protection. The latter process should be a relatively easy one with potentially valuable results. An example of this is the former garden on Trust land at Stowe Barton, Cornwall. There a detailed analytical ground survey combined with the transcription of air photographic evidence has enabled the complete layout of this important late seventeenth-century garden, as well as its predecessor, to be recovered and understood (Wilson-North 1993). However, most of the garden archaeology carried out by the Trust in recent years has been on its flagship properties, with the principal aim of assisting in the restoration of important gardens. Some of the results have been remarkable, as at Biddulph, but at the same time there are fundamental questions concerned with such restoration that must be asked, given the great costs of excavation and the destructive nature of the process.

Perhaps the most important of these questions is can gardens actually be restored to their former glory at all? It is certainly possible in some cases to get very close to the original appearance and to do it in a truly magnificent manner. This has certainly been achieved at Biddulph Grange and at Hanbury, although at both archaeology played only a small part. But at most other places this is not possible for a variety of perfectly good practical reasons. One is that, however accurately we may be able to reconstruct the hard details of former gardens using evidence from historical research as well as archaeology, it is usually impossible, except for relatively modern gardens, to replicate the original planting (Strong 1995). This is often because the exact forms of the original plants no longer exist and modern variants have to be used. Sometimes, as at Wimpole, the arrangement of the nineteenth-century borders and beds can be restored correctly after excavation, but the new planting is at variance with the documented original. Another difficulty is that today's Trust gardens have to fulfil very different functions to those of the original owners. Thus many gardens were originally designed to be at their best at only very specific and limited times of the year when the family was in residence. Such gardens were laid out and planted for an effective period of no more than two or three months at the most. Yet Trust gardens, however impeccable the evidence for earlier layouts and former planting, cannot always be run on such a basis. They are required to open on 1 April and to close on 31 October and members understandably wish to see these gardens in reasonably good condition for the full seven months.

A further difficulty is that accurate restoration can rarely be complete and is usually only partial. This is sometimes through lack of evidence from either archaeology or documentary sources. More often there are major restrictions caused by the existence of other features from different periods, such as mature trees or buildings, the removal of which would create justifiable or unjustifiable outcries and which is thus politically difficult or even impossible (National Trust 1994, 32). English Heritage faced just such difficulties in their proposals for restoration at Kenwood. All restoration is thus a compromise between the truth and the achievable. We should therefore question how far we can and should go to ascertain from destructive archaeology one aspect of truth when many others are unattainable.

Another question to be asked is to what period a garden should be restored on the basis of archaeological or historical evidence. A few gardens, which are mostly modern, are of all one date. These can be restored fairly easily to their original form if it is so desired, as at Biddulph Grange. But most gardens are not of a single period. Gardens by their very nature are usually multi-period and are either the result of constant adaptation to changing fashions or have been drastically remodelled on a number of occasions. The garden at Melford Hall, Suffolk, is an example of adaptation, the sixteenth or seventeenth-century raised terrace having been incorporated into the nineteenth-century arrangement. An example of massive and repetitive remodelling is at Blickling Hall, Norfolk, where all that is now visible, after 300 years of constant change, is the modified layout by Norah Lindsey of 1932 (National Trust 1985). Archaeological work on these types of garden could and usually does produce some evidence of parts of the adaptations and changes that took place although rarely all of them. What is mostly revealed from multi-period gardens is a mass of contradictory evidence and unexplained features as well as unexpected results. What period should be restored in such gardens is not necessarily dependent on the archaeological evidence.

Yet another question to be asked is whether large-scale excavation is in fact really necessary or whether the evidence required for either restoration or explanation can be obtained more cheaply, quicker or more completely by historical research alone. Although excavation is often spectacular, the visually less exciting work on estate papers and other sources often provides similar or better evidence at a fraction of the cost. Not that historical research can always provide the required information, but at least its potential should be examined and taken into account before archaeological work is proposed.

Although not directly part of garden archaeology, we also have to ask why we need to attempt to restore gardens to an earlier arrangement. Most gardens by their very nature are palimpsests of the ideas and aims of many people over long periods, often lovingly created to display the best of their time. This I believe is what makes gardens so fascinating. By attempting to reduce a garden to a single period in the development of that palimpsest we inevitably lose something. And are we really trying to help our members to be better informed or are we merely indulging in academic exercises at great expense? I offer no opinion on this. I merely think that we need constantly to question what we do and why.

Thus we come to the basic question, to what extent should archaeological techniques be used on Trust gardens? From what I have said so far it might be thought that I am against them. This is not so. There are many places where excavation could and should be employed either to answer very limited or specific questions or, if resources are available, to help in the restoration of exceptionally important gardens. In addition, it goes without saying that all unavoidable disturbances to gardens and former gardens should be accompanied by either excavations or watching briefs in order to recover any information likely to be destroyed. Such a policy has, of course, already been adopted by the Trust and useful results have come from it. An example is the work at Chastleton House, Oxfordshire, where the footings of the early seventeenth-century terraces were found during the construction of a soakaway chamber in the forecourt (Marshall 1995). Certainly non-destructive archaeological techniques should be used to discover and record the known and potential former garden sites as well as related features on Trust land. By doing so the value of the national heritage which the Trust holds will be better understood and thus can be better managed. Such archaeological work will also help to form the basis for protection of these sites for future generations when perhaps there will be many fewer similar sites elsewhere. The range of material which still needs to be discovered, recorded and assessed is considerable. It includes not only the remains of former gardens, such as those at Ightham Mote which have been misinterpreted (National Trust 1993), but also components of relict designed landscapes such as remains of the Bridgemanesque water features at Wimpole. It also includes relatively modern but now increasingly rare horticultural features such as the ridged daffodil fields of 1908 and later on Brownsea Island, Dorset.

Excavation can be used not only to enhance the appearance of existing gardens, but also to assist in the understanding of associated buildings. It is especially useful on some single-period gardens or where for special reasons the excavation and subsequent restoration can be achieved without the destruction of all the evidence. The classic example of this is at Mount Grace Priory in North Yorkshire. There the excavated and restored garden of one of the medieval cells, together with work on the building itself, is visually exciting, of considerable educational value, historically accurate as far as we can see, and yet leaves untouched similar evidence in the adjacent cells (Coppack 1991).

Elsewhere, and particularly on complex multi-period gardens, excavation must be justified on a number of counts. These include cost, level of destruction, potential amount of new information, educational value, aesthetic improvement and the necessity to record earlier remains which will be destroyed by restoration. There is also an important consequence of excavation and restoration to be borne in mind. The very success of what has been achieved by the Trust at Wimpole, Hanbury and Biddulph and by the Royal Palaces Agency at Hampton Court will almost certainly lead to popular demand for other gardens to be treated in the same way. This may well not be possible and may certainly not be necessary or worthwhile. The Trust will have to balance such demands against many other considerations.

At the beginning of this paper it was noted that as excavation and restoration are destructive the new parterres at Wimpole had inevitably led to the obliteration of the traces of the older ones. No criticism of the Trust is implied by that statement. The destruction at Wimpole was not 'wrong', although the remains of such parterres even if only Victorian were a rare if not unique survival. This case merely exhibits to perfection the inbuilt conflict between the desire to preserve such remains and the inevitable pressure for changes and improvements to National Trust gardens.

In conclusion, excavation should only be undertaken when it is advantageous to many aspects of the Trust's aims, not just one. For it is important to remember that excavation is not merely a clever way of obtaining new information or helping to draw in more visitors. It is an extremely clumsy and crude method of trying to understand the past which should be used with great care. In particular, excavating a garden to enable a potential restoration to be achieved could be viewed as much the same as ripping out the interior of one of the Trust's great houses on the grounds that we could make it historically more accurate and visually more exciting if we started again.

References

Allen, D. and Turtin, A. 1995. 'Basing House', *Current Archaeology*, 142, 390–2

Brown, A. E. (ed.) 1991. *Garden Archaeology*, CBA Research Report 78

Brown, A. E. and Taylor, C. C. 1973. 'The gardens at Lyveden, Northamptonshire', *Archaeol. J.*, 129, 54–60

Coppack, G. 1991. *Mount Grace Priory*, English Heritage Guide, 16–19

Currie, C. K. 1993. Unpublished notes on excavation at Hanbury Hall, held by National Trust

Dix, B. 1994. 'Garden archaeology at Kirby Hall and Hampton Court', *Current Archaeology*, 140, 292–9

Marshall, M. 1995. 'Chastleton House and the role of archaeological recording' in Thackray, C. 1995, 25–7

National Trust 1985. *Blickling Hall*, guidebook, 41–5

——, 1993. *Ightham Mote*, guidebook, 37–43

——, 1994. *Hanbury Hall*, guidebook, 30–3

Strong, R. 1995. 'William's privy garden', *The Garden*, 120 pt 6, 332–5

Taylor, C.C. 1983. *The Archaeology of Gardens*, Aylesbury

——, 1991. 'Garden archaeology: an introduction' in Brown, A.E. 1991, 1–5

Thackray, C. (ed.) 1995. *The National Trust Annual Archaeological Review 1994*, London

Thurley, S. (ed.) 1995. *The Restoration of the King's Privy Garden at Hampton Court*, London

Wilson-North, W. R. 1993. 'Stowe: the country house and garden of the Grenville family', *Cornish Archaeology*, 32, 112–27

9 Bodiam Castle, East Sussex: a fourteenth-century designed landscape

Paul Everson

Bodiam Castle in East Sussex is one of the Trust's most visited and most readily recognized properties. 'Everyone's fairy-tale castle' as the 1985 guide chose to put it (Yarrow 1985). Thousands of visitors each year delight in capturing photographic images of it, frequently striving to include a reflection of the standing structure in the surface of the broad moat and/or the rustically intrusive bough of a tree. Just such an image was chosen for the cover of the National Trust Centenary Issue of *History Today* early in 1995. Bodiam Castle even comes as a ready-made icon in a library of images available for use on computer. In this last, it stands in an exclusive club alongside Stonehenge, Big Ben, the Eiffel Tower, the Acropolis, the Alamo and their like.

The interest of this is that it is not a casual matter, and it is not merely a superimposition of modern sensibility on a value-free antiquity (though the first part is a factor at play, of course). Bodiam Castle and its setting were designed as a whole and deliberately to promote an impression and to evoke associations in a way that is quite familiar in later country houses and their settings but until recently was scarcely envisaged as relevant to the late fourteenth century. Its openness to modern reworking in related vein is itself a reflection of that original designed intent.

Evidence for these assertions has come from two distinct but wholly complementary directions. One is based in a proper evaluation of documentary sources and especially the category of licences to crenellate, one of which Sir Edward Dallingridge famously secured for Bodiam in 1385, coupled with an assessment of the standing building (Coulson 1990; 1992). Through this work, Dr Charles Coulson has cut through a long-running and, in many respects, sterile debate and argued that the actuality of the castle's ostensibly military aspects, such as the machicolations, gun loops and other elaborations of the gatehouse and barbican, is not for serious military intent but rather lies in the show and illusion of the 'modestly magnificent house ... of a successful careerist' (see fig. 9.3).

The second source of new evidence is archaeological, in the form of a survey by staff of the Royal Commission on the Historical Monuments of England in 1988 of the remarkable earthworks that surround the castle (Taylor *et al.* 1990;

Everson forthcoming) (fig. 9.1). This was undertaken at the National Trust's request in preparation for a new guidebook for the site (Thackray 1991). As such, it represents only one of a range of archaeological surveys of National Trust properties by the RCHME in recent years that mark a mutually fruitful co-operation between the two agencies and a common interest in both a better understanding of the country's heritage and a more effective communication of it to the public. These surveys have covered monuments of many types and dates, from caves with Palaeolithic deposits in the Manifold Valley to the newest acquisition at Orford Ness of the most recent forms of monument (Wainwright in this volume).[1] In the realm of gardens, parks and designed landscapes these include the formal late seventeenth-century remains at Stowe in Cornwall (Wilson-North 1993), that part of the outstanding early seventeenth-century gardens at Chipping Campden lying within the so-called Coneygree (Everson 1989), and even some aspects of the nineteenth-century garden at Benthall Hall in Shropshire (NMR SJ60SE56). At Wimpole, measured surveys recorded not only elements of Bridgeman's ornamental layout (e.g. Everson 1991, fig. 2.8), but much of a pre-park landscape including three settlements. This tendency to fossilize earlier remains is in itself typical of parklands and was frequently a designed, rather than accidental matter, as John Phibbs has suggested at Wimpole, Ickworth and Shugborough (in reports for the National Trust, and e.g. Phibbs 1991); but it can also throw light on the processes and chronology of a parkland's development, as shown by RCHME survey work at Attingham involving a lost hamlet and abortive canal (Everson and Stamper 1987).

At Bodiam, the RCHME's survey established without doubt that the majority of those extensive earthworks are the remains of elaborate gardens and water features all intended to enhance the visual appearance of the building and to manipulate access to it for maximum effect. The integrity of this designed landscape with the castle and limited evidence for post-medieval occupation argue for its being a late fourteenth-century artifice.

The castle itself is, of course, surrounded by a broad moat, held perched on the hillslope above the valley of the River Rother by a massive dam round its south and east sides. Though access is now via a bridge and outer barbican from the north, there were originally two entrances. One from the north end of the west side via a bridge to the outer barbican and thence to the principal north gate, and the other from the centre of the south side across a bridge to the postern gate. The castle stands slightly to the south of the centre of the moat, and the wide north end of the latter is not only wedge-shaped but effectively forms part

---

[1] Reports and plans resulting from all RCHME fieldwork are deposited in the National Monuments Record and are available for public consultation during normal office hours at the National Monuments Record Centre, Kemble Drive, Swindon SN2 2GZ; telephone (01793) 414600, fax (01793) 414606.

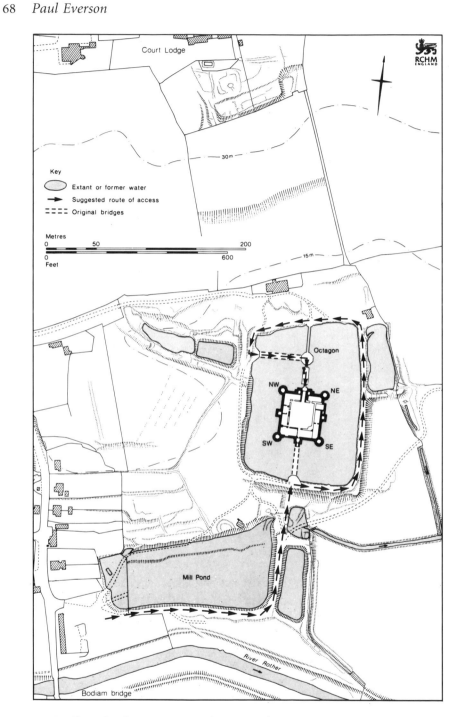

9.1 Bodiam Castle, East Sussex: interpreted RCHME site survey, 1988.
(RCHME, © Crown Copyright)

of a string of ponds once extending up the hillside to the north-west and to the east. The two ponds to the west are both badly damaged by recent activity. They occupy a natural valley, were both also wedge-shaped and have traces of terraced walk-ways on both sides. A third pond lies to the east of the moat and is now also badly damaged.

Other water features lie to the south of the castle. The most substantial is the large former pond latterly known as The Tiltyard, which is possibly a remodelling of a medieval mill-pond documented in 1386. To the east and separated from this pond by a large flat-topped bank is a smaller pond previously interpreted as a medieval harbour. Though it has been altered, certainly at its south end, in the twentieth century, there can be no doubt that it has always been a pond and could never have been connected to the river. To the north of this pond, between it and the dam of the castle moat, is an area of disturbed earthworks. The site is alleged to be that of a water-mill, but it appears also to have been the site of a bridge crossing a watercourse which led to yet another, smaller, pond to its east.

The castle and its moat thus form the centre of an elaborate modification of the whole landscape, involving the creation of a number of ponds and sheets of water whose positioning has an ornamental impact. More interestingly, it is also clear that this modification was directly connected with the manipulation of visitors around the site to experience views whose components continually change. Thus, the main approach to the castle from the west would have been along the south side of The Tiltyard pond, giving distant views of the castle across water, but as yet not perceived as itself set within water; thence along the causeway between ponds where the upper parts of the castle's south façade promise access through a central gatehouse on this axis, and crossing between further areas of water over a bridge. At this point the climb to the moat dam must have had, indeed still has, a dramatic effect, as the whole castle seems to rise up out of its moat. The visitor, denied access through what proves to be only the postern gate, was then directed east along the moat dam, then north between the moat and the one or perhaps two ponds to the east, passing what were recognizable as the principal residential apartments and chapel, and finally back west on the northern edge of the moat. At the north-west corner of the moat the approach road turned again between the moat and the two ponds to the west and finally crossed the moat in two stages to reach the main gate of the castle.

Yet this highly contrived approach is only one element of the landscape of Bodiam Castle. On the crest of the high ridge to the north of the castle, and some 30m vertically above it, is an earthwork known as the Gun Garden, for which limited excavations in 1961 suggested a medieval date. The earthworks are now somewhat disturbed but in essence consist of broad terraces backed by what may be the sites of a building or buildings. Whatever the date of the feature, it

9.2 Bodiam Castle, East Sussex. View from the Gun Garden or pleasance to the castle in its watery landscape. (BB 91/3343; RCHME, © Crown Copyright)

is obviously ornamental and grand in scale. It is most likely to have been a garden or a pleasance containing buildings and other features, but it surely must have also functioned as a viewing platform for the landscaped setting of the castle below (fig. 9.2). Whether it stood as a completely separate feature or was physically linked to the castle is now unclear. The general elongated form of the field between it and the castle suggests the latter, though the present boundaries are merely hedges.

In summary, therefore, the earthworks surrounding Bodiam Castle form an elaborate and contrived setting for the residence, of a coherence not perceived prior to the survey. Most striking is the use of sheets of water to create a staged landscape, not only to be passed through but to be viewed from above, from where the castle and its watery setting appear to float above the wider landscape of the Rother valley, and its proportions evoking certain of Edward I's north Welsh designs are seen to maximum effect.

This exciting perception indeed changes one's focus on Bodiam Castle in an important way. Whether 'old soldier's dream house' or 'modestly magnificent house . . . of a successful careerist', it should be emphasized that Bodiam was not unique in late medieval England as a noble residence, clad in chivalric garb and named accordingly, and set in watery surrounds (fig. 9.3). Cooling Castle in Kent, with its licence cast in bronze and worn ostentatiously like a medal, is perhaps another. Bodiam *is* nevertheless exceptional in the relatively intact survival of its

9.3 Bodiam Castle, East Sussex. Main gate with heraldry and gun loops. (BB 87/7999; RCHME, © Crown Copyright)

focal building, the exceptional preservation of the evidence of its context described here, and the fortuitous fact that practically the whole fragment of landscape is in the hands of the National Trust, as a body dedicated to the public's informed enjoyment and better understanding of our landscape and heritage. It is entirely characteristic that the Trust should look with care at new ideas and not simply jump at them. But here at Bodiam, there is every practical opportunity – for example, simply by managing the approach to the castle itself to replicate that outlined here and explaining the reasoning – to allow a numerous wider public to share understanding of the extraordinary nature of this designed landscape that is at present the talk of a scholarly few.

References

Coulson, C. 1990. 'Bodiam Castle: truth and tradition', *Fortress* 10, 3–15

——, 1992. 'Some analysis of the castle of Bodiam, East Sussex', in *The Ideals and Practice of Medieval Knighthood*, Proceedings of the Strawberry Hill Conference 4, 51–107

Everson, P. 1989. 'The garden of Campden House, Chipping Campden, Gloucestershire', *Garden History* 17 no. 2, 109–21

——, 1991. 'Field survey and garden earthworks', in *Garden Archaeology* (ed. A. E. Brown), CBA Research Report 78, 6–19

——, forthcoming. 'Bodiam Castle, East Sussex: castle and its designed landscape', in *Château Gaillard: études de castellologie médiévale XVII*

Everson, P. and Stamper, P. A. 1987. 'Berwick Maviston and Attingham Park', *Transactions of the Shropshire Archaeological Society* 65, 64–9

Phibbs, J. L. 1991. 'The archaeology of parks – the wider perspective', in *Garden Archaeology* (ed. A. E. Brown), CBA Research Report 78, 118–22

Taylor, C. C., Everson P. and Wilson-North, W. R. 1990. 'Bodiam Castle, Sussex', *Medieval Archaeology* 34, 155–7

Thackray, D. 1991. *Bodiam Castle*, NT guide

Wilson-North, W.R. 1993. 'Stowe: the country house and garden of the Grenville family', *Cornish Archaeology* 32, 112–27

Yarrow, A. 1985. *Bodiam Castle*, NT guide

10 A Selworthy cottage

Isabel Richardson

The National Trust established the Vernacular Buildings Survey so that its smaller buildings could be better understood and their management therefore based on sound information. Selworthy Green, with its cottages, is an example of the need for correct historical interpretation both inside the Trust and for the many visitors.

Selworthy is part of the Holnicote Estate in West Somerset, in the north-eastern section of the Exmoor National Park. The property covers 5,042 ha and stretches from Bossington Beach, facing the Bristol Channel, to Dunkery Gate, just south of the highest point on Exmoor (519m). There are several small hamlets and four villages, Allerford, Bossington, Luccombe and Selworthy, as well as scattered farms and cottages. These are mostly in the Vale of Porlock, but several farmsteads are set on hills.

Holnicote came to the Acland family when Sir Thomas Acland, seventh baronet, married Elizabeth Dyke in 1745. The estate then only included the manors of Holnicote, Bossington and Blackford.

Luccombe and Selworthy were inherited by Sir Thomas Dyke Acland (1787–1871), the tenth baronet, from the Arundels of Trerice. In 1944 the Holnicote Estate was given to the National Trust by Sir Richard Acland, in addition to the Killerton Estate in Devon. Dunkery Hill had been donated to the Trust by Colonel Wiggin (1932) and Mrs Alan Hughes (1934).

Sir Thomas Dyke Acland inherited the title in 1794 as a little boy of seven. His widowed mother left the main seat at Killerton empty and settled at Holnicote House where Sir Thomas grew up. He had been influenced as a boy by the Reverend Joshua Stephenson, who had been appointed as Rector of Selworthy.

Selworthy Green with its thatched cottages for estate pensioners has, for most of the twentieth century, been accepted as the work of Sir Thomas. Anne Acland wrote in her book 'a little group of thatched cottages had been built on the Green for estate pensioners' in her chapter on the 'Great Sir Thomas'. When therefore the vernacular survey of the Holnicote estate was initiated, it was hoped that a clearer understanding of Sir Thomas's work at Selworthy would help in assessing his influence on the buildings of the rest of the estate.

Selworthy village

The village of Selworthy is set on the south-facing slope of the hills between the

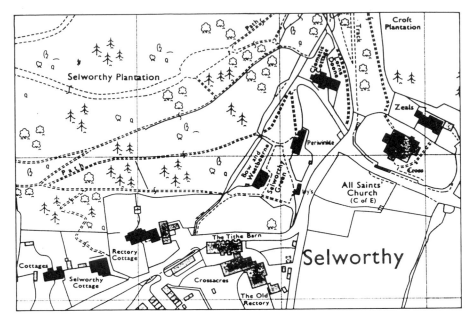

10.1 Map of Selworthy village.

Vale of Porlock and the Bristol Channel (fig. 10.1). The focal point of the village is the whitewashed church with its squat tower, set on a terrace above the old Porlock-Allerford-Selworthy road on the east side of Selworthy combe. There is one house behind the church, on a platform north-east of the churchyard, and a pair of cottages immediately to the south-east, the rest of the houses being set to the west and south-west. The Green and its six dwellings are below and west of the church, between the road and the stream, the latter flows under the road at the south end of the Green. Three more houses and Selworthy Farm are placed below this, built into the west bank of the combe. An area of land to the south of the road does not belong to the Trust. This includes the new burial ground opposite the church (on the site of the Church House), the new and old Rectories, the Tithe Barn – converted to residential use – and a few other dwellings. Apart from the Tithe Barn and part of the Rectory these privately owned buildings are all nineteenth century or later.

Selworthy is listed as a separate holding in the 1087 Domesday Book (Thorn and Thorn 1980). It was held by Queen Edith in 1066, and with East Luccombe, was awarded to Ralph de Limesi by William the Conqueror. The Luccombe family are recorded from 1201–2 onwards as holding both manors from their de Limesi overlords. In 1301, Edward I awarded both manors to Henry de Pynkeny, the Luccombes still being in possession (Chadwyck Healey 1901).

About 1330 Elizabeth Luccombe married into the St John family, and so the West Somerset properties came to them. The Arundels of Trerice acquired them by another marriage and it was an Arundel–Acland union that finally brought the property to Sir Thomas Dyke Acland in 1802. Selworthy, perhaps because it has always been held with East Luccombe, is not recorded as having a manor house.

The Vernacular Buildings Survey

The aim of the survey is to make an historical record of every building on the estate, with floor plans, notes on construction and features, and photographic coverage. Reports are compiled from the site record for each property and these are used by the Trust management.

The Selworthy houses were recorded in 1994, Selworthy Farm had been visited between tenancies in 1992. The first cottage to be recorded was Westbourne, when the tenant moved. There are six cottages on the Green. The two at the top (north) end are butting on to and angled to each other, the west cottage is single storey, the east a two-storey building. South of these is a two-storey house (this was divided into two cottages), below this is a small single-storey dwelling, and opposite – parallel to and above the stream – is a two-storey building held as two tenancies. The latter was the first building on Selworthy Green to be recorded by the survey.

Bow and Westbourne Cottages (fig. 10.2)

All the cottages on the Green are thatched with combed wheat reed and the walls are rendered and limewashed. The windows on the main elevations are leaded light casements with diamond panes. On Westbourne the front lateral stack has a projecting bake oven with a conical slated roof. The centre ground floor window is ogee-headed, as are those of the other houses on the Green, and it is advanced to the line of the front chimney. On the first floor the windows have iron frames with arched heads and the thatch is swept over them. The north porch proved to have two large oak trunks, one a pollard, supporting the porch roof and giving a picturesque rustic effect. The roof had been thatched (the line is still apparent on the wall) but about 1900 this was replaced by Bridgwater tiles. A seat between the two trunks, the back made of split timbers retaining their bark, adds to their rustic appearance. The doorway into the house has a gothic arch and is carpentry work of the nineteenth century. The porch and front door of the lower cottage also have similar two-centred arches. All these features fit comfortably into the early nineteenth-century vernacular revival and the picturesque movement.

When, however, the interior of the northern half was recorded, a structure of earlier date emerged (fig. 10.3). The main room had a transverse beam with hollow chamfer and step-runout stops, and therefore was late sixteenth or early seventeenth century, and a rear stair turret. The fireplace was blocked with a

10.2 Selworthy: Bow and Westbourne Cottages from the Green. (V.B.S.; National Trust)

modern surround and coal grate. The first floor has two rooms, one with a blocked doorway to the lower, southern cottage, the other showing the shadow of jointed crucks in the partition. It was apparent that this was a much earlier building than previously thought. When the survey of the second half of the cottage, Bow, took place there were few features of early significance on the ground floor. On the first floor, two pairs of jointed crucks could be seen, and when the roof space was inspected nearly the whole of the roof structure was seen to be smoke blackened. The three trusses, the ridge and side purlins, most of the rear rafters and some rear battens are all blackened. Unfortunately no smoke blackened thatch survives. The middle truss, which is offset from the centre to the south, is closed, the inserted wattle and daub blocking the truss blackened on the north side only. It was apparent that this was an open hall cross-passage house, originally with an open hearth fire in the hall (the middle room, Westbourne Cottage). After some years the blocking of the middle truss and the raising of the partition below it on the north side of the cross-passage meant that smoke no longer drifted down into the lower room.

In the late sixteenth century the front stack was added and the ground floor rooms were ceiled, the inserted first floor doubling the amount of living space

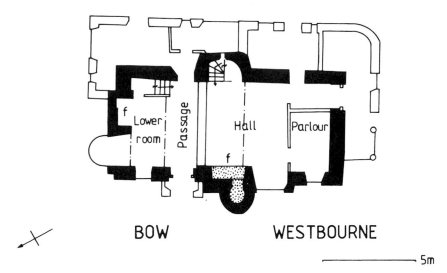

10.3 Selworthy: plan of Bow and Westbourne Cottages. (Robert Waterhouse; National Trust)

in the house. The updating of the medieval house to a two-storey building occurred under the Arundels, though we do not know whether they had the work done or merely gave permission for it. In the early nineteenth century, to create the Green, Sir Thomas Dyke Acland must have removed the farm buildings east of the house and added the lean-tos, with the other external features, such as porches, already mentioned. He also replaced the north cross-passage partition with a rubble stone wall on the ground floor, and totally removed the south partition, inserting a beam to support the first floor joists. The cross-passage thus became part of the lower room and the main living space in the southern cottage. The staircase was inserted in this room together with the bow window which gives the cottage its name.

From the early nineteenth century to the present the cottages have remained virtually unaltered, the insertion of bathrooms in the rear lean-tos in the 1960s being the major change.

Other houses on Selworthy Green

All the other cottages on the Green, like Bow and Westbourne, are thatched and rendered. All but Periwinkle have one window with ogee-headed lights, whilst all front windows have diamond leaded panes. A brief look at the historical development of other houses on the Green illustrates the methods used by Sir Thomas to create the tiny village for his pensioners.

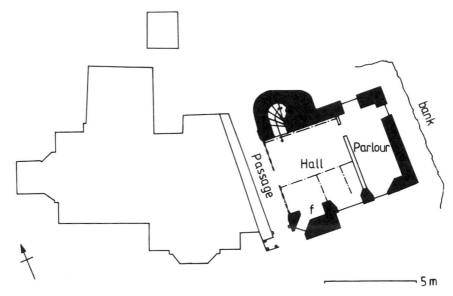

10.4 Selworthy: plan of Lorna Doone. (Robert Waterhouse; National Trust)

The top house, at the north end, is a truncated late medieval hall house with a smoke blackened jointed cruck roof (fig. 10.4). The cross-passage, hall and inner room survive, but the lower room west of the cross-passage has been removed and the partition replaced with a rubble stone gable wall. The east side of the passage survives as a plank and muntin screen, complete with top and bottom rails. The doorway in this has been moved. This little house is unusual in that evidence of an internal jetty survives over the high end of the hall, where the parlour chamber extended 0.70m into the main room, forming a canopy. In the late sixteenth century the hall ceiling was inserted when the front lateral fireplace and chimney were added.

The lower end (fig. 10.5) was probably demolished in the early nineteenth century when a single storey, two-roomed cottage was built, angled back from the front line of the original house and stepped down the hill. The room butting on to Lorna Doone has a bay window, the west room is recessed and the porch on the west end set back again. The thatched roof is irregular, with an 'L' shaped ridge, a half-hip over the bay and a full hip to the west.

The rear outhouse has since been converted into a kitchen, with a doorway cut through to it. This house is the only one with a surviving detached privy, which is thatched with a tiny Gothic window.

Lower down the Green, with its long axis north-to-south, is a seventeenth-century three room cross-passage house (fig. 10.6). It has two fireplaces, rear

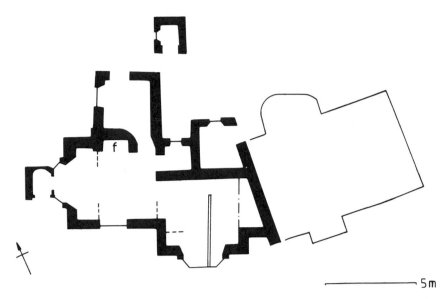

10.5 Selworthy: plan of Clematis Cottage, now the National Trust shop and information centre. (Robert Waterhouse; National Trust)

lateral on the hall and south axial on the lower room. The parlour was, and still is, unheated. It is likely that the original front of the house faced east, and that when it was divided into two cottages in the early nineteenth century the house was reversed to face on to the Green. A first floor porch chamber was added, sheltering the cross-passage doorway. The outside of the building has several lean-tos and porches, and the east hall window has been advanced so that it is aligned with the stack. There are many houses on the estate with this feature. There is a lean-to on each end and two on the west front, the south one butting on to the porch. On the south-west corner a seat is sheltered by a quarter circle thatched roof, supported on a roundwood post.

South of Periwinkle is Ivy's Cottage, a single-storey two-roomed building of irregular shape. It was built into the east bank and had an almost circular porch on the south-west corner, complemented by a similar structure on the south-east corner, which was the privy. As with the shop the rear outhouse has been brought into the cottage, this time as a bathroom and fuel store. The west wall has a low bay window on the main south room and the south window is extended forward between the porch and privy.

The survey showed that the house now known as Bow and Westbourne is one of two medieval houses on the Green, later joined by a seventeenth-century house and two single-storey early nineteenth-century cottages. In the rest of Selworthy village the houses cover a similar date range; there is a late medieval

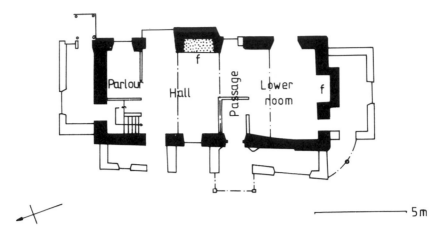

10.6 Selworthy: plan of Periwinkle Cottage. (Robert Waterhouse; National Trust)

house behind the church, two further cross-passage houses – one sixteenth and one seventeenth century – and two houses of early nineteenth-century date below the Green, whilst a pair of cottages and Selworthy farmhouse were the last additions on Trust land, built in the late nineteenth century.

Documentary research

The documentary evidence for the Holnicote Estate is not profuse. The Acland papers are held in the Devon Record Office and unfortunately were in Exeter during the devastating air-raid in the Second World War. Some very useful information for the early nineteenth century survives, but very little indeed around the crucial period of the establishment of Selworthy Green.

The 1809–12 Holnicote Estate Survey maps (fig. 10.7) are very small scale, but provide the only evidence for the area of the Green before the alterations. The 1841 Selworthy Tithe map (Somerset Record Office) (fig. 10.8) shows the Green very much as it is now; the apportionment records 'sundry poor persons' as the occupants and Sir Thomas Dyke Acland as the owner. The Selworthy map shows three small farms with a few outbuildings, and small enclosures. The farmhouses can be identified as Lorna Doone, Periwinkle and Bow–Westbourne. In the summer, the grass on the Green sometimes dries enough for parchmarks to appear, and two buildings, one skewed across the other, have been recorded. These appear to have been outbuildings serving the lowest farm, now Bow and Westbourne.

The third useful source of information is the Reverend Joshua Stephenson's diaries. He was appointed as Rector of Selworthy in 1802, during the minority

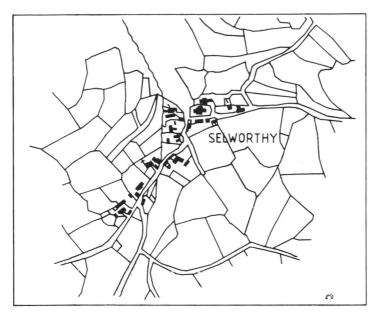

10.7 Holnicote Estate Survey 1809–12. (Devon Record Office)

of Sir Thomas, and remained at Selworthy until his death in 1863. Sir Thomas had great respect for him, he was friendly with all the family and often stayed with them. The diaries were given to him every Christmas by a member of the family, usually Lady Acland.

The Reverend Stephenson recorded several occasions when Sir Thomas met John S. Harford of Blaise Castle, and, as he had stayed at Blaise, he was familiar with the hamlet designed for J. S. Harford senior in 1809 by John Nash. Like Mr Harford, Sir Thomas added privies and wash-houses to his houses on the Green. The first mention of the Selworthy alterations is on 9 August 1828 when Stephenson records 'Sir Thomas called at the Parsonage and we looked at the new cottages'. On 5 November, he writes 'saw Sir Thomas with Mrs C. Acland and Mrs Buller at the Selworthy cottages'.

On 12 April 1829, 'Home for Sunday. In the evening called at the new Selworthy cottages'. On 18 July 1829, 'Sir Thomas Acland came to Holnicote . . . I walked with him and Captain Moresby and Mr Birmingham to look at the Selworthy cottages'. These brief references are very useful, but frustrating in that no more information is given.

Sir Thomas himself kept diaries, but none survives for the relevant period and there are very few papers indeed remaining for the crucial years. Sir Thomas's long association with J. S. Harford suggests that the idea of a Green with housing for his pensioners came from Blaise Hamlet. The design of the Green was partly

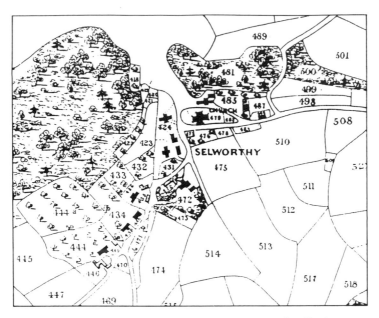

10.8 Selworthy Tithe Map 1841. (Somerset Record Office)

determined by the existing village. It may be that conversion and addition rather than a clean sweep were dictated by a need not to spend an enormous amount of money as Sir Thomas was regularly overspending his income during this period (Acland 1981). The architectural details such as thatched roofs, gothic and Tudor arches, lattice windows and round chimney uppers all were probably inspired by the cottages and houses already on the estate and from Holnicote House itself, which was very much in the 'picturesque' tradition. The mention of Mr Birmingham, the Agent, in one of the Reverend Stephenson's entries suggests that he may also have been involved in the creation of the Green. His son, Robert Birmingham, put forward designs for Holnicote House in the late 1850s, after a disastrous fire, and it is likely that his father, John, worked with Sir Thomas in the same way, producing plans that were acceptable to his employer. There is no mention of an architect connected with the Somerset estate, unlike Killerton where C. R. Cockerell designed two lodges in the 1820s and the Chapel, completed in 1841.

The Green, in its setting in Selworthy Combe, with the thatched and limewashed cottages tucked into their colourful gardens, has delighted visitors for more than a hundred and fifty years. While the interiors are not spacious, the tenants enjoy living there and value the views of the Green, with the Vale of Porlock and Dunkery stretching away to the south. In 1828 Sir Thomas had adapted the site, creating the Green and adding his own touches to the existing cottages, providing better living conditions for his pensioners than were common at the time. As suggested by Michael Havinden in 'The Model Village' (Havinden 1989) this may have been patriarchal, but for most tenants this would have been a price worth paying for a secure and more comfortable home.

Acknowledgements

I would like to thank Sheila Edwards and Beryl Coe (archaeological volunteers) for help in the documentary research, and Robert Waterhouse (Vernacular Buildings Survey, Holnicote) for drawing the maps and plans, also David Thackray for drawing the paper by Michael Havinden to my notice, and Hugh Meller for commenting on a draft of this paper.

References

Acland, A. 1981. *A Devon Family, the Story of the Aclands*, London and Chichester

Chadwyck Healey, C.E.H. 1901. *The History of the Part of West Somerset comprising the parishes of Luccombe, Selworthy, Stoke Pero, Porlock, Culbone and Oare*, London

Havinden, M. 1989. 'The Model Village' in *The Rural Idyll* (ed. G.E. Mingay), London

Law, A. and Messrs Bradley and Summers, 1809 and 1812. *Survey and Valuation of Holnicote in the County of Somerset*, Devon

Record Office, Acland Papers 1148M/add/9/6/24

Stephenson, Revd J. 1802–63. *Diaries*, Devon Record Office, Acland Papers 1148M/add/114, transcribed by Lady Acland 1974

Thorn, C. and Thorn, J. 1980. *Domesday Book, Somerset*, Chichester

Vernacular Buildings Surveys 1992–1994 (unpublished), held at the Holnicote Estate Office, Selworthy, Minehead

11 Landscape with engines

R. Angus Buchanan

My title is intended in part as a tribute to the life and work of L. T. C. Rolt, the first volume of whose autobiography was published as *Landscape with Machines*. Tom Rolt became, in the last years of his life, an outstanding spokesman for what was then, in the 1960s and early 1970s, the new study of industrial archaeology.[1] When he died, in 1974, I was appointed to succeed him as the representative of industrial archaeological interests on the Properties Committee of the National Trust. He was, so far as I know, the first person to be appointed with such a commission, and this fact alone indicates an awakening sensitivity to industrial monuments on the part of the Trust some time in the 1960s. Between us, we have tried to encourage this sensitivity for a quarter of the National Trust's century, and it is appropriate this year to take stock of what has been achieved.

At first glance, it might appear that the achievement has been slight, in so far as industrial monuments still constitute a small proportion of the Trust's huge property portfolio. However, I intend to show that a very significant holding of industrial properties has already been acquired and, still more important, that increasing familiarization with this type of heritage monument has brought a greater awareness of its potentialities to the officers and members of the Trust, and a growing readiness to consider new industrial features for acquisition. I will also try to suggest some of the directions in which this sympathetic understanding could move in the future.

It is certain that the first 'industrial' properties to be acquired by the National Trust were more or less accidental: that is to say, they were acquired indirectly, as the result of some larger property coming to the Trust, or because they were valued for their rural or rustic charm rather than for any industrial significance which they might possess. Several windmills and watermills have been acquired in this way, such as Stembridge windmill at High Ham and Dunster watermill, both in Somerset: the former was acquired as an attractive rural feature, and the latter as a by-product of the acquisition of the Dunster Castle estate. In other cases, well-preserved limekilns have come to the Trust as features in large estates,

---

1 The full autobiographical trilogy was: L. T. C. Rolt, *Landscape with Machines*, Longman, 1971; *Landscape with Canals*, 1977; and *Landscape with Figures*, Stroud, 1992. For a general survey of industrial arhaeology see R. A. Buchanan, *Industrial Archaeology in Britain*, 1972 and 1982; and for a more recent study, Marilyn Palmer and Peter Neaverson, *Industry in the Landscape, 1700–1900*, London, 1994.

such as the battery of kilns at Calke Abbey in Derbyshire; and at Erdigg in Clwyd a number of industrial items have been excellently displayed as part of the presentation of the way in which this large mansion was serviced and maintained.

At Styal in Cheshire, a much larger ensemble of industrial buildings in the shape of Quarry Bank Mill and its associated structures was acquired almost incidentally in the process of obtaining the large estate which now forms Styal Country Park (see also chapter 12, this volume). For several decades, the Trust did not know what to do with these buildings, which fell into dilapidation, but through the ingenious device of a subsidiary body, the Quarry Bank Mill Trust Ltd, acting as the tenant of the National Trust, the site has undergone a remarkable revitalization since the mid-1970s and is now one of the most successful properties in the country in terms of visitor appeal.[2] In a similar vein, the Trust took over the open rural site of the old gold mine at Dolaucothi in Dyfed, and has only recently developed its great educational possibilities as an industrial monument by erecting appropriate head-stocks on the site and by opening up some of the underground galleries to visitors.

Since the 1950s, the National Trust has made a number of deliberate acquisitions of industrial properties. The first of these was probably the 'rescue' of the Stratford Canal which was inspired in the first instance by John Smith.[3] Although successful in its primary objective, this was a salutary experience for the Trust because it brought home the considerable managerial skills and maintenance costs of such a property, so that it was returned with some relief, but as a going concern, to British Waterways. The Trust has had happier experiences with the Conwy Bridge in Gwynedd, the fine early suspension bridge of Thomas Telford, opened in 1826 and now closed to traffic; and with the Cornish engines at Pool and other places in Cornwall, acquired largely on the initiative of the Cornish Engines Preservation Society (now the Trevithick Society), an active preservation society which lacked the resources to maintain the machines indefinitely and to present them to the public. The Cornish 'landscape with engines' epitomizes what this paper is about: some splendid machines, located in dramatic engine houses, together with many empty and ruinous engine houses, of tremendous significance for the history of Cornwall and, more generally, for the history of technology (fig. 11.1). The Trust is currently collaborating with the

2. A feasibility study – *Styal* – was prepared by Dr Richard Hills in the early 1970s, and most of his scheme for the development of Quarry Bank Mill as a working museum was adopted. The Quarry Bank Trust Ltd produces first-class informative and educational literature about the site, obtainable Bat the mill, Styal, Cheshire SK9 4LA.

3. John Smith was then a member of the Historic Buildings Committee of the Trust: see Merlin Waterson, *The National Trust – The First Hundred Years*, London, 1994: 'Almost single-handed John Smith had pushed the Trust into industrial archaeology.' Waterstone also notes that in 1964 Rex Wailes was appointed an honorary Adviser on Industrial Monuments to the Trust (p. 160).

11.1 Landscape with engines: the Cornish industrial landscape of ruinous tin and copper mines is here represented by the Levant Mine on the Land's End peninsula. A steam winding engine in the building on the left was preserved by the Cornish Engines Preservation Society. It is now owned by the National Trust and has been restored. (R. A. Buchanan)

local authorities and the Trevithick Society in an imaginative project to exploit the full heritage value of this landscape.[4] The restoration of the steam launch *Gondola* on Lake Coniston has been another happy inspiration, though not without financial problems.

Another deliberate acquisition of an industrial site was that of Aberdulais Falls in West Glamorgan, obtained by the Trust in 1980. This small wedge of land in a steep-sided gorge had been intensively used for various industrial purposes, and contained the derelict remains of a tin-plate factory. It did not, at first glance, appear to be a site of high aesthetic quality. However, a decade later I hope that I am not committing a serious breach of confidence when I say that the debate over it in the Properties Committee was one of very few which had to be resolved by a vote, and that on this occasion a vociferous minority in favour of acquiring the site was converted into a small majority by the realization that Turner and other artists had been inspired to paint the waterfalls, the power of

4. The 'Trevithick Partnership' between the National Trust, English Heritage, and various local authorities and societies, was established in July 1991. It is based on the Camborne–Redruth area, but its interests extend to cover the Land's End peninsula. One aspect of the subject has been covered in *Mineral Tramways Project*, published by the Cornwall Archaeological Unit, 1990.

which had attracted industries to Aberdulais. The Trust has sensitively opened up the site, with careful excavation, reconstruction of the water-wheel, and an elegant presentation of its industrial significance. It has, moreover, found a helpful subsidiary income by installing a brand new water turbine which feeds power directly into the national grid, and this has been achieved without detracting in any way from the integrity of the site.[5]

Aberdulais has set a good precedent for the National Trust in the acquisition of industrial monuments, but not one which it has rushed to repeat. Only two uncompromisingly industrial properties have been acquired in recent years – a spade mill in Northern Ireland (which already boasted a beetling mill at Wellsbrook in County Tyrone) and a village foundry in Devon. Patterson's Spade Mill in County Antrim was taken on with some misgivings when it stopped producing spades in 1990, and seems set to become a successful tourist attraction. And even more recently, Finch Foundry at Sticklepath in Devon has been taken over as a small water-powered foundry and forge which produced agricultural hand-tools – a sort of glorified village blacksmith. Finch Foundry set another interesting precedent, as it had been run for thirty years by a small independent Trust which had rescued it from obliteration when it had closed down in the 1960s.[6] Inevitably, changes of personnel and lack of resources for long-term maintenance had caused a gradual decline in the viability of this project, and the National Trust was called upon to fulfil the role of 'safety net' in order to save a worthy but small-scale and under-funded venture from total collapse. It is a precedent with important implications for future policy, as we come to consider the way in which the National Trust could most usefully develop its portfolio of industrial properties, because many small trusts established in the early enthusiasm for industrial archaeology in the 1960s and 1970s are reaching their natural 'sell-by' date.

Another sort of industrial site which has been acquired by the National Trust in recent years has been of an incidental or accidental nature, because it has accompanied the progress of Enterprise Neptune. In the course of obtaining control over large stretches of coastline, the Trust has acquired coastal properties in North Yorkshire which have been found to contain substantial remains of the alum industry. This industry involved excavating massive quantities of alum-rich clay from the coastal cliffs of North Yorkshire, and processing them on the spot to concentrate the alum which was then shipped out to find many industrial applications. The best deposits have now been worked out and the industry has

5. The South Wales Region of the National Trust has produced several excellent site guides to Aberdulais. The approach to the site is currently being disrupted by road works which have obliterated the visitors' car park, but it is hoped that normal conditions will soon be restored.
6. Finch Foundry was acquired by the Trust in 1993. It had ceased functioning in the early 1960s and had been preserved as a working museum by a group of enthusiasts: see the short note in *Industrial Archaeology*, vol. 4, no. 3, August 1967, 285; and the supplement by J. Kenneth Major, 'Finch Brothers' Foundry Sticklepath, Okehampton, Devon' in the following issue, November 1967.

11.2 Peak Alum Works, Ravenscar. This site, an Enterprise Neptune property above the sea cliffs in North Yorkshire, has been carefully excavated by a National Trust team. It has revealed an intricate process for preparing mineral alum prior to exporting it from a jetty at the foot of the cliffs. (R. A. Buchanan)

collapsed, leaving miles of disturbed cliff scenery, the remains of alum-concentration plants, and the ruins of some primitive harbour facilities. The Trust has responded very sympathetically to the challenge presented by these remains, and at Ravenscar (fig. 11.2) in particular has undertaken a careful excavation and presentation of an alum-concentration works.[7] In the same area, on coastal properties, a Guibal fan-house associated with iron mining, and a wartime radar installation, have also received attention.

All this goes to demonstrate a long-standing sympathy for industrial monuments on the part of the National Trust. It is no longer necessary to spell out the case for treating such monuments as significant heritage features, either with the Trust or any other responsible public authority. But with the National Trust an attitude of largely benign indifference has been transformed into one of mild enthusiasm for many of the features of obsolete industrialization with which industrial archaeology is concerned. Senior officers and members have demonstrated increasing interest in the subject, and a small but well-qualified

7. The Ravenscar site has been excavated and partially reconstructed by a National Trust team led by Gary Marshall: see the excellent information sheet – *Peak Alum Works Ravenscar*, North Yorkshire Moors National Park, 1993.

team of specialist staff has been built up to deal with it. One of the big questions of this Centenary Year is thus that of what happens next in the Trust's involvement with industrial monuments. It is arguable that the phenomenal growth of the National Trust in recent years demonstrates a widespread belief that the Trust is the major custodian of the national heritage, and that this is a challenge to become more proactive in determining what it wants to acquire. In the field of industrial monuments such an attitude would involve a generous inclination to fulfil its 'safety-net' function towards those worthy small-scale bodies which have struggled over the last generation to preserve particular industrial structures from obliteration. It would also involve setting out deliberately to acquire specific kinds of monument in order to equip itself to perform a long-term heritage educational function. Consider, for example, the following list of twelve sites. Some are already in good hands, and others are not likely to become available. But all of them are worthy of consideration for acquisition by the National Trust, and if the circumstances warranted it there would be a strong case to be made for Trust intervention:

1. Chatterley Whitfield Colliery in Staffordshire. The British coal-mining industry has been transformed in recent years, and its traditional landscape is disappearing. It is most important that a few more-or-less typical examples of coal mines should be preserved. Chatterley Whitfield survived for some time as a local authority working museum, but support was withdrawn two years ago and the site now requires urgent attention.

2. Merthyr Tydfil blast furnaces. The iron and steel industry is another heavy industry which has changed out of all recognition and in which the Trust has a role to preserve heritage features. At Merthyr, a range of massive blast furnaces set in the side of the hill deserve consideration.

3. Swan Hunters' Shipyard, Tyneside. Yet another disappearing traditional heavy industry, in urgent need of conservationist attention while there is still something to conserve. Swan Hunters was one of the last, and the latest to go out of business.

4. Gladstone Pottery, Longton, Staffordshire. An admirable preservation of this, one of the last remaining sets of bottle kilns in the traditional 'Potteries', is now believed to require long-term support.

5. Cheddleton Flint Mill, Staffordshire. Another important pottery process, preserved by enthusiastic amateurs in the 1960s, this water-powered mill for grinding flints is also in need of support.

6. Elsecar Newcomen Engine House, South Yorkshire. This, probably the earliest surviving steam engine, has been preserved rather unsatisfactorily as part of a 'country park' scheme which threatens its integrity (fig. 11.3).

11.3 Elsecar Engine House. Almost certainly the oldest surviving steam engine, the Newcomen-style beam engine housed in this building in South Yorkshire provided power for pumping water from the coal mine shaft in the foreground. Its long-term preservation without impairing the integrity of the site is currently a matter of some anxiety. (R. A. Buchanan)

7. Charterhouse Lead Works, Somerset. There are large lead works on Trust property in Yorkshire and Wales, but these in Somerset are both ancient (with Roman origins) and compact – and they are threatened by neglect and by badly applied attention.

8. Saltaire Mill, Yorkshire. This huge building has been partially re-used, but its position as part of the enlightened community project of Sir Titus Salt and its vulnerability to the development of neighbouring Bradford makes it particularly significant and worthy of attention. The national stock of large textile mills is being rapidly depleted, transforming the landscape of Yorkshire and Lancashire, so it is a matter of some urgency that the Trust should examine its responsibilities in this area.[8]

9. Green Park Station, Bath. Handsomely restored by Sainsburys in the 1980s as an adjunct and car park for its store, the firm is now planning a re-location which could make the station vulnerable. The Trust

---

8. On textile mills, see the authoritative reports by the Royal Commission on the Historical Monuments of England: *Yorkshire Textile Mills, 1770–1930* (by Colum Giles and Ian H. Goodall), HMSO, 1992; *Cotton Mills in Greater Manchester* (by Mike Williams), 1992; and *East Cheshire Textile Mills* (by Anthony Calladine and Jean Fricker), RCHME, 1993.

certainly needs to consider railway stations, and this is a well-preserved specimen.

10. Star Cross Engine House, Devon. Built by I. K. Brunel as a pumping station for his South Devon 'atmospheric' Railway, this survived successfully as a museum, but that has now closed and its future is uncertain.

11. Combe Hay Locks on the Somersetshire Coal Canal. Redundant canals everywhere deserve conservation attention, but this set of 22 locks and associated works is of unusual technological significance – and neglected.

12. The Underfall Yard, Bristol City Docks. This remarkable complex of engineering workshop, foundry, steam engine, slip-way, and hydraulic engine house, was established in the 1880s and survives with many of its original features. It has been long neglected and requires attention.

This is a very selective list, and a very personal selection at that. It could be expanded many times over without exhausting all the industrial sites in England, Wales and Northern Ireland which deserve the attention of the National Trust. But while specific in its examples, it is designed to represent *types* of monument, and to remind all of us in the Trust of the sorts of obsolete industrial structures which require our sympathy – and our readiness to undertake a proactive conservation strategy in relation to this part of our national heritage in this, our Centenary Year.

12 Mills in the landscape

Marilyn Palmer

Water power is one of the most studied aspects of the development of technology, and one on which archaeologists of all periods from the classical onwards have something to contribute, as Kevin Greene has recently reminded us (Greene 1994). Jean Gimpel has suggested a power revolution taking place in the twelfth and thirteenth centuries, with water power being applied to a variety of industrial processes apart from corn-grinding, including saw-milling, iron forging and fulling cloth (Gimpel 1976). Richard Holt has shown how seignorial pressure in the thirteenth century led to the expansion of corn-milling by water power, since the lord of the manor could exercise his rights to force his tenants to have their corn ground at his mill (Holt 1988). It is precisely on this aspect of the development of water power that this paper will concentrate, since it is in its role as proprietor of many landed estates that the National Trust could make a real contribution to the study of the distribution and development of the history of water power in Great Britain.

The Trust certainly recognizes the importance of water power in the context of renewable energy resources: a water turbine has been installed on the complex industrial site at Aberdulais in south Wales and there are plans for the rehabilitation of other historic water-power sites for the generation of small-scale hydro-electric power. Of course, it also has an interest in what is now the last working water-powered cotton mill in the world as far as we know, Quarry Bank Mill at Styal (fig. 12.1). A series of water-wheels powered by the River Bollin culminated in the installation, between 1817 and 1820, of a massive 100hp iron suspension wheel, which continued to work until replaced by turbines in 1904. A similar wheel, rescued from the flax mill at Glasshouses, near Pateley Bridge in Yorkshire, was re-installed in 1985 at Styal as a working artefact. However, as in many other textile mills, water power at Quarry Bank Mill was supplemented by steam power, especially after the addition of power looms in the 1830s. Various alterations were made to the building to accommodate the engines, their boilers, flues and fuel stores. Quarry Bank Mill Trust intends to re-install an engine similar to the independent beam engine obtained from Boulton and Watt in 1836 to complete the story of powered cotton spinning on this site. The proposed alterations to the existing building in order to install this engine have been preceded by archaeological recording and excavation, which have revealed further details about the earlier forms of power (Milln 1994) (fig. 12.2). This new development at

12.1 Quarry Bank Mill, Styal, on the River Bollin. The mill was founded in 1784 by Samuel Greg for cotton spinning and this long range of brick buildings was added when powered weaving was introduced. The chimney in the distance marks the positions of the engine and boiler houses added to enable supplementary steam power to be used. (M. Palmer)

Quarry Bank Mill will be important in demonstrating how the two types of power could co-exist and correct the impression, still often repeated in textbooks, that the introduction of steam meant the end of water power.

Archaeology, nevertheless, is generally concerned with the mundane rather than the spectacular, with the spatial patterning of material culture in general rather than unique, if welcome, discoveries like the Sutton Hoo ship or the Mildenhall treasure. This is equally true of industrial archaeology, where the importance of a survival like Quarry Bank Mill must not blind us to the existence of many lesser mills on National Trust property. Landed proprietors were concerned with the exploitation of their estates, and frequently made use of water power to process materials for estate use or for sale. A good example is the little mill at Dunham Massey, Cheshire, dating back to the seventeenth century and powered from the moat. This began life as a corn mill but was adapted for saw-milling once a larger corn mill was built on the estate alongside the River Bollin in the 1860s: this latter mill has now itself been converted to flats. The history of Dunham Massey mill shows how a study of the buildings can indicate changes both in technology and in the management of the resources of an estate.

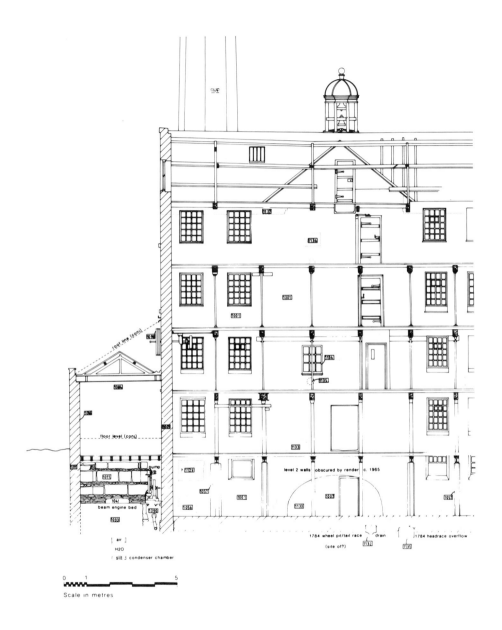

12.2 Elevational section of part of the rear of Quarry Bank Mill, showing the steam engine house on the right together with the positions of the tail races from the earlier water wheels. (Jeremy Milln)

The old mill here is preserved, like other mills at Charlecote and Erdigg, but with limited resources it is impossible to conserve all such buildings. They are, however, part of the archaeological assemblage of an estate and should be recorded as such. Whereas there is often copious documentary evidence about other aspects of a country house and its estate, items such as the corn mill or saw mill were rarely mentioned because they were so familiar. It is for this reason that archaeological recording is so important, as often only by treating the building as an archaeological section can its history be unravelled.

This paper will conclude as a brief case study with some derelict mills on the Cotehele estate in Cornwall which were recorded by the author with second-year university students. The corn mill on the Morden stream had already been recognized as part of the cultural resource of the estate, together with the adjacent estate buildings such as a saw pit and wheelwright's shop, and these are conserved and interpreted. But the Danescombe Valley to the east was let to tenants and its water power resources used for copper mining, ore-dressing, paper-making and commercial saw-milling: as such, it is an excellent example of the context of the exploitation of water power (fig. 12.3). The engine house

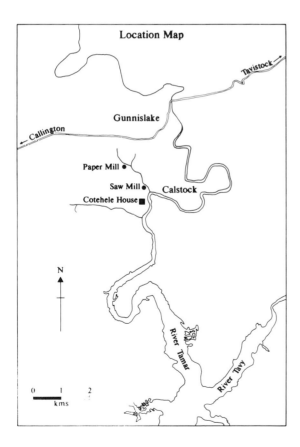

12.3 Location map of the Cotehele Estate and the Danescombe Valley.

2000	Main ground floor area
2001	Narrow corridor floor area
2002	Additional floor area, probably under lean-to roof
2003	Fragment of partition wall across main floor area
2004	Fragment of partition wall across main floor area
2005	Dividing wall
2006	Fireplace aperture in dividing wall
2007	South-east wall of corridor area
2008	Additional floor area with external access
2009	Waterwheel pit
2010	Water outlet channel to stream
2011	Flat area beside wheel pit
2012	Stone retaining wall
2013	Small walled floor area
2014–15	Walled floor areas
2016–18	Accesses to walled floor areas
2019	North-east wall of walled floor areas
2020	South-east wall of walled floor area
2021–2	Partition walls of walled floor areas
2023	North-west wall of walled floor area
2024	Walled floor area
2025	North-east wall of walled floor area
2026	South-east wall of walled floor area
2027	North-west wall of walled floor area

2040	North-east wall
2041–4	Window apertures in north-east wall, ground floor
2045	Partly infilled doorway in north-east wall, ground floor
2046	Doorway in north-east wall, ground floor
2047–52	Window apertures in north-east wall, ground floor
2053	Hole in north-east wall, external face
2054–61	Floor beam sockets, internal face of north-east wall
2062–6	Sockets in north-east wall, first floor, internal face
2067	Fireplace in north-east wall, first floor, internal face
2068	Fireplace in north-east wall, ground floor, internal face
2069	Brickcourse and stone work, probable infilling, north-east wall, ground floor, internal face
2070	Infill in doorway 2045
2071	Probable take-off for water supply leat to wheel
2072	Possible further windows or ventilated walls for top storey

2080	South-west wall
2081–8	Beam sockets in south-west wall, external face
2089	South-west wall to additional floor areas
2090	Probable window aperture in south-west wall
2091	Window aperture in south-west wall
2092	Recess in south-west wall, internal face
2093–4	Sockets in south-west wall, internal face
2095	Fireplace, south-west wall, ground floor
2096	Fireplace, south-west wall, first floor

12.4 Context numbers for part of the survey of the Danescombe paper mill.

which formed part of the copper mine has been let to the Landmark Trust and restored for use as a holiday cottage. The saw mill and paper mill were, however, ruinous and needed some attention if they were not to be a hazard to visitors. The saw mill was a single-phase building powered by a turbine and linked by a tramway to a small wharf on the River Tamar. There were no remains of the turbine itself, but a leat was taken off the stream some 160m upstream from the mill and water conducted through a rock-cut channel to a cistern some 7.87m above the mill, from which it would have fallen through a pipe to the turbine in the rock-cut pit below. The saw mill was built of the local killas with yellow brick quoins to the windows and doors. It was a single-storey building, and the curve of the end and interior partition walls would suggest it had an iron roof, which is borne out by the limited documentary evidence. The paper mill was a far more complex structure of several phases and powered by an overshot wheel, the water being conducted from a dam some 44m upstream of the mill. The wheelpit dimensions indicate that the wheel was some 14ft (4.26m) in diameter and up to 5ft (1.52m) in width. The mill itself was built of random stone with dressed granite quoins and shaped granite window sills of some sophistication. Both buildings were measured using simple equipment and recorded using context numbers as in an archaeological section (fig. 12.4), which forces the recorder to look at the building archaeologically rather than architecturally and to note anomalies such as infilled windows or straight joints indicating building extensions. The drawn record was a simple one supplemented by photographs. The survey showed that the building was originally three storeys in height (fig. 12.5), while documentary evidence in the form of an insurance policy provided a date of 1788. It is clear that a multi-storey structure of this size, resembling the earliest phases of Quarry Bank Mill, must have been a remarkable sight in Cornwall in this period, and documentary research continues. Knowledge of the sequence and functions of these buildings gives a more comprehensive picture of the economy of the Cotehele Estate as well as adding to visitor interest in the Danescombe Valley, which is on public access.

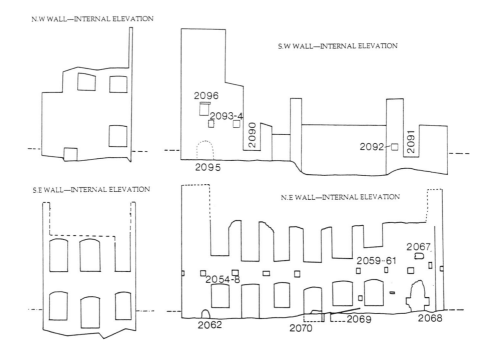

12.5 Elevations of the Danescombe paper mill.

The author hopes that Trust Property Managers and Historic Buildings Representatives will recognize the importance even of derelict structures such as these on country estates, and, where possible, arrange for archaeological recording which can reveal information about changes in space and time which are not always retrievable from documentary sources (Major 1975; Palmer and Neaverson, forthcoming). University students need training in this particular field of archaeology and can contribute at a reasonable level to the Trust's Archaeological Survey. They are a resource greatly utilized in the United States by the Historic American Buildings Survey and the Historic American Engineering Record but there are, unfortunately, no comparable bodies in Britain to organize the recording process (Burns 1989). Records should be made not necessarily for the purposes of conservation but as a means of adding to our knowledge of the extent and distribution of water-powered resources in Britain, which by no means came to an end with the introduction of steam power. We know that over 6,000 mills were recorded in Domesday Book; we have many county gazetteers of mills, generally those with some remains; and they form probably the largest class of industrial structure which has yet found its way on to Sites and Monuments Records. But we have as yet no real understanding of the topographical or technological context of the development of water power, and the archaeological resources of estates belonging to the Trust could be an important sample in this respect.

References

Burns, J. A. 1989. *Recording Historic Structures*, Washington DC

Gimpel, J. 1976. *The Medieval Machine: the Industrial Revolution of the Middle Ages*, London (first published as *La révolution industrielle du Moyen Age*)

Greene, K. 1994. 'Technology and innovation in context: the Roman background to medieval and later developments', *Journal of Roman Archaeology* 7, 22–33

Holt, R. 1988. *The Mills of Medieval England*, Oxford

Major, J. K. 1975. *Fieldwork in Industrial Archaeology*, London

Milln, J. 1994. *Power Development at the Northern End of Quarry Bank Mill, Styal, Cheshire* (Internal report for the National Trust Archaeological Survey, Cirencester)

Palmer, M. and Neaverson, P. A. 1994. *A Survey of the Former Saw Mill and Paper Mill in the Danescombe Valley* (report for the National Trust Archaeological Survey, Cirencester)

Palmer, M. and Neaverson, P. A. forthcoming. *Industrial Archaeology*, London

13 Archaeology in education

Gareth Binns

There are three areas I would like to consider in this paper. Initially, I will be looking at the development of archaeology and education. I will then set the context for education work within the Trust, and archaeology's role within it. Finally, I will consider possible future roles for the Trust in this area.

The development of archaeology and education

Archaeology and education. It really is a strange phrase to use. We tend not to hear the phrase 'history and education' or 'geology and education', yet over the last decade or so the phrase archaeology and education, or archaeology in education, has become standard within that rather small world of archaeologists who are interested in education, and educationalists interested in archaeology. It is used as if it is only at specific times, or places, such as conferences or excavation open days, that archaeology serves – or is related to – an educational purpose or goal. It has been analysed and discussed, conceptually and theoretically, sometimes to the nth degree, losing sight of the starting point. Of course if archaeology is about anything, it is about investigation and a search for understanding and meaning, and is therefore an educational activity in its own right. I hope the only debate within the archaeological profession now is not why to do it, but how and where to do it.

Where the phrase is used, it is usually in the context of formal education programmes, whether for schools and colleges, or universities. However, the main focus of discussion regarding archaeology and education has largely been centred on schools and colleges, particularly the schools. A number of individuals, units, trusts, museums and one or two universities had begun developing specific education programmes in the 1970s through into the 1980s. Thus professional archaeologists became involved in developing materials and approaches specifically to support teachers and their pupils' learning. Also, the growing field of experimental archaeology found spin-offs in technical and practical school projects. Driven by a zeal for their subject, the agenda of those involved was just as much to establish archaeology as a credible subject, gaining future support and interest in it, as it was to support learning objectives and provide a cognitive tool. These people did much to begin to break down the 'ology' syndrome which the profession had wrapped itself in, and offered effective approaches for teachers, the vast majority of whom had no current knowledge of what archaeology was about or what it could contribute.

Developments included programmes for examining artefacts and structures, and ways of putting across concepts such as stratigraphy and phasing developed, often based on active site visiting, with archaeologists and teachers working alongside each other. Many of these methodologies – such as those coming from the Schools Committee of the CBA – have stood the test of time. Occasionally there were sharp intakes of breath from the profession as youngsters actually got in the trenches to try trowelling for themselves; I wonder how many of these children have now found their way into the profession in later life.

Archaeology began to show its strengths but also its weaknesses. Its multi-disciplinary nature, bridging sciences and humanities, translated into school speak as 'cross-curricular topic work'.

Strengths included its ability to capture pupils' imaginations, and to offer opportunities for practical work. However, at times the discipline tried to present itself as all things to all people, becoming all-embracing and amorphous. Examples of this were the ever more complex topic webs based on sites or artefacts. Limited recognition of the contribution which archaeology could make came in a few official documents such as an HMI study on *History in the Primary and Secondary Years* (HMSO 1985) and *History from 5–16* (HMSO 1988). However, references only related to 'early civilisation'.

A realization dawned of how valuable an educational resource the Sites and Monuments Record was, and how quantities of unstratified pottery could actually be handled by children without harming the academic integrity of ceramic research. Awareness by the profession of marketing, sponsorship and income generation opportunities through education programmes began to grow.

The main deciding factor as to how the subject would or would not evolve in schools was the plan in the late 1980s to develop a national curriculum. This was immediately seen as both a threat and an opportunity to those concerned about the role of archaeology in education. A threat because the flexibility which had allowed teachers to develop cross-curricular projects – based largely around archaeological methodologies and material – could become lost within a rigorous straitjacket of a centrally prescribed curriculum. The opportunity, however, was to find a place for the subject within the prescribed content, most obviously within history, but also feeding into geography, science, technology and the cross-curricular themes.

A number of organizations and individuals made submissions on behalf of archaeology, a major one being the report *Archaeology for Ages 5–16* produced by the Council for British Archaeology (1989). From personal experience, I know how hard it is to define within that document, how a pupil's knowledge, skills and understanding of say chronology, or the nature of the archaeological record, should ideally develop from ages 5–16.

As document after document rolled out from the National Curriculum Council, the subject content within them developed and the debate about knowledge, skills and understanding grew. In response, a matrix tick-list mentality appeared within the archaeology and museums environment (Binns 1990). Pages were scanned for key words or phrases: 'the Anglo Saxons', 'the Vikings', 'archaeological material'. I remember a very brief phone call:

'Good news, it's in.'
'What is?'
'Handling artefacts and their value as evidence.'
'So what's out?'
'Prehistory!'

We seemed to have moved a long way from the 1988 discussion document produced by the Department of Education and Science (HMSO 1988), which suggested that by the age of 16, pupils should know of 'Early civilisation; hunter-gatherer societies, the discovery of fire and the development of agriculture'.

In the end we became grateful for what was in there, and the production of teaching packs began to roll. The word archaeology was played down and a number of creative initiatives to using material remains and investigating the historic environment were developed. On the downside, Curriculum topic webs became very stretched. Attainment Targets in Maths for numbers became related to counting pieces of Roman pottery. Archaeologists learned new phrases: 'Key Stage 2, Attainment Target 3, Programmes of Study', and all became interactive and hands-on. Just for the record, the word archaeology appears once in the History section for Key Stage 2 (7–11) (HMSO 1995) in the context of a past non-European society. The unit is, of course, optional.

The educational work of the National Trust

The National Curriculum is now fixed for five years, so what role is the Trust playing in promoting an understanding of, and interest in, archaeology through its education work? Before coming to this, it is necessary to consider the wider picture and provide some background to the range of our educational work. In 1907, parliamentary documents dealing with the purposes of the organization referred to holding property for the purposes of public instruction. However, it was not until 1987 that the Trust adopted a formal education policy. Initially aimed at schoolchildren, it has now widened to become the following: 'The National Trust is committed to the promotion of understanding and enjoyment of the properties in its care through educational use by people of all ages' (National Trust 1994).

Through the promotion of enjoyment and understanding, we also hope to make people aware of the Trust's work and purpose, hopefully to secure future support as members and volunteers. Clearly our archaeological activities and responsibilities should be a part of this.

The education work in the Trust falls within the remit of Public Affairs, is managed centrally and delivered largely through the properties. Core funding is small, but through a strategy of identifying, resourcing and promoting key sites for educational use in each region, we have created a wide-ranging programme, with over half a million schoolchildren undertaking curriculum-related visits at properties with admission points. Many more visit open-space properties and one could argue that in total, these are truly, the new figures in the landscape. Chosen sites reflect the range of Trust properties and the needs of teachers, the latter being ensured through close liaison with local authorities, inspectors and relevant organizations. Key sites will offer a range of activities and facilities including study bases, resource material and education staff. In-service training for teachers is being offered more widely, and we are able to develop special programmes which supplement and enhance the normal patterns of provision at properties, such as energy and technology projects and the use of creative arts. I hope some people are aware of the excellent record of the Trust's own Theatre in Education company (The Young National Trust Theatre), whose tour sells out each year within a very short time. We are also developing generic materials, which are applicable across a number of sites. Targeting limited resources and identifying strong curriculum links have helped us to create a convergence at properties between the varied nature of the Trust holdings and activities, and the wide and dynamic world of education.

If you doubt the need to target and be focused about what you are doing, this image might help you: the picture is of a young student from an inner-city school standing in the library of a large eighteenth-century house, decorated with Greek vases, Dutch paintings and artefacts from travels in the colonies. She looks out through a window across a restored Tudor garden, associated with an earlier, but now demolished, house. Beyond lies an eighteenth-century landscaped park with a medieval church set amidst the house platforms of a deserted village. A hillfort dominates the landscape beyond (Binns 1993). Perhaps a slightly contrived example, but it serves to highlight the complex cultural, spatial and temporal assemblage which many Trust properties represent.

Education for archaeology

What then are we doing in the educational field, which would be recognized as having an archaeological dimension to it? What happens when the multifarious subject of archaeology connects with the multifaceted world of the National Trust in an education context? One could answer this with a sweeping statement that as every Trust property is the product of past human intervention in the landscape, then by definition any education programme has an archaeological dimension to it – but I do not think that will really convince anyone.

Much of the education work on properties does have a time depth to it and there are growing opportunities to handle artefacts. Many activities include observational and recording skills based on structural evidence or signs of previous methods of resource exploitation and land management. On Brownsea Island in Dorset, the main approach for exploring the existence of a pottery in the last century is archaeological, based on pupils' investigation of earthworks and patterns of artefact distribution (Binns 1992a). A similar approach to using structural remains gives pupils a means of understanding the remains of an eighteenth-century pilchard factory on the Lizard in Cornwall. Specific programmes which take a deeper archaeological approach to evidence and processes run at Chedworth Roman Villa, the Kingston Lacy Estate in Dorset and Fountains Abbey in Yorkshire. At Bodiam and Corfe castles, pupils are offered opportunities to examine the material remains. Hypotheses can then be generated and investigated alongside other evidence such as written sources. Sites such as Aberdulais and Dolaucothi in Wales provide opportunities for pupils to focus on industrial exploitation of the landscape.

We also have pupils who study and undertake active conservation work in areas of coast and countryside under our 'Guardianship' programme – an initiative which involves the twinning of a school with its local Trust property to undertake curriculum-related projects and conservation tasks. A number of the Guardianship properties have archaeological features such as hillforts, brickworks and field systems, and one is based on a motte and bailey site. In Wales, one Guardianship specifically considers links between myth and legend and ancient monuments. A number of our property-based teachers' resource books include information and activities about material remains as do generic publications such as *Rural Landscapes* (Binns 1992b). As well as these examples, the Trust's own team of archaeologists have developed educational initiatives where this has been possible, linking, for example, with local archaeological societies, or helping with National Archaeology Day events.

Before considering where we might go in the future, it is probably helpful to consider what the building blocks for archaeology and education might be. I believe in this the Trust can offer something which is both different from, and yet complementary to, the programmes offered by others, such as governmental, local authority and charitable bodies other than itself. It can demonstrate:

1. Effective management of the archaeological resource.
2. The integration of the interests of archaeology with other activities such

as the management of access, nature conservation, visual amenity, agriculture, and forestry.

3. Through sizeable landholdings it can show how areas of landscape have evolved under human impact.

4. A wide range of archaeological sites/landscapes which connect directly with areas of the curriculum.

5. As an organization concerned with the two areas of cultural and natural heritage, the Trust has a unique role to play in explaining the links between the two, and relating those links to environmental issues and concepts such as sustainability. Archaeological sites are habitats in themselves, or components within habitats.

6. A large and growing archive of archaeological information; new stories to tell and new research.

7. Audience – over 10 million visitors to paying properties, 2.2 million members, 500,000 schoolchildren visiting and 400,000 children under family membership.

But we have to be careful. It is all too easy to try to shoe-horn archaeology into every initiative – it does not work like that. Instead we have to make connections and be aware of the potential where it exists, just as we are with ecology and history and geography. This is not to say that we should not do anything 'archaeological' unless specifically asked for, but we should be pragmatic in our approach rather than throwing the net wide. We can support educational work for archaeology, but as a subject it is just one of many we deal with such as geography, biology, geology, science, technology, history, English, art, travel and tourism, environmental education, etc.

In 1995, as a major Centenary initiative, the Trust has launched a lifelong learning programme called Minerva (National Trust 1995) – named, of course, after the Roman goddess of wisdom, patron of the arts, protectress of schools and defender of just causes – nothing if not ambitious. We hope to raise funds (£2.9m) and develop partnerships to consolidate the existing educational work with schools and extend the support we offer to higher, adult and community education providers. We plan, for example, to double our number of school visits to one million by the end of the century, and support leisure and research interests. Thus it is a timely point at which to put a marker down for archaeology.

Whilst we will not be able to do everything, the following are some areas which could be developed:

1. The wider development of creative and performing arts programmes using archaeological sites as a stimulus.

2. Developing a number of Guardianships at key archaeological sites.

3. Considering the role archaeological and historical evidence could play in providing a context for environmental education.

4. Involving more Trust properties in National Archaeology Day.

5. Build in an element for education and interpretation programmes within archaeological project funding.

6. Develop use of Information Technology for interpretative and educational purposes on and off-site.

7. Consider the role that archaeological content could play within formal and informal adult education.

8. Consider the role that archaeological content could play within informal education programmes for children, and for family learning activities.

However, there are a number of issues which will need to be considered if some of the themes above are developed.

1. How do we deal with the teacher who brings the class to study 'The Romans', with little interest in how we know what we know, i.e. the processes and techniques of archaeology?

2. How can we engage different ethnic groups in an appreciation of, or debate about, the products of a cultural past which they see as having little relevance to them? Is ethnicity an issue here, or it more about young urban dwellers seeing the Trust as irrelevant, its archaeological dimension particularly so?

3. Are we making available enough primary source material and artefacts? How far do conservation concerns override opportunities for increased access to handle material?

4. What degree of convergence is possible or appropriate between our historically based programmes and those which are environmentally based?

5. While targeted fieldwork, involving tightly defined historical periods, can help with the delivery of knowledge and understanding, it may make an appreciation of the holistic view, through cultural and environmental processes, more difficult to convey and apprehend.

6. By focusing on what is special and important, are we in danger of being elitist? It is important to balance an interest in such sites and cultural material with those with which people are more familiar or value in other ways.

I believe educational programmes are an integral and vital part of archaeology, genuinely offering valid pedagogic experiences. It is also important to the continued survival of archaeology through public support and interest. The remains and artefacts themselves can offer an exciting vehicle for arousing the interest of people of all ages. Along with others, I hope the National Trust can play its part.

References

Binns, G. 1990. 'The National Curriculum: Is there a future for teaching about the past?', paper presented at World Archaeological Congress 1990

——, 1992a. *Brownsea Island: A Resource Book for Teachers*, National Trust, London

——, 1992b. *Rural Landscapes. A Resource Book for Teachers*, National Trust, London

——, 1993. *In Trust for the Nation: The National Trust's Education Programmes*, paper presented at National Association for Interpretation Conference, Washington 1993

Council for British Archaeology 1989. *Archaeology for Ages 5–16*, London

HMSO 1985. *History in the Primary and Secondary years. An HMI view*, Department of Education and Science, London

HMSO 1988. *History from 5–16*, Curriculum Matters 11, Department of Education and Science, London

HMSO 1995. *Orders for History*, Department of Education and Science, London

National Trust 1994. *The National Trust and Education*, London

——, 1995. *Minerva Case Statement*, London

14 The tourist as a figure in the National Trust landscape

Priscilla Boniface

The tourist is a fundamental figure in the National Trust landscape. The National Trust, with its remit (in the 1907 Act of Parliament) to achieve 'permanent preservation', for the sake of generations to come, requires for its activity the wide-ranging support of today's generations. For the future it plans and desires, the Trust needs tourists now.

The National Trust is independent, and it is a charity. Its funding derives from its supporters through membership and visits to properties, and through charitable bequests and legacies; some grants are acquired from public funds, issued on behalf of society as a whole. The Trust therefore needs to communicate with, and obtain approbation for its message and belief from, a wide sector. With the UK subject to increasing decision-making by the European Union, and environmental decision-making being made on a global basis, it is necessary for the Trust to be mindful of more than merely home opinion. The Trust needs global supporters for its work to flourish and what better way to court them than by *in situ* demonstration? Though probably more by accident than design, the Japanese have been delivered into the lap of the Trust by Beatrix Potter, but a much wider spectrum of tourists from around the world are needed by the Trust. The questions of who visits the landscape of the Trust and who does not, and of how the landscape is used and is not used by tourists, are those which I would like to explore.

Who, then, is the tourist to the National Trust landscape? The classic and clichéd view probably is that the standard National Trust visitor is from the socio-economic groups ABC1, that he or she lives in the south of England and is likely to be aged more than 40. Whether this equates to the facts one does not know without consulting the National Trust information about its visitors' demography and socio-economic groupings. The National Trust kindly gave me other information and for this I am very grateful. It should be possible, by conducting a sort of archaeological analysis of the material culture of the National Trust presentation for visitors, to obtain a visitor portrait. What, therefore, are some of the products for the visitor? The archaeological first impression might be that in the second half of the twentieth century the Trust's obsession, along with decor and objects agreeable to art-historical taste, was goods bearing scent and cups of tea. The Trust's preservation portfolio, essentially, is the three Big Cs: countryside, coastline and country houses. Of these three, the country houses represent visitor attractions which require the commitment of payment from the visitor. Of course – and this represents both an excellent bargain and a strong incentive to become 'One of Us', so to speak – there is no entrance fee to Trust Members. The other principal products for visitors, as the quick archaeological survey would show, are the three Big Cs' associated facilities and income generators of shops (on or off estates), and tea-rooms or restaurants. How do all these 'look' and what do they 'say'? The Trust estate, from its inception in 1895 to the present, could be evaluated as representing a sort of stratification and archaeology of Trust ideals and concerns, of which the visitor presentation is a major and visible part. Prominent among these might be: the 'outdoor sitting rooms' provision (Octavia Hill, as reported in Fedden 1968); Kinder Scout's acquisition in 1982; the post-War Country House Scheme properties; Enterprise Neptune's shores; and the John Fowler-occasioned distinctive and ubiquitous country house interior decoration style to which Stephen Bayley drew critical attention in the 1995 Channel 4 programme, *J'Accuse*.

The Trust provides for tourists a 'time out experience'. Put very simply, traditionally this has comprised aesthetics, rambles and room-sets. The Trust has a strong culture which permeates all it does: this is its strength and weakness. For tourists, the benefit is that at Trust sites, they know what to expect with all the security attendant upon this. The disadvantage is that the Trust may only offer to the tourist what by its criteria it deems to be required and suitable. Hence, the carp about 'Nanny Trust'. The suspicion is that the Trust is not familiar with, and does not understand, what occurs and matters in the world beyond the ha-ha of its territory in the society of its visitor base. It can be argued that a major failing of, and disappointment about, the Trust, is that it is presenter, not customer, led: the Trust produces, therefore, the object of its desires, philosophy and culture not those of people who do, or more importantly if it wishes its visitor numbers to increase and diversify, do not, visit its sites.

Notwithstanding the clichéd Trust tourist portrait, as presented above, the Trust *has* courted other types of visitors. Tourists from the relevant professions visit Trust properties to study how the Trust manages its estates. Since 1966 the Trust has operated Acorn Camps which appeal to youth. In an excellent initiative, for a very small price the Trust offers to any volunteer over 18, provided they are fit and healthy, a 'Short Breaks in the Country' working holiday (National Trust, undated). So, from these examples alone, the ABC1 stereotype, if correct, is not the sole National Trust tourist form.

Representing a special type of tourism event of its own, is the National Trust Annual General Meeting week-end held in the autumn. The AGM is supposed to be a dialogue between people essentially on the same side, but it highlights the frustration and incomprehension of members as it becomes clear that they have no power to influence decisions of the Trust or to voice their preoccupations. The formality and inflexibility of the event means that the Trust misses the opportunity which the AGM offers. That opportunity is not only for the Trust to hear and consider the views of those not within the inner sanctum, but to communicate its point of view and any reason(s) behind it. A very welcome indication that the Trust does know and recognize the AGM's importance and potential for discussion with the full range of its members came during the Centennial Year. It called for 'An AGM for all' (*National Trust Magazine*, No. 75, Summer 1995, 13) and made a special effort to encourage the participation in person at the 1995 AGM of infrequent attenders, families and the young.

What are some needs in and across society to which the Trust is or is not catering? The need for an escape from everyday life is ostensibly capably met with the provision of scenes and experiences which were never, or are no longer, part of everyday life. Most of us do not indulge regularly in afternoon tea, or promenade about an orangery or a long gallery. Yet, it must be wondered, how much, for example, today's visitor to a National Trust country house actually enjoys or learns from trailing round room upon room, filled with furniture and objects chosen by the best authorities, and peopled only with stewards who require to be approached to provide information and who, because of the work's time and voluntary nature, inevitably tend to a certain sameness of type. The experience is more Necropolean than lively and vigorous. Such approaches and tableaux demand an audience attitude of reverence, and in these days of individualism, democracy and choice, for how much longer will the visitor enrol for this type of experience of heritage? It is noticeable that the general difficulty is not new to the Trust. In his book in readiness for the Centennial, Merlin Waterson reported the anger and regret at the beginning of the twentieth century of architect C. R. Ashbee at a National Trust property staying 'a mere dead lumber house with no humanity in it but just to be looked at by Tourists' (Waterson 1994, 42).

Among some of the main trends and needs in society of which the Trust, in seeking to obtain support by *in situ* demonstration, should be aware are: increased leisure time; an increase in multi-culturalism in the UK; the growing urban nature of society; non-traditional groupings, such as single parent families and a new sort of extended family; and people with special needs. Given the visitor requirements mentioned above, then the assessment should be whether the Trust has been serving them. If not, then the Trust could veer away from contemporary society, to its own and society's potential disadvantage and detriment. As has been suggested, the Trust's traditional areas have been the countryside and country houses, regarded with the attitude of a patrician landowning aesthete. One aspect of their lure is their very lack of relevance to the everyday lives of the 'masses'. With the exclusion of the Trust's capacity to provide pleasant landscape for roaming, whether garden, park or rural area, thereby meeting a growing recreational/rambling need, the Trust's 'product' might be seen as not meeting the needs of contemporary categories of people very well. For example, the Trust's slowness and reluctance to enter meaningfully into the urban environment is noticeable. Its occasional ventures – such as the Newcastle Inner City Project, and Sutton House in Hackney and its activities – by their frequent mention in National Trust communications, merely serve to underline how few of their type the Trust has to call upon for report. Town dwellers and those from minority ethnic groups may find neither interest in nor identification with the countryside and its established ways and customs as the Trust presents them; of course, it can be argued that they should do. To children of the street and shopping mall, pursuits and presentations of the country and its slower paced and still somewhat feudal lifestyle can seem tame and irrelevant. How can one compare a static country house room display with virtual reality or the dynamic interaction with information held on computer? People of the country and locals of an estate in the Trust's care may not like to think of themselves as living in a landscape of perpetuated patronage and social division. The community in the locale of a Trust property is a key visitor and witness of Trust activity, and unless the Trust can establish a sound practice of listening and understanding, such as is clearly the idea now at Osterley Park, opportunities will be lost and problems may be created for the Trust.

Of relevance to this whole matter is an advertisement in *The Guardian* (26 April 1995, 38) that was to be noticed in the Centennial Year. It represented a National Trust initiative with the Countryside Commission for a person to work 'with the aim of raising people's understanding of and confidence in their ability to visit and enjoy the countryside'. Of course, this is laudable. The respectful and serious suggestion might be made, though, that a person or persons might be usefully employed also with the objective of raising *National Trust people's* understanding of and confidence in their ability to visit and enjoy, or at least encounter, the city.

Selectivity has been apparent in the Trust's own tourism promotion, 'The National Trust Travel Collection', a joint product with Page and Moy. Clearly targeted on a certain market, 'for National Trust members and supporters', the Collection in 1995 spoke a culture of culture (*National Trust Magazine* No. 74, Spring 1995, 2). It is not necessarily to suggest that such a culture is something to deny or of which to be ashamed but to indicate, as earlier, that so strong an identity must serve to divide and deter.

These few remarks and examples together serve to indicate that the question might be asked whether the Trust is blinkered so that it does not provide to the range of tourists, as opposed to the select group, what they want, or offer something relevant and stimulating in their lives?

It should be stressed, of course, that the Trust puts much effort into being welcoming to visitors. It is unfailingly polite, caring and considerate to all who come across its threshold. It 'adheres to the English Tourist Board's Code of Conduct for Visitor Attractions, and supports the "Welcome Host" campaign, backed by the Wales and England Tourist Boards' (National Trust 1995, 14).

The Trust published a leaflet, apparently destined for children, called 'Tourism and the National Trust' (National Trust 1992). It shows how its tourism is viewed by the Trust. Two of the five points represent generalities: fee-entrance Trust properties are visited annually by over 10 million people; and access to most Trust properties – countryside and coast, etc. – is free. Another point is specific about which is the most popular Trust property with visitors – Fountains Abbey and Studley Royal. The remaining two points focus on what are either regarded by the Trust itself as essentials, or which the Trust believes to be of great import to its tourist market or watchers thereof: respectively, the numbers of shops and restaurants and tea-rooms the Trust runs, and the number of cups of tea served in Trust tea-rooms in 1991.

Since the Trust has mentioned that the site of Fountains Abbey and Studley Royal is, or at least was when the leaflet was produced, the Trust's most popular tourist destination, it seems worth analysing the particular characteristics which are present and absent for what may be revealed about the Trust and its visitors and their likes and dislikes. The site in question is in the country, it is within reasonable driving distance of conurbations and is not far from other tourist attractions. It is an outdoor location, is multi-period, and the many monuments (two of which English Heritage owns or manages) which it includes are all undeniably picturesque. The Fountains Abbey and Studley Royal site is a World Heritage Site. The place is well known: because of the joint responsibility with English Heritage, promotion of the site is through both organizations' communications channels so the site could be seen as having been more than usually publicized. Part of the site – the park and gardens – was in local authority (West Riding County Council) management until relatively recently; the Studley Royal grounds still have a slightly municipal air and this may form a part of the attraction. More recently still, almost certainly after the 1992 leaflet was published, the Trust has provided a carefully placed Visitor Centre, away from the principal monuments, at a near entrance location. If it is assumed that Fountains Abbey and Studley Royal continues its position of being the most popular property with visitors, it must be assumed too, that the Visitor Centre is now included in the package of magnetism of the place. Here then are many elements of the traditional 'National Trust day out' conforming in style to the likely tastes of the standard National Trust tourist as typified above. At Fountains Abbey and Studley Royal, it seems that Trust and Tourist know and understand one another and get on well. Yet does not this safe, bucolic and pretty scene, which we know so familiarly as a Trust product and which is replicated so often across the length of England, Wales and Northern Ireland, suggest who might not be a happy or wishful visitor there?

Probably the salient characteristics of the site are that *variety* and *spaced-off* space are offered *out-of-doors*; a contained historical theme park is represented. In the Visitor Centre, *information* and *food* and *shopping* facilities are provided. The site represents an 'open air sitting room', albeit not for the poor except on National Trust Free Entry Day. In view of the general need for the Trust to make connections on a global basis, perhaps one of the greatest omissions is that no special feature is made of the fact that the site is a World Heritage Site.

An archaeologist of the future, who was looking at the landscape of the Trust and the tourists peopling it in the opening months of the Trust Centennial might have seen this: a National Trust that in working for the future, avowedly on behalf of the nation as a whole, showed signs of having become, through lack of relevance, communication and understanding, distanced from its late twentieth-century present, and of having been unable or unwilling to develop a wide constituency. As the Centennial year got under way, and moved into the main visitor season, however, that archaeologist, if keen, would have started to notice perceptible signs of change. The 'AGM for all' call, referred to above, was one instance; the National Trust Centenary slogan 'For Ever, For Everyone' became an ever more familiar sight in a mass of places and situations; and Centennial activities at properties showed noticeable effort at broadening the Trust's range of appeal. For all this excellent sign of change to a wider base, a sign indicated also by the staff's extending range in character and type, for the moment at least, the National Trust's overwhelming style of presentation continues to be that of the country landowner, as its main subject of concern is still represented by itself as the country heritage and estate. World society, meanwhile, whose commitment, as has been indicated, the Trust needs, becomes ever more urban in manner and outlook. While the Listed Building process in the UK tries to reflect and keep up with society in extending its period and type of concern – the latest period Listed Building is a town centre office of the 1970s designed by Norman Foster – it seems inconceivable that the Trust would make moves to retain and preserve such buildings. As emblematic of the nation's recent style, it might be wondered if, as an example, the Trust would preserve and render inalienable Canary Wharf? The Trust needs to change its visitor product, and urgently and self-critically evaluate its style. The Trust needs to broaden its appeal and it seems constrained by its culture from doing so. Midway through 1995, the Trust was clearly using its Centennial Year well, demonstrating that it knew change was needed. But as a reporter commented while accompanying the first paying visitor trip to the Trust's daring acquisition at Orford Ness in June, 'The National Trust may be undergoing a philosophical revolution. But for now its customers remain a certain type' (Newnham 1995, 55).

Many love to tour the Trust's landscape. It is so perfect, predictable and safe. To the Trust, as its nurturer, it must truly seem Arcadia in which to be.

14.1 Young 'tourist figure' in a National Trust landscape at Wallington House, Northumberland.

For its own sake, though, the Trust needs to become a tourist, of the world outside. It should leave behind its usual landscape and consider another prospect on a regular basis. It will be vital in the coming years for the Trust to have sight of its tourists, existing and possible, in their home landscape as well as in its own, to listen to and watch their concerns and interests. It will not represent a Nanny–Child relationship but a dialogue between different equals.

In this impressionistic discussion, it has been sought to indicate that the whole nation and world need to have a stake in the future for which the Trust is working. The Trust must manage to keep in touch with people in the present or it will court obsolescence and risk becoming heritage itself. The Trust contrasts too strongly with everyday life. The 'landscape' which the National Trust presents to the tourist, existing and potential, must be relevant to each. In the Trust's interests, all types of tourist need to witness what it is doing, in order to appreciate the Trust's role for the future, and understand how this might cause the Trust not to meet present public needs. The Trust cannot afford to stay within the boundaries within which it feels naturally comfortable.

The National Trust has a superb story to tell of managing for the future; but to do so it needs to produce an audience. For the tourists of the future, as has been said, the Trust needs to engage those of today from a broad sector.

The symbolic young tourist figure shown in Figure 14.1, setting out across a National Trust landscape, the greensward of Wallington, to fulfil the role for which the argument has been provided, needs to represent all areas of contemporary society. If not, it is suggested, in moving towards the Bicentennial and laying foundations for it, the Trust will soon prove solely a matter for archaeology. Therefore, the tourist is a figure who is most strongly needed in the National Trust landscape.

References

Fedden, R. 1968. *The Continuing Purpose: A History of the National Trust its Aims and Work*, London, 7

National Trust 1992. Leaflet, 'Tourism and the National Trust', National Trust supported by Esso

——, 1995. *The National Trust Centenary Handbook for Members and Visitors*, 14

——, undated. Leaflet 'Short Breaks in the Country', National Trust supported by the Countryside Commission

Newnham, D. 1995. 'The wasteland' in *The Guardian Weekend*, 24 June 1995, 55

Waterson, M. 1994. *The National Trust; The First Hundred Years*, National Trust and BBC Books, London, 42

15 The vicar's dewpond, the National Trust shop and the rise of paganism

Michael Pitts

Edith Olivier wrote the following extract during the Second World War (Olivier 1941, 47–9):

> Archaeological field days mean extremely pleasant picnics. Motors arrive from all directions, and in the intervals of study the archaeologists sit about in groups eating sandwiches and mayonnaise of salmon.
>
> I well remember [a walk] ... to see an earthwork ... considered to be the only instance in this country of an exact reproduction of a Greek theatre. The clergyman led the way, and about 80 people followed him ... as we proceeded I scanned the horizon, hoping to see ... the vast ... outlines of an enormous amphitheatre. [But] the theatre was tiny. It was like an armchair in a comfortable London club ... it was not surprising that it had hitherto been overlooked ... [As the clergyman gave his address, he was interrupted by] a lady archaeologist who disagreed with him. 'It's a dew pond', she said. The old man lectured on undisturbed .... Archaeologists are among the most combative of men.

This passage captures what is still a common perception of the archaeologist in its habitat. Eating salmon mayonnaise at a time of food rationing, and arguing from no evidence about nothing of significance, two archaeologists successfully demonstrate their remoteness from daily life. So today, at public enquiry and planning meeting, the archaeologist does not tell it like it is. Old houses are not homes, but (listed) buildings. Villages are not communities but historic landscapes. And historic landscapes somehow ceased to change about a generation ago.

The archaeologist obfuscates: professional literature, like an over-thickened soup, is heavy with jargon. In theoretical combat, archaeologist lances archaeologist with tricksy phrase of obscure content. Trespassers without phrasebooks in a foreign land, both collectors (not always digging with metal-detectors) and alternative thinkers – the private diggers and theorists – attract critics. Keep off our patch: who do you think you are?

Britain today is an evil place. Crime, unemployment, roads that cover the landscape (and railways that don't), a Eurogovernment that would federalize our *falaises blanches.*

Thank goodness for the National Trust Shop. With the marketing sophistication of the businesses that dreamt up 'farm fresh eggs' – the illusion of happy hens ranging free in flowery meadows, allowing industry to get on with the job of mass rearing, streamlined slaughter and serving up hormones and antibiotics à la Kiev – tartan scarves and potpourri soothe the mind. Out there in National Trustland, all is gentle and safe. Mr Macgregor digs the turnips, bunnies eat the weeds, craftspeople lovingly turn out useful things. There are scones and jam for tea – and Keiller marmalade at breakfast.

With this mythical Edwardian past – country spells without the country smells – the present is wrapped, boxed and tied with ribbon – fossilized and hidden from sight. In this land of estate managers, tenants and artisans – everyone knows their place. As the message on the back of the National Trust lorry celebrates: 'For Ever, For Everyone'.

Not many years ago, you might – on a quiet day, with care and luck – have caught a lone English eccentric at work on an ancient monument. He – only males came out – could be identified by the woolly hat, the bulging, worn briefcase trailing wires, the pendulum, the loose bundle of charts and diagrams. From a distance, you might have thought you were watching a professional archaeologist. But close to, the expression of fevered excitement gives the game away: this is the amateur battling authority, the obsessed golfer putting his way round the course backwards.

Times have changed. This intellectual niche is no longer the preserve of the half-crazed man: the old lunatic fringe has let her hair down. They move in droves, now, sporting tailored white or coloured cloaks – or perhaps nothing at all – or, most sinister, dressed just like you or me. Many and magical are their ideas, frequently contradictory – yet there's room for all. The alternative archaeology can explain everything (sometimes with first-hand accounts of ancient times). There are people who will release you from stress, help you with your marriage, bless your home. Like the National Trust Shop, the new pagans present a vision of peace, green lanes and country walks. But there's no entrance fee to this world: anyone can join in. And there's a whiff of free sex.

But not quite yet.

Peter Ucko recently pointed out that Avebury has played a major part in raising public consciousness as to the importance of ancient monuments (Ucko *et al.* 1991, 257). Sir John Lubbock's original Ancient Monuments Protection Act of 1882 provided for the legal protection of both the West Kennet long barrow (Piggott 1962, ix) and Silbury Hill. Lubbock had struggled tirelessly against those who saw the Bill as an affront to private property (Saunders 1983). As the new owner of Silbury and part of the stone circles, he could be seen to be putting his Wiltshire property where his national mouth was. Sixty years later, the first National Trust purchase at Avebury was backed by a prominent campaign in the national press. The recent planning fiasco – three public inquiries and two bankruptcies – that led to the Trust making major extensions to its estate in Avebury, was again well covered by the contemporary media (Pitts 1990).

What I hope to show here is that Avebury can do more than help keep the public in tune with the latest in monument demolition news: the conflux of striking archaeological remains, a modern community (with a history), large numbers of visitors, private and publicly sponsored landowners – all these things stir up not just mud and mortar, but issues too. Why do we seek to preserve ancient monuments? At what cost? How can we learn about the past from them? Who determines their future? What special responsibilities do the landowners have – if any? Avebury is a cauldron where such issues have been bubbling away for generations.

The archaeologists who claim that we preserve Avebury because of what the monuments tell us about the past are deluding themselves. This may sound a contentious statement, but it is not flippant. Consider the history of research and preservation.

Undoubtedly the most thorough and informative fieldwork at the megalithic sites occurred in the eighteenth century, six generations before Lubbock's Monuments Protection Act. Indeed, it was the very destruction perpetrated before his eyes that fired William Stukeley to work with such speed and dedication. As local farmers burned, smashed and buried (a good bit of earthwork levelling went on too, but this was before he arrived), this doctor from Lincolnshire scribbled it all down. He wanted to save for posterity: to 'rescue some part from impending ruin [for] when the Country finds an advantage in preserving its poor reliques' (quoted by Piggott 1985, 50). And inspired by this activity, he developed the first complex theory of what it all meant – who made it, why and when.

Under its cloak of protection, the stone circle has of course seen some significant archaeological investigations. But how much information these works revealed is debatable. Stuart Piggott famously remarked that Keiller's excavations in the 1930s were 'more like megalithic landscape gardening than research archaeology' (Piggott 1983, 32), and indeed, given the scale of Keiller's operations, remarkably little was learnt. Avebury's great earth mover, Harold St George Gray, similarly dug for small intellectual reward. After six enormous trenches into the ditch and bank around the stones, he proclaimed the site to date from 'the Neolithic–Bronze Age transition period' (Gray 1935, 162): but this was suspected before he began in 1908, and it remained a surmise after he finished in 1922. Potentially the most informative trench into the earthwork was Sir Henry Meux's (Gray 1935, 103–5; Pitts and Whittle 1992, 206). Commanded twelve years *after* Lubbock's Act, this was a private project, done at the whim of the landowner and known only from chance gossip passed down from the supervisor and estate officer, Thomas Leslie. Archaeologists of the time seem to have taken little interest.

There have been three major programmes of excavation at Silbury Hill, all executed by coalminers. The most recent tunnel was sponsored by the BBC, but the other two, sunk from the top in 1776 and in from the side in 1849, long pre-dated any protection afforded to the Hill. As televised archaeology found to its cost, the new tunnel revealed little not already known.

To continue would labour the point: there is no direct link between protection afforded to these ancient sites and attempts, or apparent desire, to find out more about them. The archaeologist might protest that without protection, there would be little left to yield information for the future. But history shows that, while perhaps unpleasant to behold, amateur digging or even unfettered destruction can reveal a great deal. The observer could be forgiven for concluding that archaeologists want to preserve not so much to further knowledge, as to prevent others from getting the spade in first.

Shortly before his death, R. G. Collingwood blamed the masses. 'The public … cares little or nothing for historical knowledge … [For funding, archaeologists must rely on] that nostalgic self-loathing which is so characteristic of our times. "Here is a romantic ancient site", they must say, "which is about to be covered with revolting bungalows, hideous by-pass roads, and so forth. Give us your guineas"' (Collingwood 1939, 83–4). But as Sir Mortimer Wheeler showed, if Collingwood's own dictum of 'digging to answer questions' is followed, the public *does* care for historical knowledge. Preservation on behalf of the public brings with it a responsibility to increase that knowledge.

At Avebury, the process went in reverse. Most of the revolting bungalows were removed *before* the public was asked for money, and the rest would, it seemed, gently fade away. 'Condemned houses will go and they will not be replaced … all which is truly hideous shall ultimately disappear' (Avebury Preservation Fund, nd). When the Trust acquired the stone circles in 1942, on the face of it there was not much more to do than maintain the fences. For the people who lived in Avebury, however, things were very different. It all started with the cricket pavilion.

'If elected as your Councillor', wrote Jenny Baldrey in her flyer for local elections on 4 May 1995, 'I will take decisions in the interest of the whole community, not just that vocal part which prefers to see West Selkley [ward] turn into fossilised villages in a prehistoric setting.'

Mrs Baldrey was born in Avebury, and lives in a council house built as part of the Avebury Preservation Scheme. 'Do you think we could find enough people who would remember now?' she asked me. 'I'm not sure the courts would accept it after so long.'

The playing field and cricket pavilion belong to the village. At least, that's how some of the villagers see it: a gift from Alexander Keiller. After the National Trust purchase, however, they found that nothing had been written down, and what they thought of as their property was, in deed, the Trust's. This was over fifty years ago, yet it still arouses passions. 'Everyone here hates the Trust', says Jenny Baldrey. 'I don't know why, you just seem to be born like that.' Avebury cricket has a special flavour to it.

It has to be said that it is certainly not so much the National Trust in themselves that excite people, as what they represent. Before he gave them a cricket pitch, Keiller upset some sectors of the community by his activities around the stone circle – removing trees, houses, a garage, building a new garage and erecting megaliths and concrete posts (Pitts 1990, 263). His published description of part of the monument as 'the outstanding archaeological disgrace of Britain', a scene of 'indescribable squalor and neglect' (Keiller 1939, 223) was hardly designed to assuage local suspicions of this new arrival from Scotland. It was Keiller and his antiquarian predecessors who provided both the archaeological rationale and the property foundations for the Trust purchases. However, with the recent extensions to the Trust estate and the management responsibilities acquired from English Heritage, the Trust has become a uniquely large player, and will inevitably have to face the most vicious balls.

While people were rehoused outside the ancient monument, none of the facilities – the church, the shop, the pub, the men's club and the school – was touched. As the community ages (a prohibition on new housing means that expanding new families mostly have to move out of the parish), the physical distance between, for example, the Post Office (source of pension money) and the post-War housing becomes increasingly significant. There are two routes between the two: along an extremely dangerous stretch of the A4361, or across a couple of fields that are muddy and partially flooded in winter. Several schemes to construct a safe and passable footpath have come to nought.

This might seem just another story of the decline of the English village, albeit with unusual twists. But the village is not so easily separated from the monuments. In 1969, Faith Vatcher conducted the largest archaeological excavation at the circles since the first National Trust purchase. The occasion was the building of the new school: not in Avebury Trusloe, where most of the Avebury children then lived, but immediately behind the old Victorian building, adjacent to the prehistoric earthwork. Substantial archaeological disturbance occurred, the excavation was conducted under rushed and difficult conditions and remains unpublished (Pitts and Whittle 1992, 206). The club building, prominently located beside the same earthwork, qualifies as 'truly hideous', yet has refused to 'ultimately disappear'. Its relocation in Avebury Trusloe would have benefited the monument as well as the villagers who frequent the club: the suggestion now might well provoke claims of unjustified interference in village affairs.

The devious minded might almost imagine a conspiracy to depopulate Avebury. The archaeologists, concerned more with the superficial aspects of stones

15.1 Inside view of West Kennet long barrow from the local press – with pagan artefacts left by 'travellers'. (© Media in Wessex)

and dykes than what they mean, leave its prehistoric inhabitants mouldering quietly below ground. The conservationists turn their backs on the modern community, even when opportunities arise to help both villagers and monument. This is a megalithic landscape without figures – past or present.

But we are forgetting yet another group of people, vastly more numerous than villagers, conservators or prehistoric forebears: visitors. And we know about visitors. As one of the school kids puts it in an exhibition currently at the Great Barn Museum: 'Today in Avebury there are lots of tourists. They come to look around the stones. But also because of the tourists there are rubbish bins, Public lavatorys and the Stones restaurant.'

Who are these tourists? Where do they come from? Why do they travel to Avebury, and what does it mean to them? Questions like these are impossible to answer with confidence, in the absence of any published surveys.

Even the numbers are largely a matter of guesswork. The County and District Councils suggested 250,000 in 1977, while the National Trust plumped for 150,000 ten years later (Kennet District Council 1989, 14). Our experience at Stones Restaurant suggests that something in the order of 300,000 a year may be a reasonable guess (based on annual till registrations and an estimate of·the proportion of visitors who come into the restaurant). If these figures are anywhere near reality, there is a surprising implication: the common assumption that visitor numbers are inexorably rising may be wrong; at least, there is no firm evidence.

Instead, it may be that numbers rise (and fall) with events in Avebury. Keiller noted that visitor attendance rose from one or two hundred a week in the mid 1930s to 'an average of between 1000/1500 during the summer months' following his excavations in 1937 and 1938. Over 6,000 people paid to visit his new museum in 1938 (Keiller 1939, 229, 233; and see chapter 23, this volume). The BBC excavations at Silbury Hill in the 1960s created traffic chaos as viewers came to see the real thing. Ken King's advertising brought coach loads of new visitors to the Manor in 1989 (Pitts 1990). Doubtless excavations in the nineteenth century attracted visitors, as did hare coursing and hawking on the downs. By juggling attractions and facilities – especially, today, car parking – the quantity of visitors may be more amenable to management than is generally appreciated.

I was curious about our visitors, so from mid April to mid May 1995, I left some questionnaires out in Stones Restaurant. Completed forms were returned by 193 people, and what follows is based on the answers to multiple choice questions on these forms. This is a small, non-random sample, subject to none of the usual survey controls. Agreed. But it's a start.

A striking proportion of the respondents had made previous visits to Avebury. A professional survey at Stonehenge in 1978 found that 23 per cent of interviewees had been to Stonehenge before (Bainbridge 1979, 11). At Avebury, this figure was over 70 per cent, and of these more than half had visited over six times (one form was actually completed by a resident). Five people made comments emphasizing the frequency of their visits: 'twice a week', 'hundreds', 'as often as I can' and so on (if one claim to have visited Avebury but once 'in this life' has any validity, we may even yet be underestimating the return visits!).

If we imagine an annual total of 300,000 visits, then the actual number of people involved would be around 175,000. Of these, about 125,000 apparently come to Avebury with prior experience and 70,000 could be said to be regular visitors. (This is perhaps reinforced by the higher ratio of British to American respondents in my Avebury survey (5:1) than was found at Stonehenge (1.1:1, or nearly as many Americans as British: Bainbridge 1979, 6). However, there are many other factors at work here.)

We can assume that people who continue to return to Avebury like it. But for some the place has more significance than is conveyed by the word 'like', so I asked: 'Do you think the stone circles still have some mysterious power?' Even when scoring ambivalent answers as a 'no', 63 per cent - nearly two-thirds of the 186 people who answered this question - said 'yes'. If this sample were representative of the Avebury visitor, and again assuming a total of 300,000 visits, that would be over 100,000 people for whom megaliths, the village, the earthworks, the sheep, the downs – who knows what combinations? – had a special and personal meaning. Several of the respondents made a point of emphasizing their positive answer by underlining or heavy ringing. These are not day trippers out for a laugh and a souvenir: these are people for whom Avebury is part of their lives – who will notice when things change in the village – who might take a real interest in new archaeological discoveries or ideas – for whom Avebury is anything *but* a prehistoric fossil.

So what *do* they think of the archaeological remains? For what it's worth, my little survey suggests that the common thread of the more official looking and technical guidebooks, which refers to the builders of the stone circles as (to quote one) 'Beaker people [who] integrated with the indigenous neolithic communities' (Vatcher and Vatcher 1976, 7; cf. Cunnington 1936; Chapman 1947; Malone 1994) has been missed or rejected by the majority of visitors. Prompted to assign a name to the people 'who ... built the stone circles', only 13 per cent chose 'Beaker People' (one noted that this was an 'outdated archaeological theory of the 60s, since totally discredited'!): the same number who opted for either 'Druids' or 'Celts' (7 per cent). A third went for the option 'People whose names are forgotten', but 37 per cent (71 out of 193 respondents) selected 'Ancient British'.

The archaeologist authors of the guidebooks are all guarded when it comes to the purposes of the stone circles, which vary from 'religious' (Chapman 1947; Vatcher and Vatcher 1976) to 'a temple or place of worship' (Cunnington 1936); Malone (1994) offers no comment. There is a common theme of denying a funerary function. The rings were not 'a burial place' (Cunnington 1936), nor a burial ground 'in the ordinary sense of the word' (Chapman 1947). Neither was Silbury Hill a burial mound (Vatcher and Vatcher 1976). Only The Sanctuary could be said to be 'associated with burial cults, worship and feasts' (Malone 1994).

With this denial of a funerary purpose, modern visitors seem to agree, contradicting a strong tradition in the antiquarian literature that reaches back into the seventeenth century and continues to the present (Ucko *et al.* 1991, 17–24, 83, 251–2). Asked if they thought the stone circles were built 'For a burial ground', only two respondents said yes. About half selected the choice 'No-one knows', again in sympathy with the archaeologists. But it is the other half that is interesting.

About 30 people each chose to say that the circles were built 'For the Mother Goddess', 'For general fertility ceremonies' and 'As an astronomical observatory'. Fifteen thought Avebury was 'To mark a ley line', and a further 19 offered their own ideas, ranging from the simple 'Something spiritual' to the increasingly bizarre: 'A centre for magnetic field energies'; 'For people to use the energy to access their inner spirituality and knowing'; 'A landing pad'; 'A prototype crop circle'; and 'A warning' (to quote but five ideas). Not a single person chose to see Avebury 'As a war memorial' (another strong antiquarian tradition). In sympathy with Michael Dames (1976; 1977), people seem to think of Avebury more in feminine than masculine terms. Archaeologists, on the other hand, perhaps now rejecting the burial and war memorial explanations, but embracing interpretations that speak of political hierarchies, power centres and warring groups, could be said to favour a masculine interpretation (e.g. Clarke *et al.* 1985; Malone 1994, 46).

This is all very interesting, you might say, but so what? In fifty years, 'official' guidebooks (the first – Chapman 1947 – published by the Ministry of Works, the most recent – Malone 1994 – jointly by English Heritage and the National Trust) have changed little in style or content. To a certain extent, this reflects the scarcity of new research in Avebury until quite recently, although broader understanding of the prehistoric background has radically changed, as have media styles and technologies. But the public perception of Avebury is constantly on the move, and currently, in small but highly visible sectors, acquiring religious undertones. Should we ignore this? Should we, with Peter Ucko, seek a 'shift away from destructive exploration and excavation towards the educative presentation of prehistoric monuments' (Ucko *et al.* 1991, 259)? Do we agree that, no, it is not appropriate for dowsing lessons to be freely available in Avebury, 'with no cautionary advice to the contrary' (1991, 264).[1]

Today, what is freely available in Avebury goes far beyond suggestions for the use of bent coat-hangers. At the only souvenir shop inside the stone circles (is it the only such shop inside *any* stone circle?) you can find, amongst all sorts of wonderful shiny, magical New Agey paraphernalia ... magazines. *The Ley Hunter* (The Journal of Geomancy & Earth Mysteries) is currently featuring the latest update on The Dragon Project and a piece suggesting Santa Claus to be a Siberian shaman whose reindeer got stoned on mushrooms. *Pagan Dawn* (Published Quarterly at the Fire Festivals) is the official journal of the Pagan Federation, an organization open to anyone over 18 identifying themselves as Pagan. You can read about 'handfasting', and find a list of priests and priestesses willing to perform this pagan form of marriage ceremony (I suspect there have been more handfasting rites in Avebury in the past couple of years than weddings in St James' Church). The centre spread is about 'The power and pleasure of sex'. Soon the seasonal editions of *The Cerealogist* will appear, with its harvest of cropwork tales, UFO sightings and other weird gleanings. Buy *Global Link Up*, and you can plug in to a Network of Expanding Consciousness. And so on.

1.　Those in the know will realize that I exclude the efforts of John Evans, Alasdair Whittle and their colleagues, who have been researching the landscape by stealth, as it were, circling the major monuments for decades like watchful lions (see, for example, Evans *et al.* 1993; Thomas and Whittle 1986; Whittle 1991; 1993; 1994; Whittle *et al.* 1993). This superbly conceived work is independent of any policies generated by Avebury's guardians, and largely unaffected by threats of revolting bungalows or hideous by-pass roads. Very few visitors can be aware that it is happening (they will learn nothing from the official guidebook: Malone 1994).

But it's not just words on paper. In 1993, Tim Sebastian and Philip Shallcrass formed an Avebury Order of Bards – the 'Gorsedd Caer Abiri' – to be open to anyone. The following year, a small information circulation paid dividends. At the autumn equinox, representatives of King Arthur's Warband, The Secular Order of Druids, The Insular ditto, The Orders of Bards, Ovates and dittos, buskers and dancers from all over Britain gathered amongst the megaliths for a casual ceremony in which the talking stick was passed round to about a hundred people, poems were read, guitars played, Pagans and Christians sang songs together. As John Michell put it, it was 'the finest gathering of eccentrics ever seen'.

There had also been a ceremony on 30 July (Lammas), in and around the South Circle. There was a Druid Wedding ('conducted as usual at the Ring Stone'), fifteen new Bards were initiated and the company was treated to 'a spontaneous prophecy ... that a child born at Avebury would restore the sacred Kingship of both Ireland and Britain' (Shallcrass 1995, 4).

If you are interested in Avebury, but not narrowly focused on prehistoric artefacts; if Avebury is a special place for you, and you think of the megalith builders as Ancient Britons – your own, British ancestors; if you come frequently, and witness gatherings of friendly looking eccentrics singing and dancing: how do you react? Likely you will humour them, in time coming to think of them as part of the scene. If you talk to them, you will be welcomed – not preached to, admonished for your behaviour or asked for money. So you listen. And if you don't like what you hear, no-one will mind: and they will listen to you if you want to say your bit.

Where does this leave the National Trust and the archaeologist?

There can be no denying that there are today some widespread misconceptions about 'other people', which in the case of Avebury most obviously means people who once lived in the distant past. But it is not just eccentrics who misunderstand the past and the processes of archaeological reasoning. Writing about the conservation world, Tom Greeves (1989, 659) noted that 'gifted and highly educated members of modern society are unaware that tens of thousands of [prehistoric] barrows still survive ... in Britain'. *The New Internationalist* is an intelligent, established magazine with a market that likes to feel well-informed about the workings of the world. In response to a reader question 'How did human beings learn to take hard, inedible seeds, grind them up, mix them with water and cook them to get something they could eat?', another reader answered in terms that archaeologists would find less than knowledgeable. 'All such crafts for living were learned by initiate priests in megalithic times through inspiration .... At certain times when the sun forces had peculiar qualities ... earthly experience and cosmic knowledge could unite to reveal wisdom ...' (*The New Internationalist*, June 1995, 34).

Duncton Rising is a best-selling novel about moles, written by a geography graduate from Bristol University (Horwood 1992). In a key scene, Fieldfare, a female mole, stands on the longest night at the Stones of Seven Barrows (near the Uffington White Horse). She is mourning the passing of her mate, Chater.

A voice calls her, which she recognizes as that of a dead, legendary mole called Mayweed. He tells her that by standing where the seventh Stone stands on Longest Night, she has gained the ability to communicate with the world of the Silence. Mayweed takes Fieldfare's paw and leads her into the seventh Stone, where she sees Chater moving towards a mysterious Light. She asks to join Chater, but is told that there are still things for her to do in moledom. Mayweed turns to Chater, 'and together the two moles went slowly into the Stone's Light'.

There is a vaguely described 'otherliness' in this scene with which, I suggest, many of Horwood's readers can identify and which they associate with a real past, not of moles, but of people. It is an otherliness that appears in notions of a one-world pre-patriarchal female deity (Meskell 1995), or of noble Celts living in harmony with nature (Parker Pearson 1994). It might almost be seen as the central concept of an emerging archaeological fundamentalism, in which, deprived of relevant and comprehensible ideas and information, people revert to a pre-archaeological understanding whose power is increased by a touch of mysticism.

When such fundamentalism claims to interpret a real past, the integrity of other cultures is patronised (Pitts 1992, 208) – as, indeed, is the intelligence of the modern observer. But dispelling myths is not a matter of mudslinging or opinionated didacticism. The archaeologist cannot claim to 'know best', but must enter into a conference where all participants need to justify their prejudices and assertions. The archaeologist and the fundamentalist have a very different interest in the past, and it cannot be assumed that they seek the same truths.

So, too, viable archaeological research is a creative dialogue: between the present and the past. The past lives only when interrogated by the present. Accidents of discovery and research design, contemporary personalities and politics are significant contributors to the story we tell. That Avebury was not a burial ground has entered the lore of official guidebooks: it is an assertion made only because, once, it was an important hypothesis in another present. Total preservation of field remains is death to a living understanding. To cease 'destructive ... excavation [in favour of] educative presentation' is not only a contradiction in terms: it would result in communications that would bore the pants off the public (cf. Tilley 1989).

On the other hand, archaeology is not simply a matter of digging up things, putting them in museums, and digging up more things. If no-one asks why this is being done, what is trying to be established or discovered, no new knowledge is gained.

The National Trust, backed by planning legislation, may try to preserve the village and landscape of Avebury. But unless it is remembered that a village is a community, not just streets and buildings; and a landscape a living entity, not a constantly rewinding video (however beautifully filmed): then the objects of preservation will slide through our fingers like sand (cf. Fowler 1995).

The common message is: talk – and listen. Involve people. Re-figure the landscape with past inhabitants, contemporary villagers and visitors. We are all part of what Avebury is, and in the excavation, the cricket match and the pagan rite lies the route to knowledge through communication.

At the Beltane ceremony inside the stone circle, the gathering is questioned by the Herald.

> O Companions, what is your manner of pilgrimage here?

Pendragon replies on behalf of us all.

> We have come to this place of the ancient years where the Spirit was made known to man, to contact the Spirit anew.'

Who would dictate to others how they define this Spirit? But argue about it ... now that's a different matter.

References

Avebury Preservation Fund nd (c. 1940). *Avebury: An Appeal to the Nation*, privately printed pamphlet

Bainbridge, S. 1979. *Restrictions at Stonehenge: the Reactions of Visitors to Limitations in Access*, London

Chapman, D.E. 1947. *Is This Your First Visit to Avebury?* (3rd edn), London

Clarke, D.V., Cowie, T.G. and Foxon, A. 1985. *Symbols of Power at the Time of Stonehenge*, Edinburgh

Collingwood, R.G. 1939. *An Autobiography*, Oxford

Cunnington, M.E. 1936. *Avebury. A Guide* (3rd edn), Devizes

Dames, M. 1976. *The Silbury Treasure*, London

——, 1977. *The Avebury Cycle*, London

Evans, J.G., Limbrey, S., Mate, I. and Mount, R. 1993. 'An environmental history of the Upper Kennet Valley, Wiltshire, for the last 10,000 years', *Proceedings of the Prehistoric Society* 59, 139–95

Fowler, P. 1995. 'Avebury', *History Today* 45, 10–15

Gray, H. St G. 1935. 'The Avebury excavations, 1908–1922', *Archaeologia* 84, 99–162

Greeves, T. 1989. 'Archaeology and the green movement', *Antiquity* 63, 659–66

Horwood, W. 1992. *Duncton Rising*, London

Keiller, A. 1939. 'Avebury. Sumary of excavations, 1937 and 1938', *Antiquity* 13, 223–33

Kennet District Council 1989. *Avebury Draft Local Plan*, Devizes

Malone, C. 1994. *The Prehistoric Monuments of Avebury* (2nd edn), London

Meskell, L. 1995. 'Goddesses, Gimbutas and "New Age" archaeology', *Antiquity* 69, 74–86

Olivier, E. 1941. *Country Moods and Tenses*, London

Parker Pearson, M. 1994. Review of *Animals in Celtic Life and Myth* by M. Green, *Proceedings of the Prehistoric Society* 60, 463–4

Piggott, S. 1962. *The West Kennet Long Barrow. Excavations 1955–56*, London

——, 1983. 'Archaeological retrospect 5', *Antiquity* 57, 28–37

——, 1985. *William Stukeley* (2nd edn), London

Pitts, M. W. 1990. 'What future for Avebury?', *Antiquity* 64, 259–74

——, 1992. 'Manifesto for a green archaeology' in *All Natural Things* (eds L. Macinnes and C.R. Wickham-Jones), 203–13, Oxford

Pitts, M. W. and Whittle, A. 1992. 'The development and date of Avebury', *Proceedings of the Prehistoric Society* 58, 203–12

Saunders, A.D. 1983. 'A century of ancient monuments legislation 1882–1982', *Antiquaries Journal* 63, 11–33

Shallcrass, P. (ed.) 1995. *The Gorsedd of Bards of Caer Abiri Newsletter No. 3*, St Leonards-on-Sea

Thomas, J. and Whittle, A. 1986. 'Anatomy of a tomb – West Kennet revisited', *Oxford Journal of Archaeology*, 5, 129–56

Tilley, C. 1989. 'Excavation as theatre', *Antiquity* 63, 275–80

Ucko, P. J., Hunter, M., Clark, A. J. and David, A. 1991. *Avebury Reconsidered. From the 1660s to the 1990s*, London

Vatcher, F. de M. and Vatcher, L. 1976. *The Avebury Monuments*, London

Whittle, A. 1991. 'A late neolithic complex at West Kennet, Wiltshire, England', *Antiquity* 65, 256–62

——, 1993. 'The neolithic of the Avebury area: sequence, environment, settlement and monuments', *Oxford Journal of Archaeology* 12, 29–53

——, 1994. 'Excavations at Millbarrow neolithic chambered tomb, Winterbourne Monkton, north Wiltshire', *Wiltshire Archaeological & Natural History Magazine* 87, 1–53

——, Rouse, A. J. and Evans, J.G. 1993. 'A neolithic downland monument in its environment: excavations at the Easton Down long barrow, Bishops Cannings, north Wiltshire', *Proceedings of the Prehistoric Society* 59, 197–239

Questionnaire

Note: Questions and choices are listed in the order in which they appeared on the questionnaire. Results are tabulated as percentages of respondents to each question selecting a given option.

1. Who do you think built the stone circles?

Romans	1
Druids	7
Beaker People	13
Saxons	1
Celts	7
Ancient British	37
People whose names are forgotten	33
Other	3
Number of responses	193

2. When were the stone circles built?

A million years ago	3
10,000 BC	19
2000 BC	73
2000 years ago	3
Other	2
Number of responses	192

3. Why were the stone circles built?

To mark a ley line	8
As a war memorial	0
No-one knows	51
For the Mother Goddess	18
For general fertility ceremonies	15
For a burial ground	4
As an astronomical observatory	16
Other	10
Number of responses	193

(Many respondents selected more than
one option: 232 options were circled)

4. Do you think the stone circles still have
   some mysterious power?

Yes	63
No	37
Number of responses	186

5. Age

0–14	7
15–24	4
25–34	26
35–44	27
45–54	20
55 and over	15
Number of responses	191

6. Nationality

UK	77
USA	15
Germany	2
France	1
Australia	1
South Africa	1
Ireland	1
Holland	1
Spain	1
Japan	1
Number of responses	171

7. Visits to Avebury

1	28
2–6	32
more than 6	39
resident	1
Number of responses	191

16 Landscapes, archaeology and the National Trust

Timothy Darvill[1]

Introduction

One hundred years ago, in 1895, a small but dedicated group of individuals shared a common vision in which the preservation of natural beauty and historic interest could be achieved through direct ownership and management. There has been some debate about the particular stimuli and circumstances which led this group to found The National Trust (Legg 1994; Weideger 1994), but there is no doubt about its long-term success (Jenkins and James 1994).

One of the overarching themes which provided the focus to much of the Trust's early endeavours, and which has served to unite its work down the years, has been the idea of 'landscape'. In particular the rural landscape, which was a matter dear to all three founders (Gaze 1988), and, in 1993, the subject of a series of special studies as part of a countryside policy review within the Trust.[2]

Archaeology, by contrast, was not a specific primary interest of the Trust in its early years, perhaps because, at least so far as prehistoric sites went, the Ancient Monuments Protection Act 1882 provided a novel approach to the protection and management of ancient sites along the lines of what would nowadays be called Guardianship by the State (Saunders 1983). Nevertheless, as Gaze (1988, 78) has pointed out, some of the Trust's founders were active in promoting the preservation of archaeological remains, and by the early years of the twentieth century ancient monuments were regularly being brought into the Trust's portfolio of properties. Gradually, archaeology became a major strand in much of the Trust's work because of the abundance of remains that exist within National Trust properties, and the robust linkage between the land and the activities of people past and present.

Parallel to the organizational development of the National Trust, and the tremendous expansion in its membership and estate over the past 100 years, there have been many intellectual changes in the study, understanding, and appreciation of such matters as landscape, archaeology, flora, fauna, woodland and the coast

1. School of Conservation Sciences, Bournemouth University, Fern Barrow, Poole, Dorset BH12 5BB, United Kingdom.
2. The following working groups were established: aesthetics; social and economic; land-use and economic; historic and cultural; visitor values and perception; and ecology and environment. Draft reports based on the deliberations of these individual working groups were circulated in November 1993.

to identify just a few. Some subject areas have moved closer together and found common ground. Perhaps one of the most important from the Trust's point of view is the integration of archaeology with more generalizing landscape studies. This area of endeavour has moved forward rapidly not just in methodological terms but also in the academic frameworks used through the development and application of new ways of understanding and explaining observable patterns.

In recent decades, landscape archaeology has become one of the most innovative and rapidly developing sections of the discipline as a whole. Three main approaches can now be recognized, and while each represents a stage in the development of thinking about the subject they all provide important and valid perspectives (Darvill 1995; forthcoming).

The earliest, and most widely applied perspective is a functionalist or positivist one which began in the inter-war period (e.g. Fox 1933) and continued through into the 1970s to reach its zenith with the publication of two conferences on the effect of man (*sic*) on the landscape (Evans *et al.* 1975; Limbrey and Evans 1978). Throughout, the emphasis of this approach lay in the recognition of direct links between people and the natural environment. During the 1980s the focus of interest shifted to more processualist perspectives which emphasized the way landscapes change over time, and tried to identify the forces and processes which drove that change (e.g. Aston 1985; Wagstaff 1987). In the early 1990s yet further perspectives have been developing, mainly in the field of social archaeology through what can be described as contextualism. In this, landscape provides the context for social action and is therefore socially constructed (Bender 1993; Thomas 1993; Tilley 1994).

In this paper I would like to explore the way that archaeology and landscape come together in relation to the holdings of the National Trust by focusing on a contextualist approach to just two of many relevant dimensions. First, is the place of ancient monuments in the modern countryside. And second, is the exploration and understanding of what I will here call ancient landscapes. However, before pursuing these two avenues of inquiry, and in part by way of explaining their constitution, it is important to pause for a moment to consider some of the concepts which underpin a contextualist approach to landscape archaeology.

Landscape and archaeology

Sadly, the term 'landscape' has been hijacked and perverted on many occasions to the extent that it has now become seriously devalued in intellectual terms. To many it has become a synonym for the countryside in general, to others it is a trendy-sounding cover-term for what might more properly be called a settlement pattern. However, behind the façade of such a simple looking word lie some critically important concepts of which three are especially relevant here.

First, is the recognition that landscape is not a physical thing as such, rather it is constructed in people's minds as a set of values, meanings and understandings which are developed in response to what they see around them, what they are told, and their socialization (Cosgrove 1985; Cosgrove and Daniels 1988; Schama 1995). The idea of landscape is linked very closely to perception, experience and engagement, and it embraces widely applicable themes about the relationship between people, the realm of ideas and values, and the worlds that people create for themselves to live in.

Second, a landscape can only be a contemporary phenomenon which is time-space dependent and socially specific in the way it is understood and interpreted. The social categorization of space is a fundamental dimension of any landscape, and while this is something which we are overtly aware of in modern western society, anthropological and historical evidence suggests that the basic principles have wider utility (Tuan 1977; Bender 1992; Ingold 1993).

Third, and this is absolutely critical for archaeology, is the identification of a link between the landscape as a conceptual device and the structuring of space through the deployment of material culture (Hodder 1987; Tilley 1994). People live and work within a large space or environment. Within their environment they are free to move about according to socially defined rules and expectations. Every piece of such a space is identified with a series of socially constituted values and meanings because the space itself is categorized or compartmentalized in the minds of its inhabitants, and these divisions are often marked physically through boundaries, markers, or the distribution of things and associations (and see Tuan 1977). People can read these meanings like the words of a book or the signs beside the road, and develop an understanding of the place they are in.[3] Some categories superficially appear functional and straightforward: fields, pasture, house or burial ground. But behind these simplistic descriptions of places there are usually more deeply embedded understandings of space which link to belief systems and cosmologies while finding expression through emotions and feelings: burial grounds that mix images of darkness and the spirits of the ancestors; woods that disorientate and confuse; springs that give new life and link the land of the living to a supernatural underworld.[4]

3. Whether that understanding coincides with, challenges, or is simply different from the generally accepted understanding, depends a great deal on the socialization of the individual and the social context in which they find themselves.
4. Numerous good examples of the way that sacred sites and places create feelings and emotions is provided by the essays edited by Carmichael *et al.* (1994).

The values or meanings attributed to different parts of the environment dictate the way that people relate to it, move about within it, and what actually happens there. To take a rather topically modern example consider the special values placed on Britain's National Parks. Because of their perceived aesthetic beauty and their role in recreation, leisure, conservation, and the heritage in its broadest sense they are special in the minds of many people in Britain. These spaces have effectively become sacred places for today's population, and this finds expression in the material culture found in them, and the consequent limitations on what it is acceptable to do there.

Developing a social approach to landscape archaeology allows a perspective that can be applied in the two areas of concern here: the past in the present, and the matter of ancient landscapes.

The past in the present

Fifty years ago, in 1945, when the National Trust was celebrating its Jubilee, Grahame Clark contributed an essay on ancient sites to the volume edited by James Lees-Milne entitled: *The National Trust. A Record of Fifty Years' Achievement.* In it, Clark poses the rhetorical question:

> who has not thrilled at the sight of a burial mound or defensive earthwork, breaking the grim profile of a moor or dimpling and creasing the sinuous contours of a down? Who, again, contemplating the Wall, could easily dissociate Hadrian's triumph from its Border setting? (Clark 1945, 29)

And he is right. The landscape is littered with ancient remains, up to half of which may have visible traces. It has been estimated that there are 40,000 archaeological sites known to date on National Trust estates (National Trust 1988, 4), an average density of 17.3 per square kilometre, nearly six times the national average.[5]

But archaeological remains in the landscape are not about numbers and dots on maps; as Clark makes clear, what we are dealing with here are the sources of feelings and passions. When encountered, these monuments stimulate emotions, trigger memories and conjure up vivid images seemingly from nothing. They are, in a sense, places in the landscape where human minds transcend time even if only momentarily. Yet there is a tendency these days to belittle feelings and emotions while trying to objectify perception and engagement by introducing a sort of pseudo-scientific detachment to separate the observer from what is being observed, rather like the glass walls of a test-tube distancing a chemist from an experiment.

---

5. The national average *c.*3 monuments pers square kilometre is based on provisional results from the Monuments at Risk Survey (Darvill and Wainwright 1995).

Landscapes are all about people and places being together in tight-knit relationships that allow meanings to be constructed and categories contested. Far from bringing people and places closer together, many visitor centres and interpretation facilities provide such cosy and rounded visions that the people who use them no longer engage with what they actually feel but only with what they are enjoined to feel.

Being able to engage with the landscape inevitably means being able to read the signals that exist and respond to them. In the case of the archaeological remains in today's landscape the big and substantial stuff is fairly straightforward. One of the first purely archaeological acquisitions by the National Trust was the site of White Barrow near Tilshead in Wiltshire, purchased in 1909. This is a long barrow, dating to about 3500 BC, originally the burial ground of a small farming community whose settlement must lie somewhere in the vicinity. Nearly 80m long by 45m wide and 2.5m high this monument remains in good condition, has hardly been touched by excavation (Grinsell 1957, 144), and physically dominates the area around about to the extent of forcing anyone standing on it or beside it to consider and react to particular fields of view.

Equally dominating in its landscape, but very different in character, is the White Horse at Uffington, Oxfordshire, which came to the Trust in 1979. This is one of a small group of hill-figures in southern England which can be assigned with various degrees of confidence to later prehistoric times (Miles and Palmer 1995). In recent years the Uffington Horse has been a symbol of the Royal County of Berkshire, and it is generally thought to have been a territorial symbol even in prehistoric times. Close up, the shape of the horse is hard to pick out, but from the vale to the north the whole image is clear and distinctive, and can be read.

The majority of upstanding archaeology in the modern landscape is far more subtle than these two examples. The small round barrows dotted across the Downs east of Avebury in Wiltshire illustrate the point. Often now shrouded by trees, these monuments were originally white chalk mounds over important burials set on skylines to be visible from ceremonial sites and settlements in the valleys. Thousands of visitors to the great henge at Avebury look at these hillsides every year, yet very few of those eyes actually see the barrows even though their senses are stimulated by what is before them.

All these sites exist in the present in a set of arrangements and juxtapositions that only reflect the here and now. Never before in their past have they been like this, nor will they ever be like it again. It is sometimes said that the modern landscape is the sum total of all that has gone before. But this is not so and deserves to be challenged. The modern landscape, indeed any landscape, is the result of a combination of conscious and subconscious choices which have dictated what has been perpetuated or allowed to survive from earlier times, and what has been added so as to create a new, and at the time, acceptable order or structure to the world.

In doing this, the very fabric of history has sometimes been embroidered and patched so that the visibility of things or their meaning is enhanced, reduced or altered. The landscape architects of the eighteenth and nineteenth centuries were just as good at this as their prehistoric forebears. The ruins of Fountains Abbey in North Yorkshire provides an example of a medieval structure modified to suit the tastes of the Aislabie family in the late eighteenth century. William Aislabie bought the ruins of the abbey from the Messenger family in 1768 and incorporated them in the ornamental grounds of Studley Royal. He landscaped the surroundings of the former abbey, cleared parts of the ruins of debris, and built picturesque additions to them. Most of the additions were removed during the nineteenth century as tastes changed again (Gilyard-Beer 1970, 20).

Other examples still remain, but are not always obvious. The quoit at Lanyon, in West Penwith, acquired by the Trust in 1952 is a classic case. The structure seen today has come to symbolize the prehistoric archaeology of Cornwall, yet it was reconstructed in its present form in 1824 from the remains of a tumbled burial chamber at the site (Barnatt 1982, 121–4).

All these sites underline the rather important point that the landscape is not a passive thing, an object that we can stand back from, admire, and apply quasi-scientific measurements to. No. Through devices and constructions that control and manipulate perception, landscapes are active and dynamic; the things that can be seen in it, and which people engaged with, provide meanings and relationships.[6] The process known as landscape assessment provides a methodology to help unpick the landscape from a number of different perspectives in order to reveal its integrity and pattern (Countryside Commission 1993). More recently, the idea of countryside character mapping allows the documentation of shared modern values in relation to landscape and the reasons why people believe what they see and what they feel are important (Anon 1994). In a sense both approaches rob individuals of the personal nature of their feelings, yet at the same time they bring to the surface some otherwise rather deeply buried beliefs and assumptions about what is all around and taken for granted. As planning tools, both are invaluable aids to the documentation of collective perception.

But as landscape studies in the twentieth century allow a better understanding of the modern landscape and our relationship to it, it must also be recognized that the job of the landscape archaeologist includes studying and understanding the landscapes of past communities.

---

6. It is worth bearing in mind here that perception is not only direct engagement. Secondary perception is important as it is based on the experiences of others and thus creates a vivid picture which has not been directly validated by the person in whose mind it is built up.

Ancient landscapes

About twenty-five years ago, in the mid 1970s, Jacquetta Hawkes contributed a chapter on archaeological sites to *The National Trust Guide* edited by Robin Fedden and Rosemary Joekes. In the opening section she mused that it is 'almost as difficult for us to imagine the wild, sparsely populated islands of five thousand years ago as it would have been for those first little communities of farmers to picture our teeming cities or the endless rush of our traffic' (Hawkes 1977, 389). And she is right. Developing an understanding of ancient landscapes is incredibly difficult and involves far more than describing what can be seen in the modern landscape.

It is well known that no amount of new data about a problem will change understandings of it; only new models can change understandings. And so it is with ancient landscapes as I would like to illustrate by exploring briefly the case of Minchinhampton Common in Gloucestershire.

Minchinhampton Common comprises an interconnected series of open grasslands amounting to over 240 ha on the high Cotswold uplands south-east of Stroud. The land was acquired piecemeal by the National Trust between 1913 and 1936, and forms part of a much larger grouping of properties extending eastward for nearly 10km from Selsley Common on the Cotswold escarpment, via the recently acquired Woodchester Park, to Rodborough Common, and finally on to Minchinhampton (National Trust 1992, 124-5).[7] All three main commons have a fine well-developed species-rich limestone turf and open aspect. Curiously though, only Minchinhampton Common appears to be especially rich in archaeological remains, many of which are visually very impressive on the ground and from the air (fig. 16.1).

Several antiquaries mention the earthworks on Minchinhampton Common, but it was not until the survey of Cotswold Long Barrows carried out by O. G. S. Crawford in the early 1920s that much attention was paid to detail. Crawford was a careful observer of archaeological remains in the field and one of the pioneers of landscape archaeology. Although the Minchinhampton earthworks were not the main subject of his study, the map he produced of sites in the Avening area is carefully annotated with his conclusion that the main linear earthwork on the Common, known as the Bulwarks, was of medieval date (Crawford 1925, facing 7).[8]

In 1937, Mrs Elsie Clifford, a local archaeologist well-known in the Cotswolds, began examining Iron Age enclosures in the area and excavated some sections

---

7. Sadly, there is no published guide to these important and fascinating properties, which include a number of smaller connected commons and parks: Besbury Common, Minchinhampton Great Park, Hyde Common, Littleworth Common and St Cloe's Green, and Watledge Hill.
8. In this Crawford was arguing against prevailing antiquarian wisdom which gave a prehistoric date to the remains.

16.1 Minchinhampton Common, Gloucestershire. Aerial view showing the eastern side of the common with the Bulwarks visible as a sinuous earthwork. (Cambridge University Collection of Air Photographs: copyright reserved)

through the Bulwarks and other earthworks on the Common. In her report she concluded that they were late Iron Age in date, even though she found late Iron Age pottery under the bank in only one cutting (Clifford 1937). By 1961 when she published the excavations of the major late Iron Age oppidum at Bagendon near Cirencester, the Minchinhampton earthworks has become the remains of a second oppidum in the area, occupied by a sub-tribal unit of the Dobunni (Clifford 1961, 151–66). Clifford suggested that Caractacus may have been responsible for the construction of the Bulwarks (1961, 160–1), a speculation that has subsequently passed into local folklore (Palmer 1994, 2).

In 1968, Professor St Joseph of the Cambridge University Committee for Aerial Photography published a series of aerial photographs showing that in the central part of the Common there was a fine rabbit warren comprising over fifty pillow mounds and, rather rare in southern Britain, some cross-shaped vermin traps (St Joseph 1968; and see Bowen 1975, 114–16). This was followed in the 1970s by detailed surveys carried out by the Royal Commission on the Historical Monuments of England who again perpetuate the putatively Iron Age dating of the main earthworks, although add question marks to some earlier interpretations (RCHM 1976, 81–4).

Since the 1970s, interpretations of the Minchinhampton earthworks as the remains of an Iron Age oppidum have regularly been repeated and partly elaborated (e.g. Darvill 1987, 167–8; 1989), even though the construction of the earthworks is quite unlike any other oppida sites known in Britain (for example the juxtaposition of the bank and ditch are reversed) and no significant later Iron Age deposits have been found inside the enclosure despite the fact that there is a thriving town there. The extensive nature of the earthworks on the Common, and the high quality of their preservation, has promoted the view that here on this windswept piece of upland is a fine piece of ancient landscape.

In the last few years the picture has changed again, not because of any new data, but because models of the nature of the landscape have changed. Rather than taking what could be seen on the ground as the starting point for study, a more general social model of landscape and differentially categorized space has been developed.[9] In applying such a model to the later periods, historical documents help give substance to the observable archaeological features, Minchinhampton being well served by early texts and placenames (Herbert 1976), and, rather exceptionally, having an early custumal constructed in AD 1155 (Watson 1932).

What now seems clear is that although there are some prehistoric remains on the Common, including a rather fine round barrow that was missed by earlier

---

9. An interim account of some of this work was included in Darvill *et al.* 1993, 567–8, as part of a discussion of the adjacent Woodchester Valley.

workers (Darvill and Grinsell 1989, 76), most of what can be seen is medieval in origin.[10] Rather than being a major ancient landscape, Minchinhampton Common is a piece of peripheral land on the edge of a series of settlements located along the sides of the adjacent valleys and on the upland at Minchinhampton itself. To understand the landscape here means also understanding the areas all around and the way people structured it and understood it.

For most of the early medieval period, what is now Minchinhampton Common was a wood: the Custom Wood so called because of common rights to take wood for fuel and house repair. The major earthworks are wood banks separating the woodland from the field-systems of Minchinhampton to the east and Amberley to the west. Internal woodland banks also survive and there are some rather fine examples with funnel entrances to control livestock, and an intricate pattern of subdivision which hints at the former presence of coppicing. Quarrying took place in and around the wood from at least the fourteenth century, and by the seventeenth century there was an extensive rabbit warren on the highest part of the plateaux. The warrener's house still survives as The Old Lodge. Something of the peripheral and rather dangerous nature of the area can be glimpsed from the fact that in 1371 two robberies are recorded against merchants travelling through the wood.

In the mid seventeenth century the woodland was cleared or destroyed and the open grassland visible today began to form. It is possible that the woodland was lost in a natural calamity, perhaps freak storms or gales, because there are hundreds of tree-throw pits in the area formerly occupied by the wood. Other traces of the former nature of the land-use is preserved as remnant indicator species in the grassland.

Since the seventeenth century, the area has been open common, grazed by livestock. Much has been said about commons and the rights of ownership and use in recent years, but there is also an interesting archaeology of commons that has yet to be explored in detail. Minchinhampton common has a number of features such as animal creeps, dew ponds, boundary stones and a pound, but more important in many ways are the features which link the common with the neighbouring settlements. While the warren and the woodbanks became redundant in the new structuring of space after the loss of the woodland, the narrow wall-defined paths and tracks leading off the common remained in use and are still used, although badly neglected today (fig. 16.2). These structures are the articulating elements in the overall system and tie the open spaces of the high ground to the settlements on the valley sides and the industrial zones along the rivers in the valley floors (fig. 16.3).

10. There are traces of a later prehistoric field system on the plateaux and it was the presence of this which has probably given rise to relatively small quantities of Iron Age pottery from excavations and watching briefs on the Common.

16.2 Snakes Lane, Minchinhampton, Gloucestershire. A narrow walled footpath connecting the upland common with the settlements and industrial areas on lower ground. (Timothy Darvill)

There is much more to say about the Minchinhampton area but the main points will already be clear enough. As a property that has been in the hands of the National Trust for many decades it is interesting because the interpretations and understanding of what is there have changed and developed several times during that period. Against this, however, must be set the folly of trying to understand ancient landscapes within the constraints imposed by the limits of a single landholding or the islands of preservation that protect upstanding sets of the archaeological remains in isolation from the things with which they were originally connected.

Landscapes don't have edges; they are seamless webs which extend out in all directions, constrained only by the conceptual horizons of the people for whom such spaces meant something. Such horizons naturally change over the course of time. In looking back to understand ancient landscapes it is necessary to lift away the physical boundaries of the spaces relevant to today's landscape to see the scale and patterning of earlier systems.

Conclusions

Separating past from present may in some senses seem like a piece of academic

16.3 View looking east across the Nailsworth Valley towards Minchinhampton Common with Dunkirk Mill in the valley bottom. (Timothy Darvill)

alchemy given that the past runs into the present and that today's present is tomorrow's past. But there is an important philosophical issue at stake here because there are fundamental differences between a *perceptual* approach to understanding the modern landscape through direct experience and engagement, and the *conceptual* approach to ancient landscapes which can only now be accessed through models and theoretical constructs.[11] Because of the nature and richness of its estates, and its remit to preserve places of natural beauty and historic interest, the National Trust has an interest and a duty in both dimensions of landscape, modern and ancient, perceptual and conceptual, at the same time.

Other papers presented in this volume will develop case studies which the authors have been working on recently, and perhaps rise to some of the challenges to received wisdom that I have set out here. In rounding off this contribution I would like to draw out two simple conclusions.

First, archaeological monuments on National Trust estates are a fundamental dimension of the modern landscape which contribute to its natural beauty, continue to excite feelings and emotions, and influence the way today's landscape

11. Something of this distinction can be glimpsed in the recent draft policy statement published by the Countryside Commission (1994).

is perceived and experienced. As such, these monuments are not dead ruins but active agents which are as much a part of the modern world as any other components of the environment. Their contribution though is not only in terms of the estates in which they lie, but also their appearance from around about.

Second, the archaeological information locked away in National Trust estates is probably the largest and most important databank on ancient landscapes anywhere in Britain. This material is not only the visible upstanding remains, but also the subterranean traces of other features that go with them, joining them together, and in archaeological terms allowing patterns and structures to be formed. Visibility is not a very good measure of significance, nor is modern land-use an acceptable guide to scale and extent. In preserving historic interest it is necessary to examine the academic as well as the aesthetic. What is being preserved is not a physical thing so much as a set of options which will allow new meanings and understandings to be attached to familiar features.

References

Anon 1994. 'Making a jigsaw map of England', *Countryside* 70 (November/December 1994), 2

Aston, M. 1985. *Interpreting the Landscape*, London

Barnatt, J. 1982. *Prehistoric Cornwall*, Wellingborough

Bender, B. 1992. 'Theorising landscapes, and the prehistoric landscapes of Stonehenge', *Man* (ns) 27, 735–55

——, (ed.) 1993. *Landscape: Politics and Perspectives*, Oxford

Bowen, H. C. 1975. 'Air photography and the development of the landscape in central parts of southern England', in *Air Reconnaissance for Archaeology* (ed. D. R. Wilson), 103–17, CBA Research Report 12

Carmichael, D. L., Hubert, J., Reeves, B. and Schanche, A. (eds) 1994. *Sacred Sites, Sacred Places*, One World Archaeology 23, London

Clark, G. 1945. 'Ancient sites' in *The National Trust. A Record of Fifty Years' Achievement* (ed. J. Lees-Milne), 29–41, London

Clifford, E. M. 1937. 'The earthworks at Rodborough, Amberley and Minchinhampton, Gloucestershire', *Trans. Bristol and Gloucestershire Archaeol. Soc.* 59, 287–308

——, 1961. *Bagendon: A Belgic Oppidum*, Cambridge

Cosgrove, D. 1985. 'Prospect, perspective and the evolution of the landscape idea', *Trans. Inst. British Geographers* (ns) 10, 45–62

Cosgrove, D. and Daniels, S. (eds) 1988. *The Iconography of Landscape*, Cambridge

Country Commission 1993. *Landscape Assessment Guidance*, Cheltenham, Countryside Commission

——, 1994. *Views from the Past. Historic Landscape Character in the English Countryside*, Cheltenham, Countryside Commission

Crawford, O. G. S. 1925. *The Long Barrows of the Cotswolds*, Gloucester

Darvill, T. 1987. *Prehistoric Gloucestershire*, Gloucester

——, 1989. 'Shaping the Old Course', in *Minchinhampton Golf Club. Centenary History 1889–1989* (ed. D. Martin), 13–18, Minchinhampton Golf Club

——, 1995. 'Tájrégészet és a hely társadalmi használatának bizonyítéka' (= Landscape archaeology and evidence for the social use of space), in *Kultúrtáj – Történeti Táj – Műemlékvédelem. Budapest-Keszthely, 1993. Június 7–11* (ed. T. Frejérdy), 205–9, Budapest, ICOMOS Magyar Nemzetti Bizottság

——, forthcoming. 'Landscapes and the archaeologist' in *The Dorset Landscape* (ed. K. Barker and T. Darvill), Bournemouth University School of Conservation Sciences Occasional Paper

Darvill, T. C. and Grinsell, L. V. 1989. 'Gloucestershire barrows: supplement 1961–1988', *Trans. Bristol and Gloucestershire Archaeol. Soc.* 107, 39–105

Darvill, T. C. and Wainwright, G. J. 1995. 'The Monuments at Risk Survey: an introduction', *Antiquity* 68, 820–4

Darvill, T. C., Gerrard, C. and Startin, B. 1993. 'Identifying and protecting historic landscapes', *Antiquity* 67, 563–74

Evans, J. G., Limbrey, S. and Cleere, H. (eds) 1975. *The Effect of Man on the Landscape: The Highland Zone*, CBA Research Report 11

Fox, C. 1993. *The Personality of Britain: Its Influence on Inhabitant and Invader in Prehistoric and Early Historic Times*, Cardiff, National Museum of Wales

Gaze, J. 1988. *Figures in a Landscape. A History of The National Trust*, London

Gilyard-beer, R. 1970. *Fountains Abbey. Department of the Environment Official Handbook*, London, HMSO

Grinsell, L.V. 1957. 'Archaeological Gazetteer', in *Victoria County History of Wiltshire. Volume 1.1* (ed. R.B. Pugh and B. Crittall), 21–279, Institute of Historical Research, London

Hawkes, J. 1977. 'Archaeological sites', in *The National Trust Guide* (revised edition), (eds R. Fedden and R. Joekes), 389–416, London

Herbert, N. 1976. 'Minchinhampton', in *A History of the County of Gloucester. Volume XI* (ed. N. M. Herbert), 184–206, Oxford

Hodder, I. 1987. 'Converging traditions: The search for symbolic meanings in archaeology and geography', in *Landscape and Culture* (ed. M. Wagstaff), 134–45, Oxford

Ingold, T. 1993. 'The temporality of landscape', *World Archaeology* 25(2), 152–74

Jenkins, J. and James, P. 1994. *From Acorn to Oak Tree. The Growth of the National Trust 1895–1994*, London

Legg, R. 1994. *National Trust Centenary. Common Roots of 1895*, Wincanton

Limbrey, S. and Evans, J.G. (eds) 1978. *The Effect of Man on the Landscape: The Lowland Zone*, CBA Research Report 21

Miles, D. and Palmer, S. 1995. 'White Horse Hill', *Current Archaeology* 12 (no. 142), 372–8

National Trust 1988. *Subject Paper: Archaeology (Second Review)*, The National Trust Properties Committee, London

——, 1992. *Properties of the National Trust* (revised edition), London

Palmer, R. 1994. *The Folklore of Gloucestershire*, Tiverton

RCHM 1976. *Ancient and Historical Monuments in the County of Gloucester. Volume One. Iron Age and Romano-British Monuments in the Gloucestershire Cotswolds*, HMSO, London

Saunders, A.D. 1983. 'A century of Ancient Monuments legislation 1882–1982', *Antiq. J.* 63, 11–33

Schama, S. 1995. *Landscape and Memory*, London

St Joseph, J.K. 1968. 'Air reconnaissance: recent results, 15', *Antiquity* 42, 311–14

Thomas, J. 1993. 'The hermeneutics of megalithic space', in *Interpretive Archaeology* (ed. C. Tilley), 73–98, Oxford

Tilley, C. 1994. *A Phenomenology of Landscape*, Oxford

Tuan, Y.F. 1977. *Space and Place. The Perspective of Experience*, London

Wagstaff, J.M. (ed.) 1987. *Landscape and Culture*, Oxford

Watson, C.E. 1932. 'The Minchinhampton Custumal and its place in the story of the Manor', *Trans. Bristol and Gloucestershire Archaeol. Soc.* 54, 203–384

Weideger, P. 1994. *Guilding the Acorn. Behind the Façade of the National Trust*, London

17 Safe in our hands?

Nicholas Johnson

As we travel from one place to another, what we see with our eyes may change dramatically, but we are the same people we were when we started our journey.
(Horace)

Politicians are used to having their views and actions savaged almost instantaneously, and academics bite their nails, whilst their finely constructed models endure the successive assaults of students eager to shatter reputations. In contrast, those of us involved in the long-term protection and conservation of the historic heritage fondly imagine that critical appraisal of what we have achieved can perhaps be avoided or delayed by the general relief that at least the inheritance from the past is safe in the hands of the National Trust. But is it?

One answer might be 'Yes, as long as we know what it is that we are keeping safe'. We know of the value of the survival of the medieval open field at Boscastle (fig. 17.1) and through appropriate management it is being looked after very well. Nothing irreversible is taking place.

It is a fact of life, however, that as we review the past, the actions of our forebears are so often, in retrospect, seen as less than satisfactory. What impressions do visiting schoolchildren get when viewing Chedworth Roman Villa with its neat little roofs covering the villa walls and a mock half-timbered house in the middle?

We are also perhaps less enthusiastic now regarding the seventeenth-century druidic explanations of our Avebury property. Similarly the radiocarbon revolution has not only lengthened prehistory but reordered its chronology. No doubt our own constructs will similarly be changed by further discoveries in the future, but at least thinking is non-intrusive.

What about our excavation techniques and conservation methods? One hundred years ago excavations were carried out by well-meaning, learned and scholarly people in ways that today we would regard as certifiable pillage. Do we not recoil in horror at what our early supporters did to hundreds of medieval churches – in removing the box pews, straightening up barrel vaults and painting over those primitive yet saintly pictograms that adorned so many church walls? We could be forgiven for feeling uneasy about the verdict of the Bicentenary Conference when our own efforts will be judged.

How could our predecessors have missed those acres of prehistoric field systems and the innumerable earthworks in our parklands, evidence of the farming landscape swept away in the creation of a romantic idyll.

17.1 The medieval open field of Forrabury, above the beautiful Boscastle harbour. The Trust manages the strips in order to preserve their form and character. (Cornwall Archaeological Unit, Cornwall County Council)

My goodness haven't we changed! The past is so much safer in our hands – not only do we at least know what our past has bequeathed us, but also surely we know what to do about it? Well, do we? Perhaps we are just more efficient collectors, conserving our estate as best we may, believing that we are probably doing a better job than our predecessors.

I want to examine, through the experience of one region, how we have changed over the last decade in our approaches to, and in our care of the historic heritage. The changes in Cornwall mirror those in other regions. Julian Prideaux has already chronicled for us the establishment of the archaeological advisory service within the Trust and its contribution towards a more holistic view of what we hold in perpetuity, i.e. there is life beyond the parterre.

This more holistic view in the Trust is matched by a wider appreciation of the totality of landscape. The land, the physical and tangible, is made up of three basic elements. The first is the physical landscape – through geology and physical processes we have the valleys and hills and coast. Second, through the action of people over many millennia we have the historic landscape – the hedges, lanes, roads, houses, settlements, telegraph poles and so on. Third, the natural landscape – the habitats and wildlife that exist as a result of our management of the land in the past and present. We are now beginning to accept that the historic, or when given meaning, the cultural elements of the landscape are profound and everywhere. We must accept the totality of our estate, not just the physical remains but also the meaning and value which we the public give and people in the past have given it. This is stewardship that goes far beyond the economic viability of properties.

Safe in our hands? It is getting to be a tall order – not only to keep safe what there is but also safeguard what people think there is. We have already seen expressed elsewhere in these proceedings quite proper anxieties about the different values given to sites and the genuine fears of accusations of exclusivity and alienation. To counteract this the Trust is progressively advancing its recording of what it owns.

We have moved from the single monument (fig. 17.2) to monuments in their context – from monuments to landscapes. We have begun to record, as best we may, everything that we believe there is whether we understand it or not. Just as we would be foolish to buy a great house without checking that at least the floors are still in place, let alone the tapestries and pictures, so now through detailed survey, we at least know what is on offer. We also have some idea what needs to be conserved. But this is done at a price – the cost of the survey, the full horror of knowing that this wall needs rebuilding, this field must be taken out of cultivation, this ruin needs stabilising (fig. 17.3). What may be good for the historic heritage is bad news for the Chorley Formula! (The Chorley Formula is a financial device whereby the National Trust assess the size of the endowment necessary to produce sufficient revenue to support a property over time.) The more you know, the more expensive it becomes, down goes the rent and up goes the number of wardens.

Safe in our hands? The stakes are rising

The more we reveal, the more we show to visitors, the higher their expectations become and – as day follows night – the more cars we have in the countryside. There is nothing profoundly new in this message but the palms simply get more sweaty. However, if the critical path is as clear as this perhaps we should close Pandora's Box, push the experts away and settle back like Miss Haversham and let benign neglect and cobwebs slowly consume the wedding breakfast, but oh! with such dignity.

Enough of this! I detect in Cornwall, and I am sure that this is happening elsewhere, that through close attention to detail the Trust is beginning to reveal

17.2 The Rumps, a cliff castle at the eastern entrance to the Padstow estuary. The site is a popular monument along the coastal footpath. (Cornwall Archaeological Unit, Cornwall County Council)

or at least become part of a profound and gradual change in society's attitude to its historic heritage.

It starts with detailed surveys of its properties that result in repairs to small elements of the historic fabric, involving volunteers and local people – community archaeology. In Cornwall the Region has been involved in repairs to sites such as Treryn Dinas and Maen Castle promontory forts. It develops with the rediscovery of the story of the past and the part that people play, and now it usually starts in primary school with children finding out about the history of their neighbourhood. This involves real people (people they know) as opposed to 'them' elsewhere. We should never forget that every national monument is someone's backyard. Whilst courting there forty years ago, they were not marvelling at how different the chambered tomb was compared to Severn-Cotswold tombs – they had other things on their mind! In revealing our national story we are also revealing our own personal history.

This is neatly encapsulated in Cornwall's Centenary project - the St Just mining coast near Land's End. I use this example deliberately as it represents an estate fraught with difficulties and challenges. Beautiful it may be, but it is still

17.3 Consolidation in progress at Wheal Charlotte mine, St Agnes. The Trust has taken particular care to consolidate all the engine houses in its care. (Cornwall Archaeological Unit, Cornwall County Council)

very much a smashed and ruined landscape – a mirror to later deprivation – surrounded by areas traditionally reserved for flytipping, New Age Travellers and flat-roofed extensions. Yet it is home for local people, an area that in the nineteenth century was a booming mining district, then, in the 1870s and 1880s a place of emigration as foreign competition closed the mines and split families. For them mining and the relics of mining are a vital part of their sense of identity and sense of place.

Today we would call this Moral Geography – the understanding that the same place means different things to different people. St Just is not the sort of place to which the Trust would have devoted great resources perhaps ten years ago. And yet by being active here the Trust has gained genuine grass roots approval for what it is doing. Cornwall is not an easy county to pigeon-hole. There is a sense of 'them' and 'us', English and Cornish – a genuine sense of cultural loss and a loss of cultural identity that is for incomers both slightly embarrassing or intensely irritating. Running parallel to this is a loss that is symptomatic of an advanced industrialized nation – a loss of connection with the land and a loss of any sense of continuity. Since the Trust was formed 100 years ago we have lost ways of living, working and belonging that lasted for hundreds of generations past.

Our founders would be incredulous how little most of us know about the land – we have to relearn the crafts of building with cob, thatching ricks, winnowing by hand, the uses of gorse and turf for fuel, bracken for bedding, the ability to smell a storm. We have also had to learn to rebuild Uppark. In fact at this conference we also mark the passage 100 years ago from being the greatest industrial nation on earth to the uncertainties of a post-industrial society. Perhaps we are part of the post-industrial rediscovery of the meaning of our landscape – a sort of 're-connection'. This happened 100 years ago in Cornwall. Perhaps in South Wales, the Durham coalfield, Tyneside and other areas where major traditional industries have all but gone, it is too soon and too painful to contemplate the immediate past.

In a curious way, almost by accident we find that by rediscovering the patterns of past husbandry and the significance of its shape and character we are somehow bringing back to the surface a lost appreciation that land is not about things but about what we think about things and how we use them. In Cornwall this is also sharply focused on a growing feeling, at least in St Just, and I hope elsewhere, that somehow the Trust's work is helping to give back to local people their cultural heritage. Whether by design or by default the Trust is part, and an important part, of a movement that is wider, and in a sense quite separate from, the conservation of splendid views and wonderful buildings.

Of course at the Bicentennial Conference our colleagues will inevitably wonder why we did this and how we could possibly have not recognized the significance of that. We have come full circle. Techniques and explanations change and the Trust as always must keep abreast of them. Let's not worry about that aspect of 'Safe in our hands?'. We are moving with the times.

Much more important is the question of what it is all for. I sense that people are beginning to believe that what is 'ours' is truly 'theirs' as well. What might at first have been 'ours' to show 'them', is becoming genuinely 'theirs', through the discovery of cultural stewardship, and which we hold in trust on their behalf.

I suppose we have progressed from Top Down to Bottom Up in 100 years, at least I hope so. The Trust should celebrate its achievements, but only so long as we continually remind ourselves that we are merely the guardians of others' cultural inheritance. It is the shift in focus from what we see to what we are, that makes me believe that the answer to the title of this paper is 'Yes, what we hold is safe in our hands'.

18 Buildings in the landscape

Susan Denyer

The Trust now owns some 140,000 acres in the Lake District, an estate built up piecemeal over the twentieth century. This holding is spread between sixteen valleys and concentrated in the heartland of the central Lake District, where several complete valley heads are under Trust protection. Two thousand vernacular buildings have come to the Trust with this land.

To many people the Lake District is still primarily an area of great natural beauty, its historic interest only secondary. Nevertheless as early as the 1920s, the Trust accepted several valley bottom farms to safeguard the livelihood of small-scale farmers, whose land was threatened by development, and in recognition of the fact that much of the appeal of Lake District valley landscapes comes from the peculiarly satisfactory relationship between buildings, built structures and the way the land is, and has been, husbanded.

In managing its Lake District estate, nearly all of which is tenanted farmland, the Trust today has to balance competing demands of farming, access and conservation as well as justify the approach it is adopting in giving precedence at times to one element of the landscape above another. The Trust has in its hands the delicate balance of one of the world's most celebrated landscapes. How does it begin to assess the importance of the various parts which go to make up the whole and make choices? This paper will focus on one of these elements – buildings, and their relationship with the wider landscape, to show how knowledge of the way these have evolved can begin to inform the management processes.

In 1984 the Trust embarked on a comprehensive survey of its 2,000 vernacular buildings in the Lake District. In this thorough and detailed exercise, which took five years to complete, all buildings were measured, photographed and described. The surveys were conducted primarily to help with management, to create an awareness of traditional, local building materials and techniques, and to assess and evaluate the importance both of individual buildings and the holdings as a whole.

The surveys proved to be extremely successful at satisfying part of this brief, that of defining local traditions. What emerged was first a catalogue of houses, the majority of which dated from the late seventeenth/early eighteenth centuries with good contemporary joinery in the form of panelling, highly decorated cupboards and staircases; second, a similar catalogue of farm buildings; third, an analysis of plan forms which brought into focus distinctive Lake District types both in farm buildings and houses, as well as features distinctive to certain valleys; and fourth, an inventory of building methods which drew attention to the peculiarly local origin of most materials employed.

In short the surveys produced an effective assessment of buildings in architectural terms. Where they were less successful was in quantifying the importance of these buildings – or rather in defining parameters to assess importance – a problem shared, I would suggest, by the English Heritage listed buildings team when they re-listed in the Lake District in 1990. As so few buildings turned out to be either architecturally distinguished or scarce, only a small proportion were picked up for listing in some valleys and in others almost none. For instance, in Wasdale, one of the most dramatic of Lake District valleys, only a bridge, a maypole and one farmhouse are listed; there are no scheduled monuments either. In other words this visually important landscape is, apart from controls exercised by the Trust, almost totally unprotected – at least as far as manmade elements go.

Many Lake District buildings are visually appealing, particularly their symbiotic relationship with their setting, and the landscape would be the poorer without them. But how can that something, which makes a house look rooted to its place, be defined? That something was well appreciated by Ruskin who, when he came to live in the Lake District, chose to adapt a farmhouse for his own needs rather than build anew, for he recognized in the farmhouse an image of what he called 'organic, natural rightness, and wholeness with its surroundings, without the burden of taste or conscious architecture'. The shortcomings of both the re-listing and to a certain extent the Trust's surveys were that they did not recognize or evaluate this link between buildings and social and economic systems – they relied on architectural appraisals and were site-specific in their approach. What they did not do was relate buildings to one another or to the landscape and agricultural processes that spawned them – in other words they did not attempt to quantify that 'sense of place'.

In an attempt to do just this, as well as to understand the way people's husbandry of Lake District valleys had developed, an historic landscape survey team was initiated by the Trust in 1990. So far the team has worked in Great Langdale, Borrowdale, Patterdale and Wasdale Head. Seven people have worked in the team since it was set up: the two present landscape archaeologists are Robert Maxwell and Chris Whitfield.

What is beginning to emerge from this work is an understanding of the way surviving houses and farm buildings reflect part of a landscape pattern which can in some valleys be traced back to the twelfth century or possibly even earlier; to an appreciation of the value of the buildings and built remains as 'documents' which can in themselves add to our knowledge of social and economic history, and lastly to the realization that Lake District valley heads are repositories of settlement patterns which reflect slow and gradual change over the past eight centuries or so, leaving them as extremely valuable resources – historic landscapes which can be read as documents of the intervening years and ones that provide as complete a pattern as we are yet able to paint of any small-scale rural society over the last millennia: in other words, for a full understanding of buildings in the landscape one has to study the complete landscape to appreciate just what deep roots many buildings have.

The landscape surveys are based on a combination of fieldwork, archival and aural research: each piece of land is field-walked, above-ground remains systematically recorded, all relevant documents studied, and oral knowledge transcribed. The resulting, analytical, reports combine this multi-disciplinary evidence to address how people's impact on the landscape has evolved, as well as how the physical landscape has in turn constrained and defined the development of settlement patterns. Two main themes are emerging from the valleys so far surveyed: the first concerns the way the network of stone walls now covering the flat valley floors has evolved from the earliest simple dividing barrier between cultivated land and grazed fell to the complex web of walls which now exist, while the second relates to the way the numbers of farmers cultivating the valleys heads, and hence the number of houses, has declined markedly over the last three centuries. What follows is a discussion of these themes for three discrete areas: the head of Great Langdale, Watendlath and Wasdale Head.

Great Langdale

The existing houses around the head of the valley date back to the late seventeenth and early eighteenth centuries. They are sited at the edge of the main arable fields and meadows alongside what we now know to be the 'ring-garth' wall. This massive wall, built dry of glacial boulders, runs in an arc around the head of the valley at the break of slope, separating the cultivated fields on the flat bottom land from the grazed fell rising above the wall. Both fields and fell were in late medieval times managed communally and the ring-garth wall was the formal barrier between two types of farming: the small-scale farmers being both pastoralists and agriculturalists, keeping sheep and cattle as well as growing oats, barley and some hemp and flax. The wall controlled open and closed seasons on the cultivated fields. In the summer, the closed season, all animals were excluded, to allow crops and hay to grow, and were sent to graze up on the open fell; during the winter months the wall was opened and the sheep and cattle allowed in to graze on stubble. The precise days at which the wall was opened and closed were regulated by the manorial courts. The ring-garth was also a legal boundary between the two areas and allowed the Lord of the Manor to manage each separately. The Great Langdale ring-garth wall can be dated to at least the thirteenth century when it is first mentioned or implied in a written document referring to the 'inclosed land of Great Langden'; it was still fulfilling part of its function as late as 1738 when rent was collected from 'several persons who put cattle on the common on the outside of the Ring Garth'.

The common fields within the ring-garth were divided into strips or small blocks of land, with each farm having many small parcels scattered throughout the common fields and with the strips unenclosed so that in the winter months stock grazed the whole area communally. Some of the strips would have been cultivated continuously for crops, on a rotational basis, while others were dedicated meadows for hay. By the seventeenth century the common fields had begun to be subdivided with walls raised to demarcate parcels of land or 'dales' tied to individual farms, as farmers shuffled their land-holdings to achieve cultivation of larger parcels near to their farms. The name common field, however, remained – in 1745 a mortgage mentions 'two dales called Flooded Leys within Great Langdale common field'. The subdivision of the common fields continued until the early nineteenth century.

From the early sixteenth century walls also started to spread up the fell-side as farms began to enclose lower areas of fell-grazing immediately above the ring-garth wall and tie them to specific farms. The creation of these 'intakes' as they were known is recorded, for example, from 1506/7 as recent 'inclosure of three intakes containing three roods from the Lady of the Manor's waste by one Thomas Grygge'. The intakes also led to the building of drift ways or 'outgangs', walled tracks allowing animals to pass through the new intakes and out on to the open fell. These outgangs were jealously guarded and were certainly not considered rights of way. In 1654 a dispute over who had rights over an outgang, which still exists, between two farms at the head of Great Langdale got as far as the Manorial Courts, the record of a juror claiming that he could 'remember for 50 years that they of Rossett never ought to drive' anything along the outgang, thus established its existence from the late sixteenth century.

The picture emerging from the surveys is of a comparatively large number of small farms in the valley head until around the middle of the eighteenth century, when the numbers began to decline swiftly. Numbers were probably at their greatest in 1600 when as many as sixteen farms occupied the head of the valley. From the seventeenth century onwards the owners of the farms come into sharper focus in the records and the decline and disappearance of some and the survival of the few can be charted. Three farms now manage the land cultivated by eleven 250 years ago and the communal fields have been shared amongst the surviving farms. In 1750 there were four farms at Stool End; two at Middlefell Place; one at Ash Busk and four at Wallend; now there is one each at Stool End, Middlefell Place and Wallend, while Ash Busk has been abandoned.

This process of settlement can be illustrated by looking in detail at one farm group, Wallend Farm. Four holdings appear at Wallend in the list of houses eligible to provide constables for Langdale parish in 1717. Only one house now survives and this was rebuilt in its present form in 1725 by Joseph Grigg, who left his and his second wife's initials, RGIG, and the date, on a fitted press cupboard within the house. The house has hardly been altered internally since. A second house was inhabited up until 1769. Only one barn remains of the three vanished farms – its house lay at right angles to it and the footings are still visible. The barn was built according to the terms of a will made by Charles Satterthwaite, dated 11 November 1612 in which the beneficiary, his brother Robert, was obliged to erect a barn with 'three paire of trees within the terme and space of three yeeres followinge'. The barn still stands largely as built, with three pairs of cruck trusses and dry stone walls. The ring-garth wall runs directly behind the Wallend Farms and abutting it next to the cruck barn are two irregular intakes carved out of the fell-land in Tudor times, known as Bull Field and Hard Field.

The surviving buildings thus take knowledge of settlement back to the early seventeenth century; the intakes to the sixteenth century; owners are known as far back as 1571, and the nearby ring-garth wall to the thirteenth century. One further piece of the jigsaw – the name of the farm – suggests the settlement itself could be as early or almost as early as the wall. In the thirteenth century a new manor of Baysbrown was created. A document delineating the manor specified the new walled boundary in detail running from the ridge of Lingmoor Fell to the head of Langdale, down the road to Little Langdale to where it joined the enclosed land of Great Langdale. Remains of that wall still exist; and where it joins the ring-garth wall enclosing Great Langdale is the site of Wallend Farm – at the end of the manor wall – hence its name.

Watendlath

Watendlath is a sub-valley of Borrowdale. In contrast to Great Langdale, the houses form a nucleated settlement at one end of a small lake or tarn. The surviving houses date from the sixteenth to the early eighteenth centuries; all are larger than the average Langdale houses. Surveys of the surrounding landscape have revealed a pattern of expansion and then contraction in the number of small farms not dissimilar to Great Langdale. Around 1600 there were sixteen small farms; by the 1750s the number had reduced to eight; now one farm manages the land. Three houses survive; the sites of five further houses have been identified, two of which survived as ruins until the early twentieth century.

The land-management systems of Watendlath had strong similarities with Great Langdale. In medieval times farms each cultivated strips within common fields separated off from common grazing by a substantial ring-garth wall. Unlike Langdale, there is evidence for three separate ring-garth walls, the largest of which enclosed the tarn, with two others to the north and east of the houses. Since the fourteenth century, there has been a gradual expansion of open fell grazing as woodland has been cleared, and, since the seventeenth century, a gradual increase in enclosures, both within and without the ring-garth wall, as well as a decrease in the number of farm holdings – as in Great Langdale. Figures 18.1–3 define the settlement patterns at three points in time – in the fourteenth century, around 1600 and in the 1750s – and have been drawn to reflect the detailed information emerging from the surveys and are therefore as accurate as the information allows, rather than speculative.

In the fourteenth century, the low, stone houses, thatched with bracken, were clustered at one end of the tarn. Outside the ring-garth wall the fell land was heavily wooded and totally unenclosed. The common fields within the ring-garths were cultivated communally in strips and must have looked very similar to present day strip fields in southern Poland where the practice of farmers cultivating strips scattered throughout the common fields still survives. This results in a patchwork effect as the production of types of grain or hay is carried out randomly throughout the common fields rather than being grouped together.

By 1600 the common fields had begun to be divided between farms, and walls raised to delineate the 'dales'. Large areas of the lower fell had been cleared of trees and some areas enclosed by intakes as individual farms sought to attach some of the most sort after cattle grazing for their own individual use. Where woodland survived, some areas were enclosed for communal benefit, with farmers having the right to lop and top trees for leaf fodder. The small one-storey thatched houses had been substantially enlarged and some roofed with slates.

The woodland had been almost completely cleared by the 1750s, and that which survived was being carefully managed within enclosures. Intaking had increased to the point where most of the good lower grazing land was enclosed; the common fields had ceased to be common being divided between farms into walled 'dales'; while the number of houses had reduced from the high point of sixteen in 1600 down to eight and most had been rebuilt and enlarged.

In the intervening 150 years, the number of houses have shrunk even further to three; one farm now farms the area worked by sixteen nearly 400 years ago; arable crops have ceased to be grown – in the last ten even hay has been largely displaced by sileage – and the farm is now mainly pastoral. What survives in buildings and wall patterns, although a simplification of the relatively large community and the complex farming system the valley supported 300 to 500 years ago, is nevertheless a tangible link with the Watendlath of medieval times.

18.1–3 Watendlath, Lake District. Settlement patterns in the fourteenth century, around 1600 and in the 1750s.

Wasdale Head

Wasdale Head has a wall pattern of staggering complexity – at least superficially. The valley head is divided into numerous tiny irregular fields bounded by thick walls, some as much as 6ft wide. Fieldwork just being completed has revealed a sequence of enclosure similar in essence to the other two valleys so far discussed but with significant differences.

The fields in the valley bottom are encircled by a ring-garth wall with large later intake enclosures spreading up the fell-sides in a pattern similar to those of Great Langdale and Watendlath. The buildings, grouped into three clusters alongside the main track leading through the valley, at Burnthwaite, the Row and Down-in-the-Dale reveal as elsewhere a pattern of drastic reduction in numbers over the last three centuries, from eighteen small farms in 1578, to fifteen in 1674, down to the three houses and two farms surviving today. Where the pattern at Wasdale Head differs from the other valleys is in evidence revealed for settlement patterns which appear to pre-date the field patterns of the previous survey areas.

This evidence is in two forms. First, in many of the small fields large cairns of stones can be seen, some of which abut the field walls. Similar cairns, but on a smaller scale, can also be seen on the lower fell-sides on the east of the valley outside the present ring-garth wall. Such cairns, but without associated field patterns, are common on the south-west fells of the Lake District, notably around Devoke Water and, on the basis of recent surveys (by the University of Lancaster Archaeological Unit), are considered to be evidence for Bronze or Iron Age settlements. Second, at Wasdale Head there is evidence, derived from surveys of wall alignments, joints and openings, for a small enclosure at the northern end of the valley within the ring-garth, against which later fields abutted, suggesting a small ring-fence for a tiny settlement which later expanded. Taken together, the evidence from clearance cairns and the small circular enclosure could present a picture of a pre-ring-garth pattern in which crops were grown on unenclosed land from which stones had been cleared into cairns, with animals shepherded and kraaled – a pattern still extant in some parts of Europe, such as south-eastern Turkey, where similar agricultural systems prevail.

The evidence from Wasdale appears to show tangible remains and a continuity in settlement from a period much earlier than in the other valleys so far surveyed, suggesting that some of the present buildings could be associated with sites settled some time before the twelfth century.

The historic landscape survey of Lake District valleys is continuing and will move on to other areas. In time it is hoped further evidence will be forthcoming to amplify the picture so far presented. Even at this interim stage however a few observations can be offered on the impact a study of complete landscapes has on the study and evaluation of buildings in the landscape.

It is commonplace to judge buildings as objects which can be evaluated in their own right, and whose merit lies in their distinctiveness, in their association with creativity or famous occupants and in the degree to which they have been left unaltered since built. Historic landscape surveys are suggesting a more complex approach at least for farmhouses and farm buildings in Lake District valley heads, where buildings can now be seen to be part of a broader settlement pattern, and where their individuality may be of less importance than their relationship with other buildings or with the patterns of land use with which they are associated.

Such buildings need to be considered first, as part of a group or set, a set developed for particular needs, in which the importance of an individual building lies in its relationship to others in the group as well as to the group as a whole. Second, a building's form may change over time, either through repeated maintenance and use or rebuilding, but its relationship to others can still be maintained; form is only one element – function and siting are two others which need to be assessed. Third, a building may be of value for its association with past practice.

In Africa many traditional buildings are built of flimsy materials and rarely outlive a generation and yet they are built in a style that has persisted for centuries – the method and the layout are of great antiquity and are renewed each generation. Similar properties can perhaps be attributed to many Lake District buildings – they are built in local materials, assembled according to local practice, and are part of a tradition of land-management that extends back at least seven centuries, even though the buildings themselves may be only one, two or three hundred years old.

In the central Lake District, buildings can now be seen to be built reflections of a way of life that has deep roots, and care must be taken not to put value judgements on individual elements of the picture until the way the jigsaw fits together and the culture of the area is fully understood.

References

Denyer, S. A. 1991. *Traditional Buildings and Life in the Lake District*, London
——, 1992. 'A sense of place', *National Trust Magazine*
——, 1994. 'Recording farm buildings in the Lake District', in *Proceedings of a Conference on Recording Farm Buildings*, RCHM, London
——, 1994. *Lake District Landscapes*, London

19 Historic landscape studies

Philip Claris

Introduction

The growth and application in archaeology of conservation techniques and strategies for defined 'sites' is now firmly coupled to an expansion of criteria and methods for landscape study and assessment generally. The pursuit of 'historic landscape studies' has gained momentum from the need to establish more detailed criteria in support of protection measures and management practices for the historic dimension of the environment. The National Trust has developed its own approach to historic landscape studies based on an extensive survey programme, arising quite directly from its duty to manage and preserve landscape. While this role is distinctive and property-based in character, its extension and use to promote the protection of the wider historic environment is a role that the Trust is already involved in, through policy development and specific representations, and an area of great future potential.

Three elements can be highlighted which, in combination, contribute to the Trust's approach: first, the more recent development and adaptation for the Trust's management purposes of professional archaeological techniques, criteria and standards; second, the influence of inherited, historically-based traditions of property ownership and landscape management; and third, the Trust's historic founding principles of preservation for the benefit of the nation. An evolutionary trend which is now taking us into the future can perhaps best be summed up as a shift in the Trust's perception of the landscape as predominantly an 'open space' and place of 'natural beauty' towards that of 'historic interest'. The combination of these elements, and the role of historic landscape studies in shaping this evolutionary process, can be briefly reviewed by reference to three areas.

Studying the Hadrian's Wall landscape

The effect of changing balances of opinion and perceptions can be illustrated by a brief review of the history of the Trust's Hadrian's Wall Estate. The landscape setting for Hadrian's Wall and the many associated monuments has often seemed to dominate consideration of the remains themselves, although in reality the

19.1 The National Trust's Hadrian's Wall Estate. A historic landscape palimpsest: John Clayton's neo-Tudor Housesteads Farm, built on the site of an old farmstead, surrounded by the extensive Roman cultivation terraces of Housesteads Meadow, bounded by the post-medieval enclosure fields with Housesteads Wood surmounting the Wall on the skyline. (Philip Claris; National Trust)

Trust's 6-mile long estate of some 2,700 acres of farmland is, by any definition, one of the densest archaeological areas of the country, and a central component of the Hadrian's Wall World Heritage Site. It also encompasses another distinct historic landscape entity, the grouping of farms based on Housesteads and the Chesters estate which John Clayton originally bought at the beginning of the nineteenth century (fig. 19.1). Clayton's acquisitions effectively created a new landscape of Roman archaeology, to be managed and used for his own research and restoration work. This landscape and the results of Clayton's restoration of the Wall, completed by about 1887, have endured to the present day, and still provide us with our most familiar contemporary image of Hadrian's Wall. A new historic landscape study of the estate has recently been completed by the Trust (Woodside 1995).

The combination in one ownership of the Clayton group of farms, however, might well have proved short-lived. When mounting debts caused the Chesters estate to be put on the market in 1929 it was sold in individual farm parcels, and the Roman archaeological landscape was dismembered. Housesteads Fort remained unsold, and it, together with lengths of the Wall from Milecastle 37 in the west to the Knagburn gateway in the east, were given to the National Trust by Mr J. M. Clayton in 1930. Housesteads Farm was later bought by Professor George Trevelyan, intending that it too should later pass to the Trust. The present National Trust Hadrian's Wall estate was thus formed as a kind of rebirth of Clayton's original scheme of purchases, and the Trust has continued to mirror his method of gradual but systematic acquisition of farms on the line of the Wall, from 1930 to the present day.

While inheriting the traditions and methods of Clayton and F. G. Simpson (who continued to excavate and manage the Wall for the Chesters Estate following Clayton's death), a shift in emphasis of the treatment and perception of the estate by the Trust can be detected in the post-war period, as the Country House Scheme developed, and a number of the Trust's archaeological properties were placed under the Guardianship of the Ministry of Public Works. This group included Housesteads Fort, and a length of Wall down to the Knagburn gateway, which were placed in Guardianship in 1951. The Trust at this time seems to have defined the specialist treatment needed for the Wall as being better provided by others with greater resources or expertise. It is tempting also to deduce a growing absorption by the Trust of the 'country house' view of landscape, particularly landscape as 'setting' for a house or other features; and the perception and treatment of monuments as ornaments of landscape, parts of a composition but not so much organic and formative elements in the landscape as a whole. When combined with a traditional land-management emphasis on agriculture, the potential weakening of preservation strategies for the Wall as a consequence of changing perceptions within the Trust at this time is evident.

None the less the Trust did continue to do more than manage the landscape for its natural beauty and countryside qualities alone, by following the now traditional method of repair of the Clayton Wall using drystone work, rather than the cement-mortar consolidation applied by the Ministry of Works to lengths of Wall in its care, famously described by Jacquetta Hawkes as 'a copy – and one that has lost all the gifts of time'. The Trust's approach has continued to evolve so that it is now committed to both the older tradition and new standards and methods of conservation and recording, including the use of consolidation techniques on newly excavated lengths of Wall. Close collaboration with and support from English Heritage has been extremely important for this work.

A new era has recently begun with the introduction by the Trust of an archaeological database to the property. A computerized SMR was thoroughly field-tested in 1994 during the major archaeological and historic landscape survey of the Trust's Hadrian's Wall estate carried out by Robert Woodside, with supervision from Jim Crow at the University of Newcastle. The first Property-based version of the NT SMR system, to be kept by the Trust at Housesteads, has now been created, to store the results of the survey, which can be maintained up-to-date in future.

Detailed records for 597 sites have been compiled and entered into the Hadrian's Wall database, together with some 850 source and photographic records, documenting the results of historical and recent research and conservation work. Recommendations for management and future research and fieldwork are given. The accompanying landscape history describes the landscape of all periods from prehistory to the present day. Together with a boundary survey, mapping and other records the results are intended to provide not only an accurate statement but also a framework for ongoing management. A computerized site monitoring method will be applied by the estate staff from now on. In these ways a modern approach is being brought directly into contact with the existing traditions of estate management, affirming for our own time the archaeological qualities which John Clayton recognized as forming an integral part of this special landscape.

The survey has also quite deliberately emphasized the non-Roman as well as the Roman character of the landscape: 228 Roman sites as opposed to 475 non-Roman sites, and, for example, 81 features assigned to the post-medieval period from 1500–1700, characterized by the Border Reivers and seasonal pastoralism, and 111 features of the early modern period from 1700–1900, when the area became permanently settled and enclosed by drystone walls.

Management information is compiled together with the historical. 184 historic boundaries are currently maintained, 8 are recorded as not currently maintained, and 33 are relict features. More than 50 per cent of recorded features are freely open to the public (336), while the remainder are restricted or closed (63 and 98). Almost all (585) are recorded as forming part of the World Heritage Site, 221 are within Scheduled Monuments and 33 are in the Guardianship of English Heritage. The Wall itself is divided into 22 lengths for management purposes, and a total of 84 subdivisions for description and archaeological analysis. The Clayton Wall is unusually treated in effect as two parallel walls, a north and a south face: each face requires separate monitoring and maintenance as each behaves differently, being separated from each other by the Roman and later core with turf capping.

The perspective which the Trust now aims to bring is therefore based on historic landscape study in all these senses: a broad study of historic features of all periods as they survive in the landscape; an awareness and respect for historic tradition and land use; and the use of detailed survey, information technology and modern standards of conservation technique, appropriate to the outstanding value of this 'place of historic interest' in national and world heritage.

The historic quality of beauty in the Lake District

The Romantic appreciation of the Lake District was such that it is no surprise that this landscape with its particular qualities, and the many threats posed to it, should have inspired the Trust in its earliest years to seek to protect it, acquiring what is now a substantial estate of some 160,000 acres. The preservation of the landscape was the first goal, but as history has moved on it is now the preservation of the historic dimension of the landscape that is making a growing claim.

As the maintenance of traditional farming practice and community life, with their associated buildings and landscape features, has become increasingly difficult, so the need to understand the historic evolution of the landscape, if it is to be preserved, has become more accepted. The loss or alteration of stone walls and farm buildings, changes in forestry practice and the general impacts of tourism have all contributed to erosion and the piecemeal breakup of familiar features and landscape patterns. Changes in the environmental equilibrium from these causes have also had some radical effects causing the decay of archaeological sites (fig. 19.2).

Some ten years of study by the Trust and the Lancaster University Archaeological Unit have both established a record of, and demonstrated the losses occurring to, the neolithic axe factory sites of the central Cumbrian Fells. A detailed survey programme from 1984–5 provided the first accurate, measured definition of what is arguably Britain's largest field monument, an area of industrial extraction and manufacturing spread over some 5 square kilometres of the highest mountains in England, whose products were distributed widely throughout the country (Claris and Quartermaine 1989). The ritual and other archaeological contexts in which stone axes have been found indicate that they were highly valued for their symbolic as well as their practical quality. Subsequent research work by Reading University has provided a much increased level of detail and understanding of these and other aspects (Bradley and Edmonds 1993).

However, the most recent research on the environmental setting reveals quite categorically that there are serious erosion problems affecting the sites, caused by overstocking of grazing land with sheep (Quartermaine 1994). Modern agricultural practice and policies are here destroying in a few years what has been preserved for more than four millennia. Despite the success of the first trial repairs of returfing carried out by the Trust, changes of agricultural policy are needed to improve the environmental situation and to safeguard the long-term future of this rare but less visible part of our landscape heritage.

But it is the visual landscape heritage of the Lake District which is familiar to us all. Against the natural beauty of the landforms, the visual contribution of the stone walls, ancient trackways, archaeology and architecture of settlement, farming and industry, can hardly be overstated. The Trust's Historic Landscape

19.2 Great Langdale, Cumbria. A historical view from the fell-top, showing the eroded scree containing neolithic axe factory deposits in the foreground, with the surviving medieval and later valley-head field pattern below. (Philip Claris; National Trust)

Survey programme began here in 1987, and has concentrated so far on the valley heads of Great Langdale, Borrowdale, and most recently, Wasdale. So little was known before the survey began that it was hard to give a date or even a rudimentary sequence for the development of many major landscape features, let alone understand their functions or begin to place them in an historic social framework. The results have changed this picture dramatically, setting out a new historic text of the region, as described by Susan Denyer in this volume (chapter 18). The survey reports and SMR for the region which are now being compiled are intended to establish a permanent framework for ongoing research and management information.

Wordsworth's description of the Lakes as a 'sort of national property' was a clarion call for the preservation of the integrity of the landscape for the nation. Historic landscape survey of the Trust's Lake District property is concerned to identify and assess those features which make up the historical element of that integrity, and in so doing make a contribution to the case for national and international support for its continued conservation.

Archaeology of the historic coastal zone

More than a sixth of the coastline, excluding Scotland, is in National Trust ownership, and through the Enterprise Neptune campaign the Trust aims to raise awareness of the issues affecting the preservation of the coast and to raise funds for further purchases. Just as the Trust is seeking to protect the visual quality of coastal landscapes as a whole, extending from coastline to hinterland, so the historic dimension is becoming increasingly recognized for its importance in the preservation of the character of our coastline. The 'maritime cultural landscape', representing a range of ideas including the integral relationship of archaeological remains on land with those largely unseen underwater, must also be added to the historic landscape perspective which the Trust considers (Westerdahl 1994).

The historic uses of the sea are so diverse and complex, and have exerted such an influence throughout our island history, that to divorce consideration of them from the long-term protection strategies for our coastal heritage is no longer sustainable. With the development of initiatives in marine archaeology at home and abroad the Trust aims to monitor new thinking and support protective measures designed to promote marine archaeological preservation, particularly in the inter-tidal zone which abuts or is sometimes included within National Trust property.

Much of the evidence for defence, shipping, industry, coastal communications and so on is already being studied through the Trust's archaeological survey programme. New data being compiled by RCHME, English Heritage and others will be studied as it becomes available in relation to Trust holdings, and used to guide the establishment of appropriate arrangements for management or when potential acquisitions are being considered. This is an important new area for partnerships of all kinds, with the statutory agencies and research bodies, with the Crown Estate, and with partners in Europe.

As our understanding of the heritage and the criteria for conservation moves forward, so the Trust is taking account of this expanding dimension of 'historic interest', an area perhaps not so likely to have been foreseen by the Trust's founders. This is a potential area for the development of new policy and practice, extending our approaches to historic landscape study, and combining new concerns and archaeological technique with the Trust's traditional commitment to the preservation of the best of the nation's coastal heritage.

The Trust's national archaeological survey programme

Looking back, it can be acknowledged that the traditions and emphasis of property management in the Trust have, on the one hand, sometimes biased the Trust's responses to its archaeological property: changing perceptions have not always given a clear view of the requirements for specifically archaeological preservation strategies. On the other hand there is no doubt that this emphasis has also made a positive contribution to the development of the Trust's national archaeological survey programme as a whole, and has given it a character which is both pragmatic and now somewhat unusual in contemporary archaeological practice, that is, a geographically extensive approach based not on any particular set of research criteria but on the landscape or land unit itself, with all the range and diversity of landscape and historic features that the Trust's landholdings now contain. As a result the focus of each study has always been drawn to landscape areas, as well as to component parts, individual buildings or sites, the consequence of a continuing dialogue between archaeological and land management practice in the organization, and reflecting also the influence of nature conservation and other disciplines.

Ultimately the land is surveyed, in a sense, simply because it is there. The rationale for the survey programme is inherent in the existence of the landscape units themselves, groupings or individual areas of National Trust property, and the statutory duty by which the Trust holds and manages these properties, to preserve them in perpetuity for the benefit of the nation.

Landscape thus remains a potent and dominant force, providing both a visual setting and an intellectual context for the identified historic or archaeological interest of properties. It also adds that crucial dimension which goes beyond the National Trust property boundary, providing a range of opportunities and challenges for the Trust particularly in regard to the protection of the wider historic environment.

Principles of landscape management, based specifically on historic precedent and character, are increasingly adopted on the basis of survey information, and very precise data is now well accepted as being crucial to the proper execution of detailed conservation and restoration work, for buried landscapes or the strikingly visual alike.

The conclusion of this brief review is both simple and optimistic for the future: that the Trust's own historic traditions and approaches to the landscape have evolved and can provide an inherently beneficial context for the future development of historic landscape studies, both in relation to the Trust's own properties and for promoting their universal use in the management and protection of historic landscape quality in the environment, that overarching 'place of historic interest' in which we all live.

References

Bradley, R. and Edmonds, M. 1993. *Interpreting the Axe Trade. Production and Exchange in Neolithic Britain*, Cambridge

Claris, P. and Quatermaine, J. 1989. 'The neolithic quarries and axe-factory sites of Great Langdale and Scafell Pike: a new field survey', *Proceedings of the Prehistoric Society* 55, 1–25

Quartermaine, J. (ed.) 1994. *Langdale Erosion Research Programme. Project Report*, Lancaster University Archaeological Unit and The National Trust, unpublished

Westerdahl, C. 1994. 'Maritime cultures and ship types: brief comments on the significance of maritime archaeology', *Int. J. Nautical Archaeology* 23.4, 265–70

Woodside, R. 1995. *The National Trust Archaeological Survey. Hadrian's Wall Estate*, 2 vols, National Trust, unpublished

20 Ancient and modern in nature conservation

Katherine A. Hearn

By any standards, the flora and fauna of Britain has remarkably ancient origins. Unmodified by humans, it dates back to the mid-Pleistocene, to 600,000 years BP (before present) and to subsequent glacials and inter-glacials: 98 per cent of the mid-Pleistocene flora is still present today (Pennington 1969). Species such as yew, oak, hazel, hornbeam and pine, for example, are thus very ancient species. Whether they remained consistently, or migrated back and forth from parts of Europe unaffected by glaciation, is not known. Some may have remained here, given how close to the snouts of present-day glaciers some species can survive.

A substantial element of our present flora, at least 300 species, is known to have been present in Britain at the end of the last glaciation, c. 14,000 years BP. Many of these ancient species subsequently contracted their ranges in the face of competition and shade from closed woodland cover, which spread from c. 10,000 BP onwards. Thrift, for example, was once more widespread inland and in the lowlands. It is now confined to salt marshes, sea cliffs and high mountain tops, sites which were never wooded. As indicated on Table 20.1, such sites are thus among our most ancient habitats. Some still have much the same assemblage of species today as they did thousands of years ago, as shown in the pollen record, such as tall herb communities on mountain ledges (Godwin 1975). Other ancient habitats which formed before humans began to influence the landscape are also shown on Table 20.1. Some were formed by ancient processes which are no longer operative, such as post-glacial erosion on a massive scale, and rapid peat formation.

From the neolithic period onwards habitats have been created or significantly modified by humans – again, see Table 20.1. Processes involved in their creation and maintenance include forest clearance, coppicing, pollarding and grazing and browsing by domestic stock. However, although created by humans, these habitats are dominated by native species, i.e. species not known to have been introduced by human agency, and they experienced a remarkable continuity of management processes for centuries, if not millennia. They can still be regarded as ancient.

By contrast, after 1700 and particularly during the twentieth century, modern processes have operated, and creation and modification of habitats have taken

Table 20.1   Examples of habitats in Britain and their date or period of formation or creation

Period	Date	Habitat
Late Glacial (late Weichselian) Palaeolithic	*c.* 12,000 BP	Montane tall herb ledges Maritime crevice and ledge communities Grassland sites, e.g. the Burren and Upper Teesdale, i.e. open communities never subsequently wooded Natural lakes Limestone pavement Valley mires, e.g. New Forest Dunes and shingle (some sites, e.g. inland part of Murlough system, Co Down)
Palaeolithic and Mesolithic	10,000 BP	Caledonian pine forest (remnants in NE Scotland of the boreal pine forest modified by climatic amelioration elsewhere)
Mesolithic, Atlantic	7–8000 BP	Blanket mire and raised mire. Main period of peat formation, continued intermittently to *c.* 3,000 BP (e.g. Thorne Moors, post 5,000 BP)
	5–7,000 BP	Mixed deciduous forest (oak, elm, lime, alder), tiny remnants in wooded ravines in remote areas which escaped later clearance/modification?
Neolithic	5000 BP	Breckland heaths
		Chalk downlands (cleared by 3700 BP)
		Upland grasslands and heaths (e.g. Lake District fells cleared of woodland)
Bronze Age	4000 BP	Lowland heaths, e.g. Purbeck, Weald
Post-Roman		Secondary woodlands, e.g. Ashridge
Medieval-Anglo Saxon	AD 679	Meadows (first recorded at this time, but probably developed earlier)
Anglo Saxon and Norman	Mainly from 10th century	Forests, preserving at least some tree cover in remaining areas of natural woodland. Wood pasture and wood pasture commons
		Coppice woodlands (first extensive records, although in existence as a woodland management regime from the Neolithic)
Later medieval	13th century	Grazing marshes and drained fens, e.g. Pevensey Levels
	13th century	Deer parks (at peak in 1300), preserving tree cover as per forests
Post-medieval	from 1660s	Plantations – early examples, e.g. Felbrigg, 1676
	from 1761	Canals, e.g. Basingstoke Canal, 1794
	18th and 19th centuries	Upland acid grasslands on degraded and polluted peat (e.g. Pennines)
	18th and 19th centuries	Water meadows (1700–1850)

Table 20.1 (*continued*)

Period	Date	Habitat
Post-medieval	18th and 19th centuries	Reservoirs
	from 1840	Upland heath managed as grouse moor
	from 1915	Conifer plantations (extensive)
	from c. 1950	Upland grasslands created from dwarf shrub communities by heavy sheep-grazing
	from 1970	Winter cereals (extensive)
	from 1970	Oil-seed rape
	from 1988	Arable set-aside

place on a very much more major and rapidly changing scale. Dimbleby (1984) and Ratcliffe (1984) give accounts of changes before and after 1700, respectively. Wetland reclamation, deep ploughing, chemical enrichment of soils and water, plantation forestry and heavy grazing, for example, have affected over 70 per cent of the British landscape. The losses of ancient and semi-natural habitats, especially since *c.* 1950, are well documented (recently in Wynne *et al.* 1995).

Similarly, much of our fauna and flora has become increasingly dominated by introduced species. There are many ancient introductions (fig. 20.1), but there was a dramatic increase in introductions in the nineteenth century (see Table 20.2). Now 45 per cent of our vascular plant flora, for example, is introduced species (see Table 20.3), many of these being modern introductions.

Ancient habitats, or those dating from the medieval period or before, are of more value to nature conservation than modern habitats. Ancient species, i.e. native species or species introduced many centuries ago, are of more value than modern ones. Ancient habitats and species are natural, or more natural, and thus obviously the mainstay of 'nature' conservation, but there are many other reasons why 'ancientness' is of great value.

Most of our native species are found in ancient habitats. By contrast, introduced species are more characteristic of disturbed and modern habitats (Crawley 1987). It is important to conserve our native species because they are distinctive, and give Britain a special character. There is a mix of Arctic, Alpine, boreal, continental, Mediterranean and oceanic species which is unique to Britain, with the oceanic element being better represented here than elsewhere in Europe. Only 50 per cent of our flora, for example, are 'widespread/European' and of less distinction. Most introduced species come in this latter category.

Ancient species and habitats have established characteristic ranges in Britain. For example, there are *c.* 300 different plant communities, with distributions

20.1 Feral goat, an ancient introduction dating from the neolithic, and now valued as an honorary member of Britain's mammal fauna, 35 per cent of which is introduced. (D. J. Bullock)

largely determined by geology, soil and climate. These give the landscape of Britain its variety, interest and local distinctiveness. Modern communities are often more catholic in their distribution and are not so closely related to local physical conditions.

Native species, after their long period of residency, have also established characteristic ranges. With the great mix of geographic elements referred to above, it is not surprising that many plants, for example, are at the edge of their European range in Britain. Such species not only make up a significant proportion of our flora, but are of particular value in that edge-of-range sites contribute much to our knowledge and understanding of ecology. 'Modern' species contribute less in this respect.

Ancient habitats have had long periods of stability and continuity which are of vital importance to ancient species, many of which are characterized by immobility and extreme inertia (fig. 20.2); this applies even to those which can fly. Examples are given in Hearn 1994. Many of our native plants and animals, therefore, are unable to colonize modern habitats.

Table 20.2   Dates of introductions to Great Britain of various species

(a)   Mammals

Orkney Vole – pre-neolithic
Harvest Mouse – neolithic
Soay Sheep – neolithic
Feral Goat – neolithic
Lesser white-toothed shrew – Iron Age
House Mouse – Iron Age
Brown Hare – Roman
Ship Rat – 3rd century
Rabbit – 12th century (Norman)
Feral Cat – 12th century (Norman)
Fallow Deer – 12th century (Norman)
Common Rat – between 1728 and 1768[1]
Grey Squirrel – 1828 and 31 further introductions 1876–1929[1]
Sika Deer – 1860
Chinese Water Deer – *c.* 1900
Fat Dormouse – 1922
Muntjac Deer – 1922
American Mink – 1929
Coypu – 1929. Spread into E Anglia 1950s. Eradicated 1981–89
Red-necked Wallaby – 1940

(b)   Vascular Plants

Sweet Chestnut – Roman[1]
Norway Spruce – 1548
Sycamore – 1578
European Larch – 1629[2] (rare until 18th century)
Cherry Laurel – 1576
Scots Pine (introduced to England) – 1610[2]
Holm Oak – 1624 (but spread from *c.* 1900)[2]
Rhododendron – 1700s
Turkey Oak – 1735
Corsican Pine – 1759[2]
Oil-seed Rape – 1800s
Orange Balsam – 1822
Cotoneaster spp – 1824
Douglas Fir – 1827[2]
Sitka Spruce – 1831[2]
Japanese Knotweed – 1840
Canadian Pondweed – 1842
Small Balsam – 1848
Spartina alterniflora – 1870
Rosebay Willowherb – native but in *c.* 1870 started spread into disturbed ground
Pineappleweed – 1871
Hottentot Fig – 1880
Buddleja – 1890
Townsend's Cordgrass – 1890 (date hybrid *Spartina x townsendii* arose)
New Zealand Willowherb – 1904
Water Fern – 1920
New Zealand Pygmyweed (*Crassula helmsii*) – 1927

Sources:
[1] Rackham 1986. Other mammals – Harris *et al.* 1995.
[2] Hadfield 1957. Other plants mainly from Clapham *et al.* 1987, and English Nature 1994.

Table 20.3   Proportion of selected groups of the British flora and fauna which is introduced

Group species in GB	Total number of species	Number introduced species	% introduced
Vascular plants[1]	2990	1360	45
Mammals (breeding, excluding Cetaceans)[2]	65	23	35
Terrestrial and freshwater Molluscs[3]	190	30	16
Amphibians and Reptiles[4]	14	2	14
Butterflies[5]	58	1	2
Fish[6]	50	12	24
Spiders[7]	c. 700	?2	0.3?
Grasshoppers and Crickets[8]	42	11	26
Birds (breeding)[9]	208	10	5

Sources:
[1]English Nature 1994. [2]Harris *et al.* 1995. [3]Kerney and Stubbs 1980. [4]Prestt *et al.* 1974. [5]pers comm M.R. Oates 1995. [6]Wheeler 1974. [7]Duffey 1974. [8]Marshall 1974. [9]Gibbons *et al.* 1993 and Snow 1971.

By contrast, introduced species which become successfully established in the wild are characterized by mobility and rapid dispersal. The birds currently spreading most rapidly in Britain are introduced species, or recent arrivals (Gibbons *et al.* 1993), and this probably applies to many other groups (examples

20.2 Oxlip, a native species confined to ancient woodlands. Although fairly mobile, spreading at 1m per year, it will not move over open ground to colonize a new wood. (National Trust Photographic Library; Mark Yates)

20.3 Modern species Scots pine (introduced to England 1610) and rhododendron (introduced in the 1700s) invading ancient (Bronze Age) heathland. The National Trust is restoring and recreating many areas of open lowland heath on its properties. (National Trust; West Weald)

for vascular plants in English Nature 1994, and for mammals in Harris *et al.* 1995). Introduced species have various characteristics and strategies which make them successful (e.g. Noble 1989; Ehrlich 1989). Some introduced or newly arrived species are welcome, e.g. goldeneye. However, more often they are undesirable. Introduced species can eliminate native species, by many different mechanisms (outlined by Macdonald *et al.* 1989). The red squirrel, wild cat and various fish, for example, are under threat from introduced species, via competition, predation or hybridization. Whole communities and habitats can be altered, with loss of native species and biodiversity. Native species can be similarly damaging (e.g. invasive and vigorous bracken), but the majority of particularly problematic vascular plants, such as Japanese Knotweed, giant hogweed, water fern and rhododendron, are introductions (fig. 20.3). Although disturbed ground is particularly prone to invasion, some species invade pristine natural habitats, e.g. Hottentot Fig on the cliffs of the Lizard Peninsula, Cornwall.

It is not possible to correlate 'ancientness' with species diversity, as some ancient habitats are species-poor, and some modern ones are species-rich. Overall, however, as noted, ancient habitats are richer in native plant species, and the richest habitats, e.g. calcareous flushes and base-rich upland woods, are ancient and little disturbed by humans. As native plants support more species of invertebrate than introduced ones (Kirby 1992), ancient habitats are likely to be richer for invertebrates than modern ones. Finally, ancient habitats hold a wealth of historical, cultural and archaeological information, in soils, fossils and pollen, and in knowledge of the past and present distribution of species.

Ancient habitats and native species are therefore essential to the distinctiveness of Britain within Europe and the world, and to local distinctiveness within the country. They are essential to diversity, stability, continuity and knowledge. Modern processes and the continued invasions of species have resulted in an increasingly homogeneous landscape, flora and fauna. Many of our native species, probably some 70 per cent, are now rare, scarce or localized.

The essence of the World Convention on Biological Diversity, which the UK and over 150 other countries signed at Rio de Janeiro in 1992, is to conserve *native species* in their *natural ranges* (*Biodiversity – the UK Action Plan* 1994). Ancient habitats and species are thus the top priority. The National Trust owns significant proportions of valuable ancient habitats with a wealth of native species, and thus has a great responsibility for biodiversity conservation. It undertakes much work to this end. It must continue to manage habitats and repair damaged habitats; control or remove non-native species which are compromising the success of native species and encourage natural distributions of native species, for example by avoiding planting, whether trees or flower seed mixtures. Where possible, the Trust must reverse the damage imposed by humans on modern habitats, encouraging natural processes to reassert themselves, for example by allowing or welcoming flooding, marine erosion, storms and droughts, and encouraging land-use and farming which is sympathetic to the natural limitations of topography, geology, soil and climate.

Finally, the Trust must continue to recreate habitats. There are some which are impossible to recreate, such as raised mires. Others, such as ancient woodlands, would probably take at least 800 years to recreate, given the extreme inertia of many woodland species. However, there are habitats which can achieve valuable assemblages of native species quite quickly: open waters, by natural recolonization, within 5–40 years; grasslands, similarly, within 20–100, and heathlands by natural recolonization and by germination from the seed bank, probably in 10–20 years. Recreated sites are thus valuable in their own right. More importantly they provide links between isolated ancient sites. In the future they will hopefully encourage inert and immobile species to become more mobile. Already they are restoring variety to otherwise homogeneous landscapes. Ancient sites and native species must continue to be the Trust's top priority, but in many respects the modern can be used to enhance the ancient.

References

Biodiversity – The UK Action Plan 1994. HMSO, London

Clapham, A. R., Tutin, T. G. and Moore, D. M. 1987. *Flora of the British Isles*, Cambridge

Crawley, M. J. 1987. 'What makes a community invasible?' in *Colonization, Succession and Stability* (eds A. J. Gray, M. J. Crawley and P. J. Edwards), 26th Symposium of the British Ecological Society held jointly with the Linnaean Society, Oxford

Dimbleby, G. W. 1984. 'Anthropogenic changes from neolithic through medieval times' in *The Flora and Vegetation of Britain* (eds J. L. Harley and D. H. Lewis), New Phytologist, 98 (1)

Duffey, E. 1974. 'Changes in the British Spider Fauna' in *The Changing Flora and Fauna of Britain* (ed. D. L. Hawksworth), Systematics Association Special Vol. No. 6, London

Ehrlich, P. R. 1989. 'Attributes of . . . invading . . . vertebrates' in *Biological Invasions: A Global Perspective* (eds J. A. Drake, H. A. Mooney, F. di Castri, R. H. Groves, F. J. Kruger, M. Rejmanek and M. Williamson), New York

English Nature 1994. *Species Conservation Handbook*, Peterborough

Gibbons, D. W., Reid, J. B. and Chapman, R. A. 1993. *The New Atlas of Breeding Birds in Britain and Ireland, 1988–1991*, London

Godwin, H 1975. *History of the British Flora* (2nd edn), Cambridge

Hadfield, M. 1957. *British Trees*, London

Harris, S., Morris, P., Wray, S. and Yalden, D. 1995. *A Review of British Mammals*, Joint Nature Conservation Committee, Peterborough

Hearn, K. 1994. 'Habitat creation – possible or impossible?' in *Erosion on Archaeological Earthworks: Its Prevention, Control and Repair* (eds A. Q. Berry and I. W. Brown), Clwyd Archaeological Service

Kerney, M. and Stubbs, A. 1980. *The Conservation of Snails, Slugs and Freshwater Mussels*, Peterborough

Kirby, P. 1992. *Habitat Management for Invertebrates: A Practical Handbook*, Royal Society for the Protection of Birds, Joint Nature Conservation Committee and National Power, Sandy

Macdonald, I. A. W., Loope, L. L., Usher, M. B. and Hamann, O. 1989. 'Wildlife conservation and the invasion of nature reserves by introduced species: a global perspective' in *Biological Invasions: A Global Perspective* (eds J. A. Drake, H. A. Mooney, F. di Castri, R. H. Groves, F. J. Kruger, M. Rejmanek and M. Williamson), New York

Marshall, J. A. 1974. 'The British Orthoptera since 1800' in *The Changing Flora and Fauna of Britain* (ed. D. L. Hawksworth), Systematics Association Special Vol. No. 6, London

Noble, I. R. 1989. 'Attributes of . . . invading . . . vascular plants' in *Biological Invasions: A Global Perspective* (eds J. A. Drake, H. A. Mooney, F. di Castri, R. H. Groves, F. J. Kruger, M. Rejmanek and M. Williamson), New York

Pennington, W. 1969. *The History of British Vegetation*, London

Prestt, I., Cooke, A. S. and Corbett, K. F. 1974. 'British amphibians & reptiles' in *The Changing Flora and Fauna of Britain* (ed. D. L. Hawksworth), Systematics Association Special Vol. No. 6, London

Rackham, O. 1986. *The History of the Countryside*, London

Ratcliffe, D. A. 1984. 'Post-medieval and recent changes in British vegetation: the culmination of human influence' in *The Flora and Vegetation of Britain* (eds J. L. Harley and D. H. Lewis), New Phytologist, 98 (1)

Snow, D. W. (ed.) 1971. *The Status of Birds in Britain and Ireland*, British Ornithologists' Union, Oxford

Wheeler, A. 1974. 'Changes in the freshwater fish fauna of Britain' in *The Changing Flora and Fauna of Britain* (ed. D. L. Hawksworth), Systematics Association Special Vol. No. 6, London

Wynne, G., Avery, M., Campbell, L., Gubbay, S., Hawkswell, S., Juniper, T., King, M., Newbery, P., Smart, J., Steel, C., Stones, T., Stubbs, A., Taylor, J., Tydeman, C. and Wynde, R. 1995. *Biodiversity Challenge* (2nd edn), Royal Society for the Protection of Birds, Sandy

21 Tread lightly: public access and archaeology

Jo Burgon

The study of Ordnance Survey maps highlights the history of this country. The maps show the evidence of peoples' past endeavours; the way land has been utilized and fashioned; and how the countryside is criss-crossed by routes developed by the early traders and the Romans, up to the present day with the arrival of the M25, town and village by-passes, expanding seaports and airports and the Channel Tunnel.

In the twentieth century, the rapid growth in travel for commerce and leisure has been phenomenal and rapid. The pattern of travel has also changed as the countryside has become more accessible as a result of improved road networks and the increased ownership of cars. The pattern of holidays has also changed with many short breaks being taken; there is little, if no time for respite and recovery for the landscape from visiting.

This movement on a global level, now on an unprecedented scale, brings its benefits but equally its costs, both financially and culturally, to countries and communities. Many have become increasingly economically dependent on tourism, sometimes as a replacement to a declining industry. Tourism is set to become the world's largest industry by the year 2000; at the turn of the century there could be 637 million travellers worldwide on the move every year. On a world stage, to tread lightly is becoming more difficult as erosion of culture and place is happening at a rate where managing such change is likely to diminish the value of the resource and does not always bring direct and substantial economic benefit to indigenous communities. The consequences of tourism and its impact on the environment, heritage, culture and economies are now being well catalogued and addressed. The development of the tourist industry obviously has considerable bearing on how public access to the countryside is promoted and managed. The British countryside is a tourism 'asset'; the National Trust, for good or ill, is very much part of the tourism industry.

The original purpose of the wealth of tracks and paths developed as part of the working pattern of movement, for example, from village to field or quarry; trading routes for wool or salt, or the movement of cattle, sheep and geese long distances along drove roads from Scotland and Wales. Although they have long since gone, they remain an essential part of the history of the countryside; every path has a story to tell; routes with their associated banks, ditches and structures are of archaeological interest. These routes are now valued and used extensively

21.1 Trail ride. Riding the Ridgeway near White Horse Hill, Oxfordshire.

for recreation and leisure. Many of the National Trails established by the Countryside Commission over the last thirty years are based on old routes such as the Ridgeway over the Wessex Downs and the Peddars Way in Norfolk. Their value for walker, rider and even the trail rider is often their historic interest, coupled with sites and features which abut, such as the hill figure and hillfort of White Horse Hill (fig. 21.1) or the long barrow, Wayland Smithy, on the Ridgeway.

Efforts to have all 140,000 miles of Rights of Way defined and open by the year 2000 in England and Wales is a challenging one. It is important for these routes to be kept open and valued to enable access into the countryside as well as protecting their historic interest. In recent years the National Trust has placed a greater emphasis on its responsibilities for Rights of Way and in its centenary year has launched an initiative to create new routes which help to serve a new purpose for today's traveller. No doubt, in time these will be seen as part of the archaeology of recreation and leisure in the late twentieth century!

Walking is the most popular recreational activity with 20 million people walking regularly. Between 1986 and 1993 5.5 million mountain bikes were sold in Britain. Horse riding is undertaken by over 3 million people twice a month. An estimated 50 million visits a year are made to National Trust countryside properties, with sites such as Dovedale receiving 2 million visits; Box Hill 1 million; the Carneddau 500,000 and the Giant's Causeway 450,000 visits. These are substantial numbers and the pressure on the local road network and on parts of the site are considerable. How can the fabric be maintained, and the quality of the visit not eroded by congestion? There are places where being part of a crowd is part of the experience, there are places and times where solitude and remoteness are the most valued part of a visit. The challenge is how it is possible to enable all these experiences to be pursued which are in harmony with the sense of place – *genius loci.*

The Trust is spending, for example, over £500,000 per annum on upland path repair in England, Wales and Northern Ireland. In the Lake District the Trust and the National Park Authority have identified 90 upland paths in need of major restoration. The Lake District has 20 million visits per annum. The introduction of car park charges at some countryside sites is one means of generating income for countryside management. Income from car parks in the Lake District is now at £120,000 per annum.

Public access is not just about the physical impact that large numbers of feet and hooves can bring but also about the impact on the senses — 'tread softly because you tread on my dreams'. The current debate in Parliament, during the passage of the Environment Bill which will establish independent National Park Authorities with revised purposes, about whether quiet enjoyment should be explicitly stated in these purposes is an example of how the value of peace and quiet should be sought in a highly urbanized, noisy and restless society. National Parks and National Trust properties are places where the pace of life, at least for the visitor, can change for a short period of time. The landscapes in the care of the Trust are valued for their natural beauty and historic interest but also as a space for activity – active and passive: riding a mountain bike, having a picnic, gazing at a view, standing in the waves looking out to sea; climbing a challenging crag or learning a new skill. There are over forty recreational activities that take place at some time, somewhere on Trust land.

These and many other activities, pursued in the green lungs of the countryside, are at the heart of what the Trust is all about. The origins of the Trust are rooted in the battle to protect green space from the effects of the industrial revolution and the enclosure of commons. The National Trust Act 1907 (sec.4(2)) empowered the Trust to acquire or 'assist in the maintenance and management of lands as open spaces or places of public resort'. The Act imposed a specific duty on the Trust in respect of commons 'to keep such property unenclosed and unbuilt on as open spaces for the recreation and enjoyment of the public'. The challenge remains a continuous one of 'promoting the permanent preservation for the benefit of the nation of lands ... of beauty and historic interest' (National Trust Act 1907 sec.4(1)) while promoting 'access to and enjoyment of such ... places ... by the public' (National Trust Act 1937 sec.3(c)).

Today support for the Trust's work, financially and politically (with a small 'p') is dependent on its members and the public at large. Access to Trust properties remains a critical means of retaining and building on support. At the same time the degree to which access can be granted is crucial if conservation *with* access is to be sustained. Access to archaeological sites encourages public support for their protection and conservation, not just for Trust sites but to the countryside as a whole. Improving understanding and appreciation of these historic landscapes has been covered elsewhere in these conference papers; it is an important aspect of the quality of access for people. Not that every site should automatically be interpreted, explained, every question answered; elements of mystery and the voyage of self-discovery should remain, although the powers of observation and questioning may have been enhanced.

The physical impacts of access on archaeological sites are chiefly ones of erosion and removal of artefacts. The protection of sites through erosion control measures is now well established and techniques have improved steadily. Where is erosion acceptable? The holloways of the English landscape are the result of centuries of erosion on unpaved roads, use by horse and cart and other traffic. There is a tendency to view all human-induced erosion as being 'a bad thing' and therefore should be kept to a minimum except where it is necessary to protect other interests such as access on hillforts or maintaining the landscape integrity of an upland fell.

The planning of access in the countryside needs to be an integral part of conserving the significance and local distinctiveness of landscapes. This involves not just maintaining Rights of Way or creating new routes but also how, for example, car parks and visitor facilities are designed and located so that they do not intrude into the quality and sense of the place. The location of car parks can be a major influence on the overall management of erosion and appreciation of a landscape. At White Horse Hill in Oxfordshire the removal of cars in the late 1970s, just prior to Trust ownership, from immediately below the hillfort has played a major part in spreading access out so that there are many routes people now take to different parts of the site. The removal of cars and scrub from Badbury Rings on the Kingston Lacy Estate, Dorset (fig. 21.2), has also prevented further damage being caused to this hillfort but the cars are still in a sensitive archaeological area; locating them further away would currently be unacceptable, particularly to local people who have enjoyed a tradition of parking in and close to the Rings. Ultimately, with consultation, the aim should be to move cars off this archaeological site and visitors will have to walk a little further.

These and other issues of access and conservation management have been subject to a two-year review by a Trust working party. The report *Open Countryside* has been considered and endorsed by the Trust's Council and Committees. The implications of its findings are now being considered by the Trust's Regions as it is aimed to provide guidance and support for local managers. The recommendations in the report are based on three principles:

21.2 Restoration of Iron Age hillfort at Badbury Rings, Kingston Lacy, Dorset.

1 The duty and primary purpose of the Trust in the countryside is to promote permanent preservation for the benefit of the nation. It will regard access as a fundamental way of providing this benefit and as a principal purpose.
2 The Trust's Acts establish the responsibilities for conservation. If serious conflict arises, conservation will take precedence over access.
3 The Trust will ensure that the countryside retains characteristics which afford the widest range of experiences and will enable people to enjoy access to its properties.

These principles, sensibly and reasonably applied, should ensure that current and future generations can continue to enjoy the rich diversity of the countryside in the Trust's care. The Trust cannot work in the countryside in isolation; it is part of the local community and economy; Trust properties are not islands in the countryside and from an access perspective the Rights of Way network provides the basis on which the traveller can enjoy and experience the historic and natural qualities of the landscape. The cumulative impact of foot, hoof and tyre may mitigate against the assertion that it is possible to 'tread lightly', but the desire and will should be there.

Postscript

Although there may be more logic and planning in countryside access today, it is still based on the historic evolution of tracks and routes maybe started by a solitary calf!

The Calf Path

> One day through the primeval wood
> a calf walked home as good calves should;
> But made a trail all bent askew,
> A crooked trail as all calves do.
> Since then, three hundred years have fled,
> And, I infer the calf is dead.
> But still he left behind his trail
> And thereby hangs my moral tale.
> The trail was taken up one day
> By a lone dog that passed that way;
> And then a wise bell-wether sheep
> Pursued the trail o'er vale and steep,
> And drew the flock behind him too,
> As good bell-wethers always do.
>
> And from that day, o'er hill and glade,
> Through those old woods a path was made,
> And many men wound in and out
> And dodged and turned and bent about,
> And uttered words of righteous wrath
> Because 'twas such a crooked path.
> But still they followed — do not laugh —
> The first migration of that calf,
> And through this winding roadway stalked
> Because he wobbled when he walked.
>
> This forest path became a lane
> That bent and turned and turned again;
> This crooked lane became a road
> Where many a poor horse with his load
> Toiled beneath the burning sun,
> And travelled some three miles in one;
> And thus a century and a half

They trod in the footsteps of that calf.
The years passed on in swiftness fleet,
The road became a village street;
And this, before men were aware,
A city's crowded thoroughfare.
And soon the central street was this
Of a renowned metropolis;
And men two centuries and a half
Trod in the footsteps of that calf.

Each day a hundred thousand rout
Followed this zig-zag calf about;
And o'er his crooked journey went
The traffic of a continent.
A hundred thousand men were led
By one calf near three centuries dead.

They followed still his crooked way,
And lost one hundred years a day;
For thus such reverence is lent
To well established precedent.

(*Samuel Foss, 1895*)

References

Croall, J. 1995. *Preserve or Destroy – Tourism and the Environment*, London
National Trust 1995. *Open Countryside – Report of the Access Review Working Party*, London

22 The archaeology of an industrial society?

Richard Keen

Industrial archaeology in Wales may be said to have come of age following the heady days of the 1960s and 1970s. Then, passionate individuals sought to preserve buildings and machines, sometimes in the face of ferocious opposition. The landscape presented an embarrassment of riches for the industrial archaeologist, and eighteenth- and nineteenth-century remains were still visible in abundance. The industrial monoliths of coal, iron and steel declined after the First World War, decline becoming an intensely felt depression during the 1920s and 1930s. This depression in the inter-war years allowed the survival of buildings and features associated with industries of an earlier era.

The Second World War brought relief as the demand for Welsh industrial products increased. The post-war period saw diversification of the industrial base and a general lifting of standards and aspirations. It was a time of contradictions. Vital new industries required space occupied by the old, and society urged the removal of dereliction, a demand that intensified after the tragedy of Aberfan in October 1966. Funds for the reclamation of derelict land were made available, and the onslaught on industrial archaeology began in earnest. From the 1970s onwards the Lower Swansea Valley Project, for example, swept away hundreds of acres of derelict buildings and polluted land, to create a new business park and leisure facilities. In social and economic terms there was every need to do so, but their removal from the landscape obliterated virtually all physical traces of a fundamental period in the history of that locality. There was little time or manpower available even to record areas such as the Lower Swansea Valley before they disappeared. Now there are more people involved in industrial archaeology in Wales, but less to record and save.

A balance between retention of industrial remains and creation of new businesses is not easily achieved. New employment is undoubtedly needed in a fragile economy such as Wales, yet new industries often require land occupied by important industrial archaeological remains. Attitudes are changing, however, and some industrial remains are now perceived as having their own integrity and being worthy of preservation. Time lends perspective, and a newer generation views the era from a more dispassionate standpoint.

Some aspects of industry are now perceived as tourist assets. A small number of men who once worked at the coal or quarry face now try to evoke for visitors the reality of work in a mine or quarry (fig. 22.1). Where once output was measured

22.1 Penyrorsedd Slate Quarry, Gwynedd, 1988, showing aerial ropeways used for lifting loaded trucks from the quarry floors. (National Trust)

in tonnages it is now judged by numbers of visitors through turnstiles. Industrial archaeology has become part of the visitor experience in Wales and a visit to a preserved coal mine is accorded the same validity as a visit to one of Edward I's castles. What does a visit to either tell us of the history of Wales? The castle, as one of the main and most visible remnants of its age, necessarily conveys only part of the story. So much of the landscape evidence other than castles and churches is not readily accessible. How much better our understanding would be if examples of complete medieval landscapes were available. The preservation of a coal mine in isolation from its community again only tells part of the story. Yet total industrial landscapes are still extant, and the opportunity yet exists for us to convey to future generations a fuller picture of the period.

That there is a growing interest in industrial history is indisputable, but the criteria that govern preservation require further analysis. Is it enough to merely preserve a pottery or a brickworks, without asking how those places of production affected the surrounding landscape and society? There is justification for carefully dismantling a row of workers' cottages and re-erecting them on a suitable greenfield site, close to good visitor facilities, where they may form part of a larger visitor experience, but only if *in situ* preservation were not possible. Can half of a colliery winding sheave mounted on a concrete plinth on the graded, grassed slope of a former colliery waste tip be anything more than a symbol?

22.2 General view of Rhondda Fawr, Mid Glamorgan, 1987, showing a typical coal-mining landscape, now minus its collieries. (National Trust)

Industrialization involved social upheaval, a struggle for independence of thought and life, the overturning of standards, enlightenment of the greater mass of the population, and the emergence of a new class of people. Where are these elements written upon our landscapes? The machines, buildings and other places of production are a vital, but incomplete, representation of industrialization. In industrial archaeological terms the opportunity still exists in a few places in Wales to bring together the wider elements, to form a cohesive whole that would give a better insight into the complexity of a great era.

Sensitive interpretation of an industrial period is essential, because many of its defining elements are impossible to preserve. Take away the actual process of production and so much is lost. A disused iron furnace cannot in itself convey the intensity of heat, noise and fumes that was an everyday part of iron manufacture.

Again, explanation of the wider social context of a preserved industrial site relies heavily upon good interpretation. Over-simplification, the substitution of cliché for truth, and the sanitization of grim reality are potential pitfalls. Coal mining, for example, is often characterized by images of noble, hard-working men and boys singing in harmony as they leave the pit and return to families clustered outside spotlessly clean cottages. Or, industrial life is represented by a simulated pit explosion or workers' uprising. Grinding, unremitting toil and bleak living conditions do not easily lend themselves to the information 'sound bite' and are often ill served by lumpen, life sized, models in workers' clothing, 'authentic' weariness and depression moulded upon their rubberised features. In due course, perhaps a host of lifetimes will be effectively compressed into ten minutes of computerized 'virtual reality'.

For the present, perhaps only when one looks down upon a landscape such as Rhondda (fig. 22.2) or Blaenau Ffestiniog does the true scale and complexity of industrialization begin to emerge. Only then does the totality of the landscape come across so powerfully. It is the 'archaeology of industrialization'.

23 Interpreting Avebury: the role of the Alexander Keiller Museum

Rosamund M. J. Cleal

The Alexander Keiller Museum is a small museum within the Avebury part of the Avebury and Stonehenge World Heritage Site. The building is owned by the Trust, the collection within it by the nation, and its management has recently passed to the Trust from English Heritage. This short case study highlights the changes which have occurred at Avebury over the last few years and particularly within the last twelve months, and outlines the ways in which it is envisaged that the Museum's role within the property will develop.

The major part of the property at Avebury was acquired in 1943, when it was purchased by the Trust from Alexander Keiller. Keiller had first been drawn to the area to excavate at the causewayed enclosure on Windmill Hill, and by the time of the sale to the Trust owned Avebury Manor and much of the surrounding land. He excavated within the henge, and along the West Kennet Avenue in the 1930s, principally to enable the re-erection of buried and fallen stones.

The estate purchased by the Trust included the henge monument, the West Kennet Avenue and the Windmill Hill causewayed enclosure. It also included the building which housed Keiller's archaeological collection, which had been open to the public since 1938, and this is still the museum. The purchase did not include the collection itself, which was later given to the nation by Keiller's widow, although it remained in the building. The Trust did not take over the running of the museum, that role being filled by the Office of Works and its successors the Ministry of Public Buildings and Works, the Department of the Environment, and English Heritage. Similarly, both the major monuments owned by the Trust, and others not owned by it (i.e. Silbury Hill, West Kennet long barrow and the Sanctuary) were managed by the same successive bodies.

The Trust added little to its holdings at Avebury for most of the next half century, but this picture has changed dramatically in the last few years. Since 1988 the Trust has purchased 262 hectares at Avebury and further acquisitions are being considered. In particular it has acquired almost all of the West Kennet Avenue, Avebury Manor and its estate, and West Kennet farmhouse and buildings, the latter lying over part of a recently discovered complex of prehistoric palisaded enclosures. At the beginning of April 1994 the Trust took over the management

23.1 Alexander Keiller and his excavation team at Windmill Hill. Mrs Veronica Keiller sits to his right and her sister, Dorothy Liddell, also an archaeologist, is on his left. (Alexander Keiller Museum, Avebury)

of the properties formerly managed by English Heritage, including the museum (under a 25-year management agreement), and the sites not owned by the Trust. All these remain in Guardianship of the Secretary of State for National Heritage.

To enable the Trust to manage these new responsibilities there has been an increase in property staff at Avebury from, in 1992, a single area warden, who also covered other open space properties in north Wiltshire, to a Property Manager with a team of eighteen full, part-time and seasonal staff which includes wardens, gardeners, a full-time curator's post at the museum (filled as a job-share), and museum custodians. At present three of these positions are filled by archaeologists.

The museum lies in the heart of the village of Avebury, just outside the henge monument, and occupies the former coach house of the manor. The displays in the small single gallery – which were redesigned by English Heritage in 1991 – concentrate on the major prehistoric monuments of the area but also touch on the later history of the village and on Alexander Keiller and his work.

The future for the Alexander Keiller Museum

Because the Museum has only been in the Trust's care for a year, and the Curators have been in post for less than that, work so far has been concentrated largely on developing plans for the future and formulating some guiding principles for that development. Our first principle is a simple one, and is that it should be the role of the Trust to provide the visitor to Avebury with information on the archaeology of the area and to make that information easily available. Our second is that the museum is an integral part of the property and its development will be bound up with that of the property. To this end the museum features in the property management plan, prepared during 1995, and the Museum's own Forward Plan is included as a supplement to that property management plan.

Guided by these two principles we have both short and long-term aims. Our immediate aims are coloured by the recognition that in the short term we can do little to remedy our lack of gallery space, but we do aim to increase the number of visitors to the museum by drawing in a higher proportion of those already visiting Avebury. Visitors to the site are currently estimated at around 400,000 to 600,000 per year, although figures are difficult to establish as there is no charge for entry to the monuments. Visitor numbers at the Museum are in the region of 45,000 each year, suggesting that only 8–10 per cent of the visitors to the site visit the museum.

Given the small size of our building, however, it is clear that as well as aiming to increase visitor numbers to the museum we must also attempt to reach visitors outside the museum building. To this end the museum staff participate in the development of leaflets, display panels, travelling exhibitions and saleable material both for the property and elsewhere and it is envisaged that this involvement will continue.

Two other areas which we feel have to be tackled in the short term are that of improving educational facilities at Avebury, and that of improving access to the archive. As part of a World Heritage Site we feel it is particularly important that we encourage and facilitate the use of the site for educational purposes, and this includes making more easily available the rich resources of the museum's archive.

Education

Prehistory is poorly served by the National Curriculum, particularly in the subject – history – with which museums are traditionally associated. The study of the remote past of our own country does not appear to qualify as history in this context, and although schools continue to utilize Avebury it is clear from contacts with teachers that many who have used Avebury in the past are finding it more difficult to continue that use. It is the aim of the Museum, therefore, to make the task of utilizing Avebury easier, both in terms of the Museum and of the sites. Already we have established contact with local teachers, some of whom are providing assistance in planning our educational strategy, and this will continue in future.

23.2 Alexander Keiller Museum, the gallery in Keiller's time. (Alexander Keiller Museum, Avebury)

In terms of the present presentation of the museum we are fortunate that the current displays were created with regard to the requirements of the National Curriculum, by English Heritage. As described by one of the team who designed it, 'it was my prime concern that the re-displayed museum would relate as closely as possible to the constraints, attitudes and opportunities imposed and offered by the new National Curriculum. This especially meant focusing on the nature of historical (archaeological) evidence and the subjectivity of interpretation based on such evidence' (Stone 1994, 193). In view of this, and of the fact that the display is only four years old, re-displaying the gallery is not one of our short-term aims.

Accessibility of the archive

Our other major short-term aim is linked to education, in that use of the archive as – among other things – an educational resource must be linked to its ease of use. The archive includes the excavation records and finds from the major excavations at Windmill Hill neolithic causewayed enclosure, the excavations within the henge, and those along the West Kennet Avenue. As well as archaeological artefacts there is an extensive photographic archive, including Alexander Keiller's colour transparencies of the excavations in the 1930s. It is intended that for each major excavation in the archive there should be a 'User's Guide', detailing the material available, and reproducing much of the original plans, sections and notes in a more organized form than they are at present. For the henge itself this task will be completed during 1995 by an intern provided by the US branch of ICOMOS. It is also the intention to make the most of the research potential of the archive, and to publish those parts of it not already published, as this too is very much part of increasing accessibility.

Summary

There are three areas, therefore, in which there are aims which should be achievable in the short term: reaching the visitor – both inside and outside the museum; improving educational facilities; and increasing ease of use of the archive.

It has to be recognized, however, that there are limits to what can be achieved and to the type of provision which can reasonably be made for the visitor if the museum remains confined within the present building. The present museum and its display, though very effective in conveying a large amount of information in a small space, simply cannot do justice to the long and complex history of the area, the international importance of which is recognized by its designation as a World Heritage Site. The very richness and diversity of the archive could only be barely exploited in the present display, but there is much more which deserves to be made available to the visitors. In the last few years, research – mostly by the University of Wales, College of Cardiff – has increased knowledge of the complexity of the area, and at the same time developments in information technology mean that such information can be made readily available to the visitor at a number of different levels, for instance through interactive displays.

For these reasons we feel that our long-term aim for the museum must be to provide alternative or additional accommodation for the museum within the property. It should be stressed, however, that this is not envisaged as a visitor centre through which all visits to the site should be channelled, and it is certainly not our intention that Avebury should become an experience largely defined by the National Trust. Avebury will always, we hope, be there for the visitor to experience in her or his own way, but at present there is almost more available for the visitor on 'alternative' interpretations than there is on the archaeology, and that is a situation which it should be and is our aim to remedy.

At present, therefore, although the Alexander Keiller Museum is only one element of the Trust's estate at Avebury, the part it plays in that estate is far out of proportion to its physical size. Not only does it contain an archive of national, and arguably international, importance, but it is set to make an even greater contribution to the interpretation of Avebury than it has done in the past.

Acknowledgements

I would very much like to acknowledge the assistance of my job-share partner in the post of Curator at the Alexander Keiller Museum, Clare Conybeare, who has greatly assisted in the preparation of this paper. I would also like to acknowledge Christopher Gingell, who kindly read and commented on the paper at various stages.

Reference

Stone, P. G. 1994. 'The re-display of the Alexander Keiller Museum, Avebury, and the National Curriculum in England' in *The Presented Past Heritage Museums and Education* (P. G. Stone and B. L. Molyneaux), London, 190–205

24 Orford Ness

Angus Wainwright

At Orford Ness, a wild landscape of shingle and marsh, justly valued for its geological and biological interest as well as its stark beauty, is combined with relics of military and scientific research. It is a landscape symbolic of our conflict with nature, as well as the conflict of nation with nation. This is a landscape for today.

In some ways, when the National Trust takes over a new property it is like an arranged marriage; neither partner knowing much about the other, portraits must be exchanged and dowries discussed if the first meeting is to be prelude to a fruitful and loving relationship. My job, along with Jeremy Musson (Assistant Historic Building Representative), was to paint a portrait of a new property called Orford Ness for the National Trust.

Management plans are the basis of the responsible management of National Trust properties. These plans draw together the results of specialist surveys, describe the aims of management and explain how the property is to be managed within the constraints of finance and specialist interests. The production of these surveys and plans is particularly important for new properties where owing to unfamiliarity it is easy to take decisions which damage unrecorded details at once or set in train policies which can be damaging in the future. The defining and describing of the aesthetic qualities of properties has not been developed to the same extent as the surveys of other aspects. In most cases this deficiency has not been detrimental to the aesthetic qualities of National Trust properties as the preserving of important historical or biological elements and processes has coincidentally preserved aesthetic attractions. But the fact remains that the sum of the objects described in these surveys does not adequately capture the essence of a landscape.

This problem is well illustrated in the case of a property such as Orford Ness. Here the landscape has a disturbing effect on the viewer partly owing to the violent contrast of its manmade and natural elements and partly owing to its exposed and somehow hostile nature, so typical of the East Anglian coast. Some of the features that go to make up this unique landscape have historical or biological importance but others do not. Arguing for the preservation of many of these features has been difficult. It is easy to argue for the preservation of historically unremarkable but attractive features, it is more difficult to argue for the preservation of ugly features when they are rare, and nigh on impossible when they are common. Unfortunately it is just such ugly and seemingly commonplace features that are an essential part of what makes Orford Ness a unique place to visit.

Many who visit Orford Ness dislike it on first meeting, a reaction which includes many decision-makers within the Trust. Around the time of acquisition there developed a school of thought which believed that the place should be 'tidied up' and converted back to a 'wilderness'. This was a shocked reaction of those used to judging the rural charms of bucolic lowland farms or wild upland moors. Our job was to step beyond such gut reactions and endeavour to understand Orford Ness on its own terms, to appreciate the order in disorder and the beauty in ugliness. We had to listen to its stories, learn to savour its attractions and finally persuade others to fall in love with it. The following account summarizes how we went about developing our case and how the management and presentation of the property was effected.

Orford Ness lies more or less on the eastern extremity of England, on the Suffolk coast between Felixstowe and Aldeburgh. The shingle spit that comprises most of the property stretches for about 10 miles (16km) south of Aldeburgh (the southern half is not owned by the Trust); protected behind it is a thin strip of grazing marsh and mud flat, and dividing the spit from the mainland is the River Ore. In geological terms it is a great rarity being one of the three major shingle formations in the British Isles and is the only one which comprises both a shingle spit and cuspate foreland. The shingle surface preserves a complex pattern of ridges deposited over many centuries and recording the stages in the formation of the land form. Orford Ness is the largest vegetated shingle spit in Europe as well as being the second largest but best preserved area of vegetated shingle in Britain. It has an internationally rare and highly specialized flora, and this botanical interest is enhanced by the variety of habitats present which include mud flats, salt marsh, reed beds, brackish lagoons, shingle beach and neutral grassland. The property is also notable for its bird life, being an important overwintering and breeding ground for sea birds, waders and wildfowl. The national and international importance of the geology and biology of the property is reflected in its designation as a Grade One Site of Special Scientific Interest, a RAMSAR site and a proposed Special Protection Area.

The salt marshes were reclaimed during the Middle Ages when Orford was an important port protected by the impressive twelfth-century keep of Orford Castle. The port lost its importance during the Tudor period probably because of the rapid extension of the spit which made entering the harbour difficult. The only surviving early building on the Ness is the Light House which was built in 1792.

The military connection began in 1915 when the Armament and Experimental Flight of the Royal Flying Corps was transferred to Orford Ness. Research work was divided into three subject areas: machine guns and gun sights, testing of bombs and bomb sights, and navigation and aerial photography. Other work included the development of aerial combat tactics. By 1918 the staff numbers had reached over 600 and a wide range of buildings had been constructed including two large Belfast Truss hangars. Orford Ness even had its own prisoner-of-war camp.

After the First World War Orford Ness was put on a 'care and maintenance' order until 1924 when it was reopened as a satellite of the Airplane and Armaments Experimental Establishment at nearby Martlesham Heath. The Ness was the firing and bombing range for all the armament testing work on guns, bombs and gun sights flown over from Martlesham. During this period the airfield was only used on an occasional basis. Buildings from this period include the Bomb Ballistics Building, which housed equipment used to record the flight of bombs in order to improve their aerodynamics and to provide data for the production of the tables used to improve bomb aiming. Another interesting building from the period is the Marine Navigation Beacon. This timber tower held a transmitter which was used at first to aid marine navigation but seems to have been in actual fact a disguised prototype for an airfield navigation beacon.

An important incident in the history of Orford Ness was the brief residence during 1935–6 of Watson-Watt and his team working on the development of RADAR or what was then known as Radio Direction Finding. The first demonstrations of the possibilities of RADAR as a practical air defence system were made here before the team moved down the coast to a larger site at Bawdsey Manor. Given the pivotal role of RADAR in the defence of the British Isles during the Second World War it is chastening to think that the history of the world might have been quite different had it not been for the faltering efforts of a few young men using out-dated equipment in three dilapidated wooden huts at Orford Ness.

During the Second World War the pace of work increased, now under the auspices of the RAF combined with a strong civilian scientific contingent. Experimental work concentrated on Bomb Ballistics and Firing trials. Bomb Ballistics experiments increased in sophistication as the speed and height of aircraft increased; bombs grew larger too, culminating in the 22,000lb 'earthquake bomb'. Firing trials looked at improving the lethality of allied ammunition and improving the protection of allied aircraft against German ammunition. Whole aircraft or individual parts such as fuel tanks, oxygen tanks or running engines were subjected to carefully controlled and recorded simulations of attack.

Trials continued after the war when rockets became a particular subject of work. Model simulations were developed where reduced scale 'shapes' of bombs or other missiles were fired through an indoor range and their flight characteristics recorded using 'spark photography'. The Royal Aircraft Establishment finally handed the site over to the Atomic Weapons Research Establishment in 1959 although forerunners of the AWRE had a presence since the great flood of 1953.

Initial work on the Atomic Bomb concentrated on the ballistics of the weapon and the telemetry required to record other properties of the bomb in flight. Later, enormous concrete test cells were built on the shingle to carry out environmental tests on the whole weapon and its constituent parts. These tests were designed to mimic the rigours which a weapon might suffer before detonation; they included vibration, extremes of temperature, shocks, 'G' forces, etc. Although the weapons did not include any fissile material the high explosive initiator was present; a test failure might result in a catastrophic explosion. For this reason the tests were controlled and recorded remotely and the cells were designed to absorb and dissipate an explosion without affecting the other facilities or the nearby village of Orford. AWRE finally relinquished the site in 1971 when development work was concentrated on their site at Aldermaston. Much of the work carried out at Orford Ness remains secret.

Between 1971 and 1973 Orford Ness briefly became RAF Orfordness with the construction of an immense Anglo-American over-the-horizon RADAR installation known as Cobra Mist. This system was either ineffective or was rendered obsolete. Part of the building is now used by BBC World Service. This part of the Ness does not belong to the National Trust.

Between 1967 and 1986 the Ness was home to No.2 Explosive Ordnance Disposal Unit (RAF). This team slowly cleared the bombing range of unexploded ordnance in advance of construction work on Cobra Mist. Training and the disposal of out-dated ordnance was also carried out to the detriment of some of the buildings.

Between 1986 and the acquisition of the property in 1993 by the National Trust the site was open to the devastating effects of the triple forces of easterly gales, scrap metal merchants and vandals.

The history of the first half of the twentieth century was dominated by wars of a previously unimaginable scale; the second half has been dominated by the Cold War, carrying with it the threat of a 'hot war' on such a scale that the destruction of whole nations was a possibility. The effect these events have had on our culture must be immense, although difficult to detect from such close proximity in time. The staggering advances in science have produced weapons which have rendered the conventional view of the battlefield redundant, threatened civilian populations on an unprecedented scale, and have produced unlooked-for threats to the natural environment.

What will be the memorials to the turbulent decades of the later twentieth century? In earlier periods when the nation's wealth was expended to fight off real or imagined threats, buildings were used both strategically and as a means of displaying power, a classic example being Orford Castle which was built to the latest design by King Henry II to counterbalance the power of the Barons in the region. By the end of the Second World War such buildings had been rendered

24.1 Orford Ness, AWRE Lab 4 used for vibration tests (1961). Colloquially known as 'the pagoda'. (Juliet Yates; National Trust)

redundant by the increase of the range, accuracy and destructive power of contemporary weapons (the result of the scientific work carried out at such places as Orford Ness). Subsequently it was by parading this technology that power was displayed. Redundant weapons are preserved in various museums but these will never have the hold on the imagination that the great medieval castles do. Much of the appeal of these structures stems from the contrast between the dominating scale of the architecture and the effects of time and nature on their fabric. Some castles are still capable of holding us in awe especially where their imposing form is set in opposition to the forces of nature such as at Dunstanburgh on the windswept Northumbrian coast. The impact of this castle in its landscape is closely comparable with that of the AWRE test cells standing in the shingle wastes at Orford Ness (fig. 24.1).

Like the castles of Wales and the Scottish borders the buildings at Orford Ness can be looked at in a number of ways, as part of the documentation of past events, as symbolic of deep-seated urges within our culture, or as dramatic forms in the landscape.

Like the ruins of medieval castles these buildings also say a lot about our continuing confrontation with the forces of nature and the ability of these forces to adapt to our structures and, given time, to destroy them. In the harsh environment of Orford Ness the destructive powers of nature are most evident either in the form of disintegrating iron and concrete or in the form of the massive shingle banks thrown up or scoured away in the course of a stormy day.

Defining and promoting the aesthetic, symbolic and historical importance of the property was the first step in the production of a management plan, the next stage was to identify those features which contribute most.

When describing Orford Ness one is apt to use adjectives such as 'bleak', 'mysterious', 'secret' or 'hostile'; although these words describe the over-riding impression of the shingle areas they do not describe other areas of the property. For aesthetic purposes the property can be divided into character areas, that is definable areas with unique aesthetic characteristics. In the case of Orford Ness these character areas gain their distinctiveness from their particular geology and past history of management, for this reason they may well be meaningful in nature conservation and management terms as well. To a large extent they also define areas with distinctive histories. The three main character areas are:

> The old airfield
> Kings Marsh and Lantern Marsh
> The shingle

Obviously these areas can be sub-divided; for example, the shingle might be divided into the narrow spit to Aldeburgh, and the broader area of the Ness itself at the south-west end of the property, and the quarried area between. Other character areas, such as the saltings, might be added.

The old airfield

This is the first area seen by the visitor after alighting from the boat. A visitor primed to expect an exposed windswept site will be surprised, as the initial impression given by this area is of a rather enclosed piece of well settled and unspectacular pasture. This feeling is created by the high river banks which cut any view of the sea on one side or the countryside on the other and the arrangement of small pitched-roof buildings spread around the perimeter of the grazed fields. That the site is near the sea is only revealed by the occasional bulky container boat passing near in-shore. The visitor walks across the old airfield on one of the concrete roads and into the main site which dates mostly from the First and Second World Wars. Before the property opened, this area gave the impression of a ghost town as what appeared to be occupied buildings were revealed on closer inspection to be dilapidated and in a state of collapse. The visitor will now be aware of the Stony Ditch river wall and the AWRE concrete buildings beyond and will be tempted to investigate these by crossing one of the bridges to reach the shingle.

Despite the obvious signs of human activity in this area, the feeling of mystery and secrecy which imbues much of Orford Ness is evident here. This is

24.2 Orford Ness, First World War guardhouse, *c.* 1917. (Juliet Yates; National Trust)

due to the silence broken only by bird calls and rattling corrugated iron; the dilapidated and overgrown buildings; and the incomprehensibility of the function of many of the structures.

Without an understanding of the history of military buildings and the specific work which took place at Orford Ness it would be easy to dismiss these dilapidated buildings (fig. 24.2). From the historical and archaeological standpoint various criteria can be used to decide which buildings and structures were most important both here and elsewhere on the property. These are:

(a) Rarity. This category includes such unusual buildings as the model bombing range and older buildings such as the First World War eighty-man barrack hut.

(b) Functional Group Value. Buildings forming part of a group devoted to a special function. Buildings associated with the bombing range fit in to this category.

(c) Aesthetic or symbolic value. Buildings with a special aesthetic value either individually or as part of a group. Structures with a symbolic function might include the concrete perimeter fence, which is one of the few signs that the area was once a secret site.

(d) Buildings with special historical associations. These could be associations with important technical developments such as the development of early Radar or with historical events such as the early Atom Bomb tests.

The buildings clustered around the airfield seem to us rather unremarkable; we are familiar with this sort of plain and functional, prefabricated architecture from any number of industrial estates and farms. It is difficult now to appreciate how revolutionary these structures were when they first appeared and how important the technical advances made in their design and manufacture were to post-war architecture. These advances were made during the 'hot house' conditions of two world wars when immense numbers of easily constructed, permanent or movable huts were required. The designers had to produce designs that could be mass produced, easily transported, easily erected and did not use scarce resources. The result was such remarkable inventions as the familiar Nissen Hut originally developed during the First World War. Orford Ness is remarkable in preserving a variety of different First World War examples of hut types; added to this is a range of similar buildings of all periods up to the 1950s. Buildings of each period are to some extent characteristic of the styles and concerns of their period. It is essential that this rich and varied building stock is preserved.

Kings and Lantern Marshes

These two marshes are effectively divided by the Cobra Mist building with the associated BBC transmitter masts (this area is not owned by the National Trust), and the Pig Pail dyke and its river walls. Like the airfield, these are enclosed areas, but here the atmosphere is more lonely. This is the preserve of waterfowl attracted by the flooded borrow pits, craters and ditches and the haunt of the silent barn owl.

The marshes are difficult to penetrate due to the many ditches and the tall tussock grass making its area seem greater than it is in reality. Towards the top end of Lantern Marsh, the marsh narrows considerably and is colonized by salt marsh plants where salt water penetrates the shingle beach. This stretch is overshadowed by the immense bulk of the artificially raised shingle ridge. This is one of the few areas where it is obvious to anyone that the sea is eating into the land and driving the beach forward over the marsh. Both marshes are dominated by the monolithic presence of the Cobra Mist building, its featureless grey surface only enlivened by the shadows of passing clouds.

The shingle

Access to this, the most distinctive part of the property, is gained at the time of writing via two bridges at the south end of the airfield site; access is straight to the heart of the AWRE site. The original access, first to the Light House and later to various bombing-range buildings, was by a footbridge and later a vehicle bridge at the north end (the High Light Bridge); this bridge has since been removed.

The bridges give access to a network of concrete roads leading to the AWRE buildings.

The disposition and peculiar shape of the buildings and the flat, almost featureless landscape they inhabit lead to a disturbing compression of perspective and a difficulty in judging distances. The visitor is drawn from one building to another; only during the long walks between the buildings is their monumental scale appreciated. As they loom larger and larger anticipation grows; this slow process is one of the attractions of the place. The scale of the buildings is overbearing and in this exposed landscape the individual can feel overpowered and reduced in their presence. Once a building is reached, the sense of mystery increases rather than diminishes. What are now silent, shadowy, rubble-strewn and roofless interiors give little clue to what only a few years ago were the home of banks of shining and humming machinery tended by an army of white-coated technicians. The ruinous condition, scale and inscrutability of the structures conjures up comparisons with the temples and funerary monuments of past civilizations. Secrecy is strongly implied by the effective obliteration of any evidence of function and the heavy metal grills through which one looks – the visitor is left to ponder. The areas between the buildings are scattered with debris, and close inspection reveals the concrete and iron to be disintegrating, lichens have colonized pieces of broken asbestos roofing, whilst horned poppies and other plants are establishing themselves amongst heaps of bricks. This process of colonization and decay of the 'manmade' by nature is one of the key aesthetic qualities of Orford Ness.

The Light House and the sea beyond will probably be the next target for a visitor with any energy left. The Light House is an obvious landmark with a well-known and reassuringly benevolent function. The coastguard station next to it, though sadly dilapidated, is still redolent of tradition and Great Britain's 'marriage' to the sea (fig. 24.3). It is a building on a domestic scale and with domestic details, a friendly face after the rigours of the windswept beach and the vast and incomprehensible AWRE buildings. To the north of the Light House is one of the better-preserved areas of shingle ridges; here is one of the few places where it is possible to gain some impression of what the Ness was like before the 1950s. In contrast, around the head of Stony Ditch and further to the north the scene is one of devastation. Here the shingle has been bulldozed out for the construction of Cobra Mist. However, this destruction has created an attractive habitat for waterfowl and seabirds; flocks of hundreds can be seen on the pools in winter. Northwards the shingle narrows to an artificially raised ridge stretching away to Aldeburgh whose Martello Tower is just visible three miles off.

To sum up the aesthetic qualities of a place is difficult but some key qualities can be defined.

24.3 Orford Ness, late nineteenth-century coastguard look-out. (Juliet Yates; National Trust)

The key aesthetic qualities are the sculptural impact of the buildings in a spacious landscape and the contrast of the manmade with the natural.

The key symbolic significance of Orford Ness is its ability to symbolize the role of technology in the late twentieth-century warfare and the awesome destructive forces it unleashed as well as the political, moral and social repercussions.

The key natural process is the colonization of and the destruction of manmade artefacts by nature.

Other aesthetic qualities can be summed up by such words as exposed, hostile, disturbing, mysterious, inscrutable, conflicting, bleak, solitude, peaceful, stillness. Words such as 'wilderness' often applied to the Ness are not, and probably never will be, applicable.

Following the analysis of the aesthetic qualities of the property a general philosophy of non-intervention has been adopted. This stems from a need to protect both the fragile aesthetic qualities described above and features of nature conservation and geomorphological value such as breeding bird colonies and shingle ridges. The challenge for the National Trust in the management of the property will be to both preserve the evidence of the past use of the site and at the same time to allow natural processes to run their course. The philosophy will be applied with varying degrees from character area to character area according to practical constraints and a management aim to enhance the natural history value of the property.

On the shingle spit this philosophy will be held most rigidly. No form of tidying will take place and on most of the buildings no form of conservation will take place.

From an archaeological point of view it has to be admitted that in allowing the natural decay of these buildings we are allowing the loss of the structural detail which contributes to their archaeological value. However, much of this detail will be preserved in the form of architects' plans and documentation. The main structure of the buildings and their impact on the landscape should survive for many years; thus its symbolic value will be maintained for future generations. Added to this, the process of decay which is such an important part of the aesthetic interest of Orford Ness would be allowed to run its course.

An unfortunate side effect of the implementation of this philosophy will be to bar unattended access to the area. This is because Health and Safety requirements would necessitate the removal of many dangerous ancillary structures and the blocking of all entrances. Such actions would be greatly to the detriment of the architectural and historical value of the buildings.

The distinctive aesthetic character of Kings and Lantern marshes will be somewhat altered in the future after grazing is reintroduced. This change has only been allowed because it will increase the value of the property to nesting and overwintering birds. Fences should be kept to a minimum to maintain the open aspect of the area. Of course, there is an historical precedent for grazing; some of the marshes were grazed from at least the medieval period up to recent years.

Intervention and change of character will be most evident on the airfield site. This is where Orford Ness's new life as a National Trust property will be centred. The smooth running of the estate required a range of buildings including Warden's accommodation, vehicle stores, volunteer dormitory, education room and interpretation area. Wherever possible these functions have been married up with the most historically important buildings as a practical way of preserving them. As this will be the main public part of the property the requirements of Health and Safety legislation mean that some dangerous buildings will have to be removed. Where buildings are to be removed wall footings and concrete bases will be left so that the keen expert can still 'read' the site, and buildings will be recorded before demolition. Rubble will be piled in localized areas so as to avoid covering any significant features. Despite these changes and the inevitable activity which will be centred around the area it should be possible to maintain something of the dilapidated and 'ghost town' atmosphere. As elsewhere, tidiness is not to be an end in itself, but only a method of ensuring visitor safety and the smooth running of the property.

The original public access route to the shingle spit was not ideal. Crossing the AWRE bridges over Stony Ditch and into the centre of the site with the buildings ranged from left to right displays them to least aesthetic benefit. From here visitors are likely to fan out in both directions causing maximum disturbance to the shingle and wildlife and maximum visual disturbance. Any movement can be plainly seen from any point on the shingle, in fact figures can be seen on the shingle even from the Quay at Orford. It is most important both for nature conservation and visual reasons that at least some areas are kept as free as possible from human intrusion. A better route has been created by rebuilding the Bailey Bridge at the old High Light bridge site at the north end of the airfield, this gives access to the top of the AWRE site and Light House. This building will probably be the target point for most visitors to the property.

This route takes the visitor past or near to three interesting buildings: the Bomb Ballistics Building (1933), the Marine Navigation Beacon Tower (1928) (see above) and the Coastguard Lookout. Owing to their extra height these buildings all give commanding views across the site, making them ideal interpretation centres.

In developing the use of these buildings and restricting access to a narrow corridor it is hoped that the expectations of the visitor will be satisfied and the air of solitude of the rest of the area will be preserved. But in restricting the areas of access we are restricting the ability of the visitor to appreciate the special aesthetic of the place. Thought should be given to opening a choice of routes in the future.

It is worth noting that because access to The Island is restricted to a ferry from Orford, the time available for a visit will be limited. A restricted area of public access will ensure that visitors do not get stranded at the extremities of the property.

There are many challenges in the interpretation of Orford Ness. One problem will be catering for diametrically opposite views of the historic significance of the place. Depending on your view of the Cold War the buildings could be symbolic of the West's successful defence of freedom against the communist menace or as symbolic of the subversion of a political system and scientific endeavour by unbalanced leaders. In its interpretation the Trust should endeavour to provide fuel for the debate but not be seen to come down on one side.

Orford Ness engenders an immense range of reactions apart from these political standpoints. Artists react to the aesthetics and ornithologists to the bird life. Those who worked on the site remember the exciting technical work with which they were involved and social life of the 'Island', a memory which contrasts violently with the dereliction and silence of the place today. As a reminder that Orford Ness is about people as well as nature and science it might be appropriate for such personal reactions and impressions to be the basis for any display material.

The powerful but fragile aesthetic of the place must be open to appreciation by the visitor. Signs and direction markers should be carefully designed so as not to erode this quality. Directions are to be stencilled on to the concrete roads and where they are necessary signs will use a plain MOD pattern typeface rather than the National Trust's more friendly style. Signs of National Trust ownership should not be overt, the individual should be allowed to develop their own personal interpretation of the meaning of the place.

Information should be confined to boards within a number of buildings around the site. The high viewpoints provided by the Bomb Ballistics Building and Marine Navigation Beacon are obvious candidates as they provide visual access to restricted areas. Leaflets might be provided so that the visitor can interpret the history of the site as they walk round. Important aspects of the history are all but invisible; these include the use of the site as an airfield and the evidence of the RADAR work.

The problem of visitor expectations is one which will have to be addressed. Firstly, there will be a strong expectation that the visitor will be able to see the AWRE test cells. Even though this is not possible at the moment I believe that these buildings are such a significant part of the experience of Orford Ness that some sort of access to them should be an aim for the future. There may also be an expectation that a visit to Orford Ness will be much like visiting most other National Trust properties – a safe experience. By contrast, a visit to this property can be both physically and emotionally rigorous. Once on the Island many visitors will be shocked by the apparent neglect of some of the buildings and the heaps of rusting metal left lying about; information will be provided to counteract the expectation of National Trust tidiness and to explain the management philosophy.

This paper has gone some way towards defining the fixed and changing elements which go towards making Orford Ness a special place. No one element of this landscape is more important than any other, all work together in a dynamic relationship giving Orford Ness a personality which is both exciting and challenging. For the first time Orford Ness is to be managed by an owner conscious of these special qualities, let us hope this will mean that they will still be there to challenge future generations.

25 The National Trust and World Heritage Sites

Tiffany Hunt

This paper examines the purpose and value of World Heritage Site designations at properties in the ownership of the National Trust. It addresses the question: is the award of World Heritage Site status comparable with that of an Oscar or a wooden spoon? My answer is based on some personal experience as a National Trust staff member involved in the management of World Heritage Sites and on observations and comments made by colleagues.

By definition a World Heritage Site must represent outstanding universal value and meet criteria defined in *The Operational Guidelines for the Implementation of the World Heritage Convention*. Essential qualities include the representation of a unique artistic achievement or a masterpiece of creative genius and being an outstanding example of a type of building, human settlement or land use. Additionally a World Heritage Site must meet the test of authenticity in design, material, workmanship or setting and have adequate legal protection as a safeguard. Once classified and included on the World Heritage Site list it is expected that the values and conditions which give a site universal significance will be maintained.

The Convention concerning the protection of the World Cultural and Natural Heritage was adopted by the General Conference of UNESCO in 1972. The United Kingdom became a party to the Convention in 1984 and by 1992 was one of 131 states who recognized in Article 4 'the duty of ensuring the identification, protection, conservation, presentation and transmission to future generations of the cultural and natural heritage.' This aim in intent mirrors closely that of the National Trust's fundamental purpose of protecting places of historic interest or outstanding natural beauty in perpetuity. It is another centenary accolade to our founders that they anticipated at a national level what nearly a century later was to become a world concern.

Why, though, is it desirable for the Trust to seek or accede to World Heritage Site status for certain of its properties, especially as Article 5 of the Convention makes it clear that there are encumbent responsibilities attaching to their care? In view of the exceptional quality of many Trust properties it was perfectly understandable that the Trust should be involved in the management of several of the key sites initially nominated by the United Kingdom government, namely the Giant's Causeway and Causeway Coast, Fountains Abbey and Studley Royal, Hadrian's Wall, Stonehenge, Avebury, and associated sites and properties in and around the City of Bath.

The Trust has therefore been in at the beginning. A brief look at some of the past and current management issues at these properties highlights the ways in which World Heritage status has affected the Trust's approach.

All the designated properties have attracted visitors over a long period of time. The curious geology of the Giant's Causeway for which it qualifies as a World Heritage Site drew visitors from at least the early 1700s. Between 350,000 and 400,000 people now visit throughout the year and, according to the visitor book, comprise some 50 different nationalities.

Visitors, however, have little or no awareness of the property's World Heritage Site status. Efforts are being made to remedy this and reference is made to the designation in the recently revised interpretive displays in the Visitor Centre. It is hoped also that this will contribute to the visitors' understanding of why the Trust recently has had to close a 1 mile (1.6km) stretch of the lower path to the Causeway due to the ravages of natural and human erosion. This action was the result of a survey carried out by Queen's University, Belfast, sponsored interestingly by the Department of the Environment and the Tourist Board. Careful footpath management is critical here as at the Trust's other World Heritage Sites. A three-year footpath management plan now forms part of the forthcoming management plan which is required by the Trust and ICOMOS, acting on behalf of the World Heritage Committee.

It is the classic conundrum of balancing the best interests of conservation and access which governs the central management issues at Trust World Heritage Sites. Stonehenge is a paramount example. One of the most intriguing archaeological excavations I recall seeing revealed the layers of different footpath surfaces leading up to the monument which had been tried over time with varying degrees of success. They were exposed as Professor Richard Atkinson was searching, it must be said, for more erudite material evidence during the late 1970s.

The problems associated with the management of past and present human interests at Stonehenge seem particularly intractable. In the words of the Trust's Regional Director for Wessex, a 'big bang solution' is required to reunite the monument and its surrounding features so that they can take their rightful place in a landscape devoid of twentieth-century clutter. Progress hinges at present on proposals to redirect the A303. English Heritage and the National Trust are working together towards achieving the key objectives of removing both the intrusive road system and existing visitor facilities in order to provide more appropriate practical and visual access.

The issues surrounding access are also exercising the Trust and others within the City of Bath. As at Stonehenge the Trust is keen that car parking provision should not detract from the handsome eighteenth-century landscape garden at Prior Park. Rather than introduce a new car park the Trust is working closely with the City of Bath with a view to developing a strategy for a park and ride scheme.

25.1 Hadrian's Wall as it slides across the Crags just west of Housesteads Roman Fort and on over the escarpment. (National Trust)

Arguably, the controversial debate surrounding sites such as the City of Bath and Stonehenge has helped to raise the profile of World Heritage Site status. This is certainly the case at Avebury. Successful battles have been fought to prevent unsuitable developments on the Ridgeway Cafe site on Overton Hill and at West Kennet Farm and in rescuing Avebury Manor from conversion into an Elizabethan experience. Tellingly in the case of West Kennet the developers' proposals were turned down following a public inquiry. The decision by the Secretary of State recognized the importance of the World Heritage Site designation in supporting the physical preservation of the archaeological remains rather than preservation by record or burial.

Although under the same World Heritage umbrella, the Trust recognizes important differences in character between Stonehenge and Avebury. The monument at Avebury must be managed in empathy with the needs of the local community of which it forms a crucial part. A World Heritage Site management strategy has been drawn up and a management working group representing interested parties, including local councils at all levels, has been set up to carry this forward.

Overall management responsibility for the Avebury monuments now rests with the National Trust. However, a key and often complicating factor in the management of World Heritage Sites is the number of owners and statutory

25.2 Fountains Abbey. (National Trust)

authorities involved. English Heritage, with the Trust's participation, have helped to address this issue at Hadrian's Wall. A steering group comprising representatives of the many and varied interested parties has been set up to produce a World Heritage Site management plan for Hadrian's Wall. The resulting draft document is to be launched by the Chairman of English Heritage on 27 June 1995 for public consultation. Whether this document will prove to be the instrument that pulls together the complex and often conflicting strands in the management of Hadrian's Wall remains to be seen, but the aim of a more coherent, better informed and integrated management must be right.

In talking to colleagues both within and outside the Trust I have heard Hadrian's Wall referred to as 'a sacred cow', 'the ultimate Chinese puzzle' and 'labyrinthine in its challenges'. Whatever the preferred metaphor, Hadrian's Wall exemplifies many of the taxing issues facing World Heritage sites. For one thing no precise boundary line was ever drawn. Its location is given as a zone which 'lies east to west across England from ... Newcastle upon Tyne ... to ... Carlisle with extensions south-west into Cumbria'. Such uncertainty perhaps reflected the vagueness surrounding the meaning of World Heritage Site status when it was designated in 1987. Since then substance has been given to the designation. Once again this was in respect of a planning application. In December 1990 ARCO British Ltd submitted a planning application for oil exploration close to the Wall.

It was approved by the Northumberland County Council, but the Department of the Environment instituted a public inquiry. Professor Peter Fowler led the opposition to the proposal contending that proper account had not been paid to the World Heritage Site status of the site. As a result the application was refused by the Secretary of State who noted that 'in the absence of consideration of the World Heritage Site aspect of the application there would be no strong environmental case against the proposals.' Since then a similar application for opencast mining at Old Stagshaw Colliery which forms part of Hadrian's Wall's landscape setting has also been turned down.

The threats to Hadrian's Wall are possibly even greater above ground. The wear and tear of visitors' feet, particularly on the central section of the Wall in the Trust's ownership, cause continuing problems of erosion. Ironically for a structure built for defensive purposes, Hadrian's Wall is one of the most fragile of all National Trust properties. If we are to remain the responsible inheritors of both Hadrian's and John Clayton's archaeological legacy utmost care in the investment of conservation resources will be vital, especially with the advent of the new National Trail.

The Wall's world renown is something of a mixed blessing in attracting large numbers of visitors to a place whose spirit derives from its dramatic and remote open landscape setting.

However, encouragement can be drawn from Fountains Abbey and Studley Royal where the Trust's new visitor reception building on the Swanley Grange site has enabled us to spread the visitor load and lessen the impact of visitors on the Abbey ruins.

Fountains Abbey and Studley Royal is another internationally important site. Here World Heritage Site status is used increasingly as a marketing tool to support both the conservation and commercial dictates of the property. Symbolically the World Heritage Site commemorative plaque was used as the foundation stone for the visitor reception building designed by Edward Cullinan.

I well recall my difficulty as Regional Information Officer in Yorkshire in 1987 in trying to explain the significance of World Heritage status with very limited information to go on until the local media caught hold of the idea that Fountains Abbey and Studley Royal was now on a par with the Taj Mahal and the Great Wall of China. This engendered both local pride and possessiveness. Whilst the Trust is doing much to try to demonstrate the benefits of its ownership and management for local people it is not always easy to achieve a harmonious balance at a property which attracts a worldwide audience.

Additional funding was not offered originally to help protect World Heritage Sites. Whilst there is now a World Heritage Fund, it is unlikely that sites in the United Kingdom would or indeed should qualify as beneficiaries in the face of World Heritage Sites in countries where resources are far scarcer. Whilst all the

World Heritage Sites referred to in this paper would undoubtedly welcome additional funding, it will be a matter of future judgement as to the weighting which World Heritage Site status should be given in determining priorities for resources.

Perhaps in two years' time we shall find ourselves celebrating a tenth rather than one hundredth anniversary to mark the introduction of World Heritage Sites in the United Kingdom. On balance I think this should be a matter of celebration not regret. In answer to the question posed at the outset of this paper, World Heritage Site status should be valued as an Oscar, but is an award which must be regularly cleaned and repaired to ensure that it does not degenerate into a wooden spoon.

26 Past significances, future challenges

David Thackray

A phrase which is gaining in currency and has been used on several occasions in these proceedings is 'Historic Environment'. This is a valuable term, although we may think of better. It embraces a number of areas of activity which have too often been seen as separate. In particular, I refer to the assumed distinction between archaeology, landscapes and historic buildings, where archaeology is apparently restricted in its application to ruins, earthworks and anything below ground. This distinction is unfortunately reinforced by the different legislation that relates to archaeology and to Listed Buildings and by the way that it is implemented.

Although it must be true to say that that perception of a dichotomy still exists within the National Trust, it has gone a long way towards demonstrating the basic integrity of historic disciplines within the organization. That this continues is very important as it is an overarching principle which the Trust must accommodate in its own management, and wishes to promote more widely. It is part of what we need to understand in order to sustain the distinctive qualities of place, whether remote, rural landscapes, or the historic house and its immediate environs.

Now, at the start of its second century, the National Trust has accumulated a great deal of experience in the management of historic sites. In common with other managers of historic sites, this experience is continuously growing and expanding, and within the framework of the historic environment, new values and expectations are continuously emerging. Witness, for example, recent work nationally on garden archaeology (Brown 1991), the archaeology of standing buildings (Wood 1994) or landscape archaeology.

Twenty years ago, the Trust's work in archaeology was almost exclusively site-specific, although it was a time when archaeologists were becoming increasingly involved in work on wider landscapes (e.g. Taylor 1970). Such important practitioners of landscape archaeology as Collin Bowen, Desmond Bonney and Peter Fowler had a profound influence on the Trust's first professional steps in archaeology, but for the Trust as a whole this work was in its infancy.

The importance of landscape contexts gradually became clearer. By the 1980s the Trust could acknowledge that the breadth of its landholdings enabled it to preserve many of its sites within their landscape settings. The methods for understanding the historic significance of these contexts, and how their component parts related and articulated in a significant way, either spatially or temporally, are now widely accepted and used to inform property management. Today, the Trust examines more closely not just the sites, but the historic landscapes of its properties as a normal part of the process of preparing archaeological surveys, and as a management tool which is generally recognized to be essential (Darvill 1987).

Similarly, it now employs archaeological techniques for recording historic gardens and designed landscapes, or historic buildings, in association with other professional skills, in repair, conservation, rehabilitation or restoration work on the historic fabric of its properties, as a matter of course.

The Trust also acknowledges the importance of integrating conservation disciplines to provide a broader, holistic approach to property management (Waterson 1993). Archaeologists work with ecologists and nature conservationists, agriculturists, horticulturists and garden historians, foresters, managers, those responsible for visitor services or the provision of information, planners, building surveyors and architects, engineers, and artefact or building fabric conservators, and others. All these disciplines have developed sophisticated working practices, often designed to achieve conservation ends, upkeep and renewal of properties, and to make them accessible to people. Archaeology sits, or stands, fairly and squarely alongside them at the drawing board, in the field, or at the site or planning meeting.

What is happening in the National Trust is a reflection of the world of applied archaeology throughout the country, in English Heritage and Cadw, local authorities, archaeological units, even universities where cultural heritage management is practised (Cleere 1984; Council for British Archaeology 1993). And quite rightly, as its responsibility for property management in all its senses is so wide, and, in its entirety, is imbued with history.

In looking to the future, a number of areas emerge which will further inform, enhance and ask questions of the three broad areas of archaeological activity which form the Trust's present *modus operandi*; the identification and understanding, the protection and the promotion of the cultural heritage.

Identification and understanding

Identification and understanding has been one of the primary functions of the Trust's archaeological work to date. It is clear about the need to know what it has on its properties through the processes of survey and research, so that we can manage them effectively and preserve the particular features of value.

The Trust has developed an archaeological survey methodology over the last fifteen to twenty years, and continues to refine it through practice and experience. The value of survey as a means of identifying and describing sites, structures, and landscapes, of historic importance and with recognized archaeological potential is now well established. Surveys have been completed for approximately two-thirds of all properties, covering perhaps 140,000–150,000 hectares of the Trust's present landholding of *c.* 240,000 ha.

Concomitant with this programme of survey is the requirement to manage that vast body of survey data in the most effective way through information technology. A Sites and Monuments Record has been developed to enable the Trust to handle, analyse and disseminate information for management purposes, and as an important planning tool.

At present the surveys of archaeological sites, cultural landscapes and vernacular and other buildings are supported by some research; indeed this is essential in collecting data on and understanding the historic character and components of properties. The Trust is not primarily a research organization; it cannot afford to be and research is not its purpose. The Trust's primary objectives for the permanent preservation of its properties are dependent on its considerable skills in property management. Yet it acknowledges that these skills are often informed by research, and systematic secondary research is undertaken as a matter of course in a large number of disciplines, not least in those concerned with the historic environment.

The Trust has, of course, built up excellent working relationships with organizations involved in research, for example, the Royal Commissions on Ancient and Historical Monuments for England and Wales, where it has benefited from their direct research, through survey, carried out in the landscape. But, I believe that the Trust should look for more opportunities to align itself with research organizations, universities, colleges or individuals in order to benefit from the skills and facilities which they have, and which otherwise the Trust may not have access to. Further, I would like to think that it can enter into regular partnerships with such bodies, in which the Trust's archaeologists participate in research projects related to the history and archaeology of its properties.

It is at this point that we should perhaps begin to ask further questions about our understanding of the archaeology and history of the Trust's properties, and the processes that have caused them to develop. I believe we need to understand how much these processes are cumulative, alive and continuing, and will lend further value to the diversity of our landscapes in the future. There is a need for cross-cultural research to explore this question and also to examine the meanings and values of places and of cultural heritage (Lipe 1984). This is a fundamental challenge which will enable the Trust to gain far greater insight into the importance people place on sites and landscapes, whether through brief association on a visit, or more intimately through their significance to the communities in a locality.

The challenge to the Trust will be in managing a consensus of the significance people ascribe to a place. We will inevitably need to consider and try to balance the conflicts that might arise between the local distinctiveness of a place as perceived by those who live there, and other perceptions held by visitors and perhaps promoted by the tourist industry and the national and international designations placed on a site or area; the World Heritage Site at Avebury is an example where such conflicts are being addressed.

Such research could also include work on the determination of aesthetic values, on the presence or absence of symbolic or spiritual values of place, on the sense of stability and continuity of human culture that can stem from the awareness of the age and history of the landscape, and on the respect and attachment for the place, and perhaps also for oneself and others, that may also derive from such understandings.

A deeper knowledge of some of these values is essential in developing and enhancing relationships with others with whom we work. It will also be important in understanding people's response to the processes of change that inevitably and relentlessly occur.

We need, too, to identify and understand those processes of change, themselves, however derived, that will affect and modify our management of our historic sites and landscapes over time. We need only think of the implications of such changes as urban or industrial development or decline, agricultural change in response to political situations, increasing promotion for tourism, increasing cultural homogenization, demographic or social changes, neglect or the natural processes of decay.

Next to change, continuity is also very important and we need to identify those processes where continuity is of direct relevance to the conservation of historic sites, structures or landscapes. Understanding of the traditional knowledge, skills and methods that produced our historic objects or buildings is essential to their ongoing management and conservation and the continuing application of such traditional techniques will itself perpetuate both the processes and the products (Jokilehto 1994).

In short, therefore, identification and understanding embraces survey and research, but also requires review, reassessment and re-evaluation of meanings; we need to acknowledge the importance not just of the extraordinary, but also of the ordinary, historic features of our landscapes which may perhaps be the most vulnerable to change.

Protection and conservation

The second broad area of responsibility with which we are currently concerned and which follows directly from the first, is the protection and conservation of the cultural heritage. Here, too, lie important challenges, particularly in the promotion of integrated, or holistic, conservation philosophies and practices.

Archaeological heritage management, or more broadly, cultural heritage management, will continue to evolve as a core function of the Trust, as property management becomes increasingly sophisticated in response to increasing pressures or knowledge. This is inevitable, and must be planned carefully so that the processes that are bringing it about can be managed.

Integrated conservation management is increasingly being achieved by the Trust in all areas of its practical conservation activities, relating to buildings, artefacts, landscapes and nature conservation. In these, archaeology and history are core subject areas as are ecology, aesthetics and environmental studies (Thackray *et al.* 1995).

Principles of sustainable management, environmental protection and the minimizing of environmental impacts are assuming increasing importance, and in the future will underline all the Trust's work. This, too, raises critical questions, and we need to be clear about how we reconcile conservation and livelihood in the countryside and elsewhere.

One area in which we can expect to see development of this integration is in Whole Farm Plans, which establish priorities for farms and farmland following an assessment and evaluation of all relevant interests. The Trust, working with its tenant farmers, is at present pioneering these to determine the optimum long-term land use of an area to benefit soil, water, wildlife and cultural interests and, of course, the livelihood of the farmer. Where conservation constraints may result in a reduction of income for the tenant, the Trust must consider providing some compensation, such as reduced rental, or payments on the lines of, for example, ESA payments.

Other agri-environmental changes, particularly the increase in land going out of production, are providing opportunities for habitat recreation (Harvey 1995). These might involve, *inter alia*, the creation of new woodlands, the restoration of traditional management regimes, including grazing and grassland management, woodland management, hedge-laying or stone-walling. The creation of wilderness or non-intervention areas might provide valuable opportunities for monitoring and researching processes of natural change on the human-made features of the landscape.

Indeed, conservation and site protection provide many opportunities for technical research, much of which is ongoing internationally, and which is constantly developing. The Trust needs to be aware of, and closely involved in these developments. Where appropriate, these too need to be interdisciplinary, in order to make them of the widest possible value. Such research, aimed at achieving improvements in conservation methods, would have direct practical application, and would include such subjects as building technology, visitor management techniques, site stabilization techniques, habitat management techniques or visitor attitudes, values and perceptions (Trotzig 1993). Further, research into the authenticity of sites, structures and techniques will promote the integrity of conservation principles related to form, design, materials or function, the context, setting or sense of place, and traditional practice or techniques (Fielden and Jokilehto 1993; Stovel 1994).

In developing its countryside policies the Trust needs to provide a framework for future landscapes in which existing and past values can be accommodated and in which new values can accumulate (Jacques 1992). The Trust needs to set the limits and scale of acceptable change for its properties, but needs to be flexible as the true effects of change are realized.

Promotion and involvement

The third area of interest, which contains many challenges, is that of the promotion of the historic and archaeological interest of the Trust's properties. In this we must seek the means of involving people and sharing understanding in order to build on our knowledge.

Throughout the lengthy process of preparing surveys of Trust properties, it has amassed an enormous amount of data, much of which is on subjects which are of popular interest. Survey reports contain a wealth of archaeological, local historical, topographical, regional or architectural historical information and research. This may well be disseminated to only a very few people. It might be argued that this introverted gathering of data, although essential for property management, is not used wholly effectively and is even perhaps elitist, or at best inconsiderate of wider public interests. What a resource! What an opportunity! We want to raise awareness, to make the information and the subjects accessible, but how do we do it? What are the most effective ways of sharing this knowledge? Because that is what we must do.

But, before we rush out, enthusiastically, to promote our subject, the Trust needs to consider some basic questions and to plan carefully in conjunction with educational and public affairs colleagues, both within the Trust and in other organizations such as English Heritage, who have already gone through this thinking and gained experience in these questions.

We need to consider first of all who the information is for, and then what sort of information do they want; what is relevant to particular groups. We must also look at our resources and consider the most effective way these can be used. It is possible that opportunities may be found through partnerships or co-operation with other bodies, schools and education authorities, universities and colleges or other training agencies.

It is perhaps arbitrary to suggest a distinction between education, training and informing, but, if you accept the distinction, I believe we have opportunities in all three although there is clearly considerable overlap. The educational opportunities are obvious. Archaeological and historical information is core subject data in all levels from primary to tertiary education. It is directly relevant or can be adapted for many National Curriculum subjects. Many local schools have direct involvement with their local Trust properties, some even adopting properties to visit, study and participate in the management. Increased archaeological involvement in these partnerships should be developed.

At tertiary level the Trust's sites and landscapes are used for field-trips and for teaching, and to a small extent Trust properties are studied for undergraduate dissertations. Closer direct relationships with appropriate university departments would enable the Trust to build on these relationships, and would also create and offer opportunities to promote properties for post-graduate research, either in the sciences or humanities. Investment from the Trust in the promotion of archaeology in education would have direct benefits, able to be felt at property level, either through increasing interest in and support for the properties, or through the results of new research. It would also have wider indirect benefits in enabling deeper understanding of the history and development of the countryside, an experience which lasts a lifetime.

Similarly, I believe we can promote further the potential and opportunities for training provided by Trust properties and the skills of its staff. Again, this is nothing new to the Trust, where work experience and training have been core activities for many years. But archaeological involvement in this has only been on a small scale in the past. To raise awareness and instil a breadth of knowledge of the historic environment, resources should be put into developing a structured approach to training staff and volunteers, and planning to use the Trust's properties as a resource to train others, particularly in conservation skills (Wood 1993). Ideas such as internships, student placements, short, commercially-run training courses and even a summer school, all providing an integrated package of subjects applicable to the Trust's work in cultural heritage management, should be investigated. In considering these sorts of ideas we should again be looking at possible partnerships with such bodies as the Society of Antiquaries, ICOMOS, the Countryside Commission, CCW, English Heritage, Cadw, or individual universities or colleges, including, of course, agricultural colleges. The Trust should also consider using its specialist skills to extend its influence not just in Britain, but in Europe and elsewhere.

Promotion of course is not entirely to do with learning or training, but is also concerned with raising awareness or interest in a less intensive way. Many of the Trust's members and other visitors are unaware of the breadth of the Trust's work in archaeology, nor are they necessarily aware of the many fine sites of international, national or local importance which they can visit on Trust properties. In addition to those members of the public interested enough to join or visit, there are many more to whom the Trust's messages are not penetrating. In particular, perhaps the Trust should promote the multi-cultural history of our landscapes, including urban landscapes. It is a clear responsibility to make the Trust's archaeological sites and historic landscapes more accessible and to provide information where appropriate, which will interest the visitor and help promote the value of the cultural heritage generally. The Trust's archaeologists should be contributing to guidebooks, developing non-technical, popular publications and otherwise using the historical information we are accumulating to promote the history of Trust properties to general interest audiences.

The Trust's properties can be promoted in the same way through the involvement of local communities, many of whose members have a particular and often deep-seated interest in the heritage of their locality. The further development of relations with local communities to promote historical and archaeological interest may be reciprocated by local research or conservation initiatives, involving volunteers, and feeding back historical information or providing practical help or monitoring. On a less academic scale, such endeavours as parish, or in the Trust's case, estate maps might foster this relationship of sharing properties with individuals and communities.

Improving communication skills and promoting the historic and archae-ological interest of Trust properties is perhaps our most powerful challenge, as through promotion we can meet others interested, address areas of mutual concern, such as achieving a sustainable balance of tourism, unlock resources, develop educational, research, training and conservation initiatives and increase interest in and respect for people and place, for past and present.

References

Brown, A. E. (ed.) 1991. *Garden Archaeology*, CBA Research Report 78

Cleere, H. 1984. 'Great Britain' in *Approaches to the Archaeological Heritage* (ed. H. Cleere), Cambridge, 54–62

Council for British Archaeology 1993. *The Past in Tomorrow's Landscape*, London

Darvill, T. 1987. *Ancient Monuments in the Countryside, An Archaeological Management Review*, HBMC

Fielden, B. and Jokilehto, J. 1993. *Management Guidelines for World Cultural Heritage Sites*, ICCROM, Rome

Harvey, H. J. 1995. 'Nature conservation in the National Trust', in *The National Trust and Nature Conservation: One Hundred Years on* (eds D. J. Bullock and H. J. Harvey), Biological Journal of the Linnean Society

Jacques, D. 1992. 'The welcome complexity of cherished landscapes', *Paysage et Amenage-ment and Landscape Research*, Blois Conference Proceedings

Jokilehto, J. 1994. 'Questions about "Authenticity"', in *Conference on Authenticity in Relation to the World Heritage Convention* (eds K. E. Larsen and N. Marstein), Bergen

Lipe, W. D. 1984. 'Values and meanings in cultural resources' in *Approaches to the Archaeological Heritage* (ed. H. Cleere), Cambridge, 1–11

Stovel, H. 1994. 'Notes on Authenticity' in *Conference on Authenticity in Relation to the World Heritage Convention* (eds K. E. Larsen and N. Marstein), Bergen

Taylor, C. 1970. *The Making of the English Landscape, Dorset*, London

Thackray, D., Jarman, R. and Burgon, J. 1995. 'The National Trust's Approach to Integrated Conservation Management' in *Managing Ancient Monuments: An Integrated Approach* (eds A. Q. Berry and I. W. Brown), Clwyd Archaeology Service, 37–48

Trotzig, G. 1993. 'Applied research – the backbone of Archaeological Heritage Management' in *Archaeological Heritage Management* ICOMOS, Sri Lanka, 108–11

Waterson, M. 1993. 'The Whole Picture', *The National Trust Magazine*, No.70, 22–3

Wood, Jason (ed.) 1994. *Buildings Archaeology Applications in Practice*, Oxbow Books

Wood, John 1993. 'So important – but how should we do it? Education, training and professional development for Archaeological Heritage Conservation' in *Archaeological Heritage Management*, ICOMOS, Sri Lanka, 130–41

27 Secured for the future?

Geoffrey Wainwright

I have always regarded it as a great compliment that over thirty years ago as an aspiring archaeologist I was accused of resembling a National Trust Agent. I immediately discarded the cap but retained my admiration for an organization which regarded my profession as central to its concerns. It gives me particular pleasure to be invited to provide a summary and overview of the achievements and opportunities set out for us in this centenary conference which has seen some twenty-six papers delivered over the course of two days. I will not attempt to summarize what has been said – it would be inappropriate to do so, and what follows is a series of personal impressions of the major themes which have emerged.

The impression dominant in my mind is the genuine pleasure felt by the large and distinguished audience in joining with Trust staff in celebrating the centenary of an organization which has been a powerful influence for good in the conservation movement. The scope of archaeological activities set out for us in the papers and in the excellent exhibition which accompanies this conference has been a revelation to many, and the National Trust and the Society of Antiquaries of London are to be congratulated on the concept of the conference and carrying it through to such a successful conclusion. Throughout the two days there has been a powerful sense of goodwill emanating from the audience and an impression of self-confidence in the way in which Dave Thackray and his staff go about their business which has never degenerated into complacency.

For me, four main themes emerged consistently over the two days – communications, partnership, a sense of vision and the delivery of the opportunities represented in those themes. I am concerned in this conclusion with the content of the message the Trust wishes to communicate, not with the medium of communication. The conference would have benefited perhaps from an international perspective where experiences in other countries would have identified the recipients of the message which the Trust is attempting to convey as including multi-ethnic inner-city dwellers as well as the more traditional supporters. We all have a stake in our heritage and the National Trust (and English Heritage) need to evaluate the style and content of the message they wish to convey. As part of that process it is vital to establish common ground with the public and invite their participation in defining that message. Remarkably few attempts have been made to extend such invitations and the examples of St Just and Avebury described by Nicholas Johnson and Mike Pitts were notable on that account. Any organization which is in the business of conserving and presenting the nation's heritage is in danger of becoming divorced from the concerns and aspirations of society in the last decade of the twentieth century unless that dialogue takes place.

This necessary partnership with the public is echoed in the way in which the Trust goes about its work. No organization working in the conservation field can do so without partners and this approach is currently embodied in the management of historic landscapes, local agreements with English Heritage and local authorities and by surveys of monuments with the Royal Commissions. To ensure value for money it is incumbent on all of us – including the National Trust – to review our activities and evaluate areas which might best be done by others or where a combined approach is necessary for success. Education is surely one area where the wheel is in some danger of being reinvented by separate organizations. The management of our industrial heritage is a major issue facing us all where a clear definition of responsibility and a joint approach is essential. In addition, there is the issue of Stonehenge – mentioned by several speakers – where a formidable partnership between the Trust and English Heritage is attempting to rectify the current arrangements at this World Heritage Site, which the Public Accounts Committee of the House of Commons has rightly called 'a national disgrace'. I make no apologies for recalling our joint objectives for this project. They are:

(a) to restore the monument to its landscape with the closure of the A303 and A344;
(b) the establishment of a visitor centre outside the World Heritage Site and the removal of the present facilities;
(c) the creation of an appropriately managed landscape within the World Heritage Site with visitor access.

International opinion is awaiting the outcome of our joint negotiations, the success of which is regarded as a litmus test of the regard which the Government has for our heritage.

I have already made a distinction between delivery mechanisms and the messages which they convey. In my experience more debate is likely about the former than the latter – a sense of vision is more painful to acquire than a knowledge of Internet. It is not surprising therefore that more emphasis has been placed at this conference on the solid achievements to which the Trust can draw attention rather than the opportunities for the future. Speakers have referred to the need for a more pro-active policy in respect of our industrial heritage, the challenge posed by post-industrial landscapes and the need to encompass maritime archaeology and defence sites of the twentieth century. All these are issues which will or are being debated by the Trust and will be taken forward with partners in the most effective, efficient and economical way. The vision of the next century has to revolve around the relevance of the National Trust to a society which must encompass multi-ethnic culture and the inner cities. The challenge for the Trust – and their archaeologists who will play an important role in the process – is to define that vision in consultation with all elements of society and to deliver that in partnership with others, through the portfolio of properties which you have in your care. Your great strengths, which have come across so clearly at the conference, lie in the high quality of your advisers and staff and in particular the goodwill to succeed which you have from all of us.

Do we all feel a sense of relief that a property has been secured for the future when it passes to the National Trust? Before the conference I would have agreed with Nicholas Johnson that I *think* so. Now I share the confidence of the audience that this is so and look forward with optimism to the next hundred years.

INDEX